W9-BXQ-873

Presidential Impeachment and the New Political Instability in Latin America

This book documents the emergence of a new pattern of political instability in Latin America. Traditional military coups have receded in the region, but elected presidents are still ousted from power as a result of recurrent crises. Aníbal Pérez-Liñán shows that presidential impeachment has become the main instrument employed by civilian elites to depose unpopular rulers. Based on detailed comparative research in five countries and extensive historical information, the book explains why crises without breakdown have become the dominant form of instability in recent years and why some presidents are removed from office while others survive in power. The analysis emphasizes the erosion of presidential approval resulting from corruption and unpopular policies, the formation of hostile coalitions in Congress, and the role of investigative journalism. This book challenges classic assumptions in studies of presidentialism and provides important insights for the fields of political communication, democratization, political behavior, and institutional analysis.

Aníbal Pérez-Liñán is an assistant professor of political science and a member of the core faculty at the Center for Latin American Studies, University of Pittsburgh. Born in Argentina, Pérez-Liñán has conducted extensive research in Bolivia, Brazil, Colombia, Ecuador, Paraguay, and Venezuela. He has published articles in academic journals in Argentina, Brazil, Chile, Egypt, Great Britain, Spain, the United States, and Uruguay. His most recent articles have been published in the *Journal of Politics*, *Electoral Studies*, and *Comparative Political Studies*.

Cambridge Studies in Comparative Politics

General Editor
Margaret Levi   *University of Washington, Seattle*

Assistant General Editor
Stephen Hanson   *University of Washington, Seattle*

Associate Editors
Robert H. Bates   *Harvard University*
Helen Milner   *Princeton University*
Frances Rosenbluth   *Yale University*
Susan Stokes   *Yale University*
Sidney Tarrow   *Cornell University*
Kathleen Thelen   *Northwestern University*
Erik Wibbels   *University of Washington, Seattle*

Other Books in the Series

Lisa Baldez, *Why Women Protest: Women's Movements in Chile*
Stefano Bartolini, *The Political Mobilization of the European Left,*
   1860–1980: The Class Cleavage
Mark Beissinger, *Nationalist Mobilization and the Collapse of the Soviet State*
Nancy Bermeo, ed., *Unemployment in the New Europe*
Carles Boix, *Democracy and Redistribution*
Carles Boix, *Political Parties, Growth, and Equality: Conservative and Social*
   Democratic Economic Strategies in the World Economy
Catherine Boone, *Merchant Capital and the Roots of State Power in Senegal,*
   1930–1985
Catherine Boone, *Political Topographies of the African State: Territorial*
   Authority and Institutional Change
Michael Bratton and Nicolas van de Walle, *Democratic Experiments in*
   Africa: Regime Transitions in Comparative Perspective

Continued on pages following the Index

Presidential Impeachment and the New Political Instability in Latin America

ANÍBAL PÉREZ-LIÑÁN

University of Pittsburgh

CAMBRIDGE
UNIVERSITY PRESS

CAMBRIDGE UNIVERSITY PRESS
Cambridge, New York, Melbourne, Madrid, Cape Town, Singapore, São Paulo

Cambridge University Press
32 Avenue of the Americas, New York, NY 10013-2473, USA

www.cambridge.org
Information on this title: www.cambridge.org/9780521869423

© Aníbal Pérez-Liñán 2007

This publication is in copyright. Subject to statutory exception
and to the provisions of relevant collective licensing agreements,
no reproduction of any part may take place without
the written permission of Cambridge University Press.

First published 2007

Printed in the United States of America

A catalog record for this publication is available from the British Library.

Library of Congress Cataloging in Publication Data
Pérez-Liñán, Aníbal S.
Presidential impeachment and the new political instability in Latin America / Aníbal
Pérez-Liñán.
    p. cm.
Includes bibliographical references and index.
ISBN 978-0-521-86942-3 (hardback)
1. Impeachments – Latin America.   2. Political corruption – Latin America.   I. Title.
JL959.5.C6P47   2007
328.8′07453 – dc22   2006035960

ISBN   978-0-521-86942-3 hardback

Cambridge University Press has no responsibility for
the persistence or accuracy of URLs for external or
third-party Internet Web sites referred to in this publication
and does not guarantee that any content on such
Web sites is, or will remain, accurate or appropriate.

To my mother, for her strength and generosity

Contents

Tables and Figures

Tables

Figures

Preface and Acknowledgments

The 1990s were an era of great hopes for Latin America. After the demise of authoritarian regimes in the 1980s and the early 1990s, major economic reforms were undertaken in most Latin American countries in order to reduce chronic inflation and promote sustained growth. For many contemporary observers, the confluence of democracy and free markets signaled a break with the past, the dawn of a new era of civil liberties, prosperity, and political stability.

More than a decade later, it is hard to look back at this period without a mixture of nostalgia and sarcasm. The legacies of the 1990s varied from country to country, but they can be generally described as notable achievements overshadowed by missed opportunities. In the economic realm, hyperinflation was eventually defeated, but economic growth remained elusive and poverty resilient. In the political arena, the military eventually withdrew from politics (not a minor feat), but elected governments, surprisingly, continued to collapse. Starting in the early 1990s, presidents were removed from office in Brazil, Venezuela, Guatemala, Ecuador, Paraguay, Peru, Argentina, and Bolivia – in some countries recurrently. This outcome frequently represented the triumph of an indignant society over a corrupt or abusive executive, but it seldom prevented the occurrence of new abuses in later administrations. By the early years of the twenty-first century, it was clear that the particular circumstances of each crisis represented only parts of a broader puzzle – a new pattern of political instability emerging in the region.

This book explores the origins and the consequences of this novel pattern of instability, emphasizing the critical events that defined the new trend between 1992 and 2004. During this period, civilian elites realized that traditional military coups had become for the most part unfeasible and experimented with the use of constitutional instruments to remove unpopular presidents from office. Presidential impeachment thus became a distinctive mark of the new political landscape in Latin America.

The recurrence of presidential crises without democratic breakdown challenged many dominant views among political scientists. Latin American democracies proved to be simultaneously enduring and unstable, willing to punish presidential corruption but unable to prevent it, and responsive to popular demands only in the context of massive protests and widespread frustration. My attempts to understand these facts initially relied on well-delimited theoretical perspectives that proved rather disappointing, and I was forced to embark on a long exploration across the disciplinary boundaries of political sociology, communication, political behavior, institutional analysis, democratization, and the study of social movements. Others who have studied these topics more thoroughly than I may be reluctant to recognize their subject in the chapters that follow, but I hope that they will forgive my intrusion. In the course of this exploration I have wandered through the academic fields of many colleagues and collected a large number of intellectual debts along the way.

Intellectual debts, Theodore Lowi once wrote, are never paid in full. Over the course of the years many people and institutions have endowed my work with ideas, guidance, support, and helpful criticism. This book grew in the fertile ground provided by the Department of Government and International Studies (now Political Science) at the University of Notre Dame and was finished in the Department of Political Science at the University of Pittsburgh. Scott Mainwaring coached this project from beginning to end; Michael Coppedge, Robert Fishman, and Guillermo O'Donnell imparted enthusiasm and sound advice. The lively intellectual environments of the Kellogg Institute for International Studies at Notre Dame and the Center for Latin American Studies at the University of Pittsburgh nurtured the ideas presented here.

I am particularly grateful to people and institutions who, in many ways, contributed to my research in five countries. In Brazil, I was hosted by the University of Brasília and the Catholic University of São Paulo. Fernando Abrúcio, Marta Assumpção-Rodrigues, Regis de Castro Andrade, Márcia Cavallari, Paula Cencig, Claudio Couto, Ney Figueiredo, Ricardo Fiuza, David Fleischer, Zé Gomes da Rocha, Fernando Limongi, José Lourenço, Félix Mendonça, Rachel Meneguello, Luiz Moreira, Edison Nunes, Mauro Paulino, Carlos Pio, Brasilio Sallum, Aaron Schneider, Gustavo Venturi, Anderson Vieira, Marisa Von Bulow, and others who asked not to be identified shared with me their knowledge of Brazilian politics and helped me to develop my project in other ways.

Corporación de Estudios Para el Desarrollo generously hosted me in Quito. My knowledge of Ecuadorian politics greatly benefited from the insights, information, and collaboration offered by scholars, friends, and public officials, including María Lourdes Alarcón, Raúl Baca Carbo, Adolfo and Elsa Bucaram, Karla Bucheli, Flavia Freidenberg, Ramiro García, José Hernández, Gabriel Martínez, Andrés Mejía Acosta, Paco Moncayo, Simón Pachano, Frank Vargas Pazzos, Blasco Peñaherrera Jr., Marco Proaño Maya, Omar and Tatiana Simon, Alexandra Vela, and others who asked to remain anonymous.

In Venezuela, I was a visiting Fellow at IESA (Instituto de Estudios Superiores de Administración). Many people helped me with, or agreed to be interviewed for, this project. Luis Christiansen, Imelda Cisneros, Gloria Cuenca de Herrera, Beatriz di Totto, Francisco Figueroa, Hugo Grooscors, Janet Kelly, Luis Lander, Margarita López-Maya, David Myers, Miguel Henrique Otero, Michael Penfold, Carlos Andrés Pérez, María José Rodríguez, Miguel Rodríguez, Andrés Velásquez, Italo del Valle Alliegro, and Luis Vezga Godoy provided valuable help, information, and insights. Other people, who asked not to be identified, deserve my recognition as well.

In Colombia, the Department of Political Science at the Universidad de Los Andes and the Comisión Colombiana de Juristas provided institutional affiliation, and many people offered useful data and ideas. I am especially indebted to Alexandra Anchique Bohorquez, Gloria Arango, Myriam Bautista, Ana María Bejarano, Andrea Benavidez, Jaime Bermúdez, Andrea Bolaños, Alvaro Camacho, Michael Donovan, Gustavo Gallón, Benjamín Higuita, Ana María Iturralde, María Lucía Lara, Carlos Lemoine, Jorge Londoño, Carlo Nasi, Alonso Ojeda, Eduardo Pizarro, Rosario Pradilla, Javier Restrepo, Luis Alberto Restrepo, Rodrigo Rivera, Pilar Rueda, Germán Ruiz, Ernesto Samper Pizano, Andrés Sánchez Thorin, Horacio Serpa, Yanis Tamayo, Arlene Tickner, and Elisabeth Ungar Bleier.

The research institute Desarrollo provided institutional affiliation for this project in Asunción, Paraguay. Mauricio Aguilera Coronel, Luis F. Canillas, Francisco Capli, Enrique Chase, José María Costa, Marcelo Duarte, Derlis Ferreira, Rafael Filizzola, Aristides González, Federico A. González, Eduardo González Petit, José Molinas Vega, José A. Moreno Rufinelli, José Nicolás Morínigo, Federico Narváez, Emilio Pérez Cháves,

Gonzalo Quintana, Francisco J. Recalde Trujillo, Miguel A. Saguier, and Angel R. Seifart provided valuable information.

In addition to these people, other scholars and friends read drafts, discussed ideas, shared data, and supplied generous encouragement. Manuel Alcántara, David Altman, Samuel Amaral, Barry Ames, Adriana Bacciadonne, Jody Baumgartner, Andrea Castagnola, Rossana Castiglioni, Brian Crisp, Douglas Dion, Susan Eckstein, Andreas Feldmann, Agustín Ferraro, Andrew Gould, Agustín Grijalva, Carlos Guevara Mann, Russell Hahn, Fred Hansen, Susan Hansen, Gretchen Helmke, Rodney Hero, Victor Hinojosa, Mark Jones, Naoko Kada, William Keech, Charles Kenney, Marcelo Leiras, Néstor Legnani, Margaret Levi, Rissig Licha, Germán Lodola, Andrés Mejía Acosta, Martha Merritt, Scott Morgenstern, Kajal Mukhopadhyay, Robert Muncaster, Gerardo Munck, María Matilde Ollier, Benjamin Radcliff, Juan Carlos Rodríguez Raga, Sebastián Saiegh, Alberta Sbragia, Mitchell Seligson, Peter Siavelis, Susan Stokes, María Clara Tena, Sanford G. Thatcher, Brian Turner, Silvio Waisbord, Kurt Weyland, Laurence Whitehead, Dina Zinnes, and Carlos I. Zúñiga Guardia all made, in very different ways, significant contributions to this enterprise.

Research for this five-country project was supported by several donors. The University of Notre Dame granted a Philip Moore Dissertation Year Fellowship. The Kellogg Institute for International Studies awarded a Seed-Money Grant for the project to take off and a Dissertation Year Fellowship for it to land smoothly. The Social Science Research Council and the American Council of Learned Societies contributed with a generous International Field Research Fellowship to complete research in Brazil, Ecuador, Colombia, and Venezuela during 1999 and 2000. The Center for Latin American Studies at the University of Pittsburgh supported field research in Paraguay during 2002 and additional data collection during 2003. It goes without saying that without such vast support, this book would have never been possible.

Pittsburgh, Pennsylvania
August 2006

1

Institutional Crises in Presidential Regimes

The president's seat represents the dream job for most politicians. Presidents are power brokers, party leaders, role models, the daily focus of public opinion. Presidents speak for the nation, they are *primi inter pares* among national political figures. "They say," former Chilean president Patricio Aylwin once joked, "that the most difficult task after being president is getting used to not being president." Presidents, however, are not free from failure. And the completion of their terms, particularly in Latin America, is never guaranteed.

This book deals with an extreme form of political failure: presidential impeachment. Impeachment transforms the luck of the most successful politician in the country into a model of defeat. Presidents are deprived of honor and power, deserted by former allies and voters, prosecuted as ordinary citizens, and many times incarcerated or forced into exile.

In the 1990s, an unprecedented wave of impeachments swept Latin America. Dwellers of presidential palaces, from Carondelet to Miraflores and from Planalto to the House of Nariño, unexpectedly confronted this threat. In just over a decade, between 1992 and 2004, six presidents faced an impeachment process, and four of them were removed from office. Brazilian President Fernando Collor de Mello in 1992 and Venezuelan President Carlos Andrés Pérez in 1993 were accused of corruption and ousted on impeachment charges. In 1996, Colombian President Ernesto Samper was charged with receiving illegal campaign funds from the Cali drug cartel. Congress ultimately acquitted Samper, but his political leverage was greatly diminished as a consequence of the scandal. The following year, the Ecuadorian Congress confronted President Abdalá Bucaram and, in order to avoid the institutional intricacies of impeachment, declared the president mentally impaired. Paraguayan President Raúl Cubas Grau confronted an

1

impeachment after releasing from prison a popular military leader accused of conspiring to kill the vice president. Cubas resigned and fled to Brazil in 1999, after a harsh confrontation with Congress. His successor, Luis González Macchi, was accused of corruption two years later. In a desperate attempt to prevent his fall, his party majority in Congress forestalled an impeachment and finally acquitted the president in early 2003.

These episodes inaugurated a new pattern of presidential instability in the region. Anticipating an impeachment process, Peruvian President Alberto Fujimori fled the country in November of 2000. Ecuadorian President Lucio Gutiérrez narrowly escaped an impeachment in November of 2004 and was ousted in April of 2005. Opposition protests forced the resignation of Argentine President Fernando de la Rúa in 2001, and of Bolivian Presidents Gonzalo Sánchez de Lozada and Carlos Mesa in 2003 and 2005.

Until very recently, the Latin American crises of the last fifteen years were treated in isolation rather than as part of a regional trend (for exceptions, see Bermúdez 1999; Carey 2005; Coslovsky 2002; Hochstetler 2006; Kada 2002; Pérez-Liñán 2000; 2003a; 2005; Valenzuela 2004; Whitehead 2002, 102–107). The concentration of multiple impeachment crises in a few years, however, has opened important questions that are difficult to ignore. Is this pattern indicative of a major change in Latin American democracies? Are impeachments a functional equivalent of old-fashioned military coups? Are we witnessing a turn in executive-legislative relations throughout the region? And if this is the case, why are some corrupt presidents impeached while others are not?

The lack of a comparative theory of impeachment has complicated the search for answers to these questions. Because impeachments are rare events (and have been particularly infrequent in this region in the past), the traditional literature on Latin American institutions for the most part disregarded them. A classic textbook of the 1950s noted in passing that "although there are a few instances in which presidents have been removed through this procedure, those cases are exceptional and in most countries no president or vice-president has ever been impeached" (Pierson and Gil 1957, 240). Published in 1992, the year in which Fernando Collor was removed from office, Shugart and Carey's seminal book on *Presidents and Assemblies* – which devoted a whole chapter to discussing constitutional deviations from the principles of dual legitimacy and fixed terms in office – virtually ignored the issue of impeachment (Shugart and Carey 1992, Chapter 6).

This book argues that recent impeachments constitute the tip of the iceberg of a much broader emerging trend in Latin American politics. Latin

America is confronting a distinctive pattern of political instability, one that represents a break from the past. As in previous decades, democratically elected *governments* continue to fall, but in contrast to previous decades, democratic *regimes* do not break down. Several reasons explain this paradox of democratic regime stability in the midst of government instability. Among them are the end of the Cold War, changes in U.S. foreign policy, the political lessons derived from the dramatic experience of military dictatorships in the 1960s and the 1970s, and the new role of international institutions. Because in this context civilian elites cannot invoke a military intervention, they have been forced to find constitutional mechanisms to solve their disputes. Presidential impeachment has emerged as the most powerful instrument to displace "undesirable" presidents without destroying the constitutional order.

Opposition politicians, however, are not always able to unleash an impeachment process against the chief executive. In the following chapters, I show that impeachments are likely when the mass media systematically investigate and expose political scandals *and* when the president fails to keep tight control over Congress, either because the ruling party is very small or because it is under the control of an adversarial faction. At the same time, the ability of the legislature to remove the president from office ultimately hinges on the degree of popular mobilization against the government. When a broad social coalition takes to the streets to demand the resignation of the president, the fall of the administration is usually in sight.

The new pattern of instability poses a major theoretical challenge for comparative studies of presidentialism. For more than two decades, the conventional wisdom in the field claimed that extreme forms of executive-legislative confrontation are likely to destabilize presidential democracies. Recent crises, however, have led to the downfall of elected presidents without triggering democratic breakdowns. In order to explain this phenomenon, some scholars have argued that Latin American presidential democracies are developing "parliamentary" traits (thus making presidential impeachments akin to votes of no confidence), while others have claimed that social movements are expanding the realm of democratic citizenship by fighting against neoliberal policies and toppling unpopular presidents. These interpretations are partly correct, but, as the following chapters will show, the contribution of recent presidential crises to the process of democratization has often been ambiguous, and we should probably avoid any overly optimistic assessment of this trend.

This introductory chapter serves three purposes. In the first section, I explian why a better understanding of impeachment is essential if we are to update our theories of democracy and presidentialism in Latin America. The second part introduces my approach to impeachment as a particular outcome of executive-legislative crises. In the last section, I summarize the argument of this book and outline the contents of the coming chapters.

Impeachment as a Theoretical Puzzle

Recent cases of impeachment have challenged much of the common wisdom about democracy in Latin America. For years, the conventional view was that Latin American presidential democracies were unable to resist much executive-legislative conflict. In contrast to parliamentary regimes, where the prime minister (through the dissolution of the parliament) and the parliament (through a vote of no confidence) have constitutional tools to avert government deadlock, presidential regimes, where the two branches are popularly elected and their terms in office are fixed, were seen as prone to stalemate. According to this argument, attempts to overcome such stalemate in Latin America had usually led to political polarization and created the conditions for military intervention (Lamounier 1994; Linz 1990; Stepan and Skach 1993; Valenzuela 1994).

In the mid-1990s, this argument was recast in terms of an excess of "veto players" in presidential systems. George Tsebelis argued that "in regimes where government change is impossible (except for fixed intervals like in presidential regimes), policy immobilism may lead to the replacement of the leadership through extra-constitutional means (regime instability)" (Tsebelis 1995, 321–322). Thus, while divided government was expected to create policy stability in advanced presidential democracies, it was expected to promote regime instability in weakly institutionalized ones.

The critics of this perspective argued that some forms of presidentialism were more prone to interbranch confrontation than others, without questioning the underlying assumption that extreme executive-legislative conflict was dangerous for democracy (Jones 1995; Mainwaring 1993; Mainwaring and Shugart 1997a; Shugart and Carey 1992; for an interesting exception, see Cheibub 2002). Some of these studies even acknowledged the role of impeachment as a constitutional instrument allowing Congress to remove the president from office without disrupting the democratic process, but they claimed that this highly restrictive procedure was virtually impossible to activate in the context of an institutional crisis (Linz 1994, 10; Shugart and Carey 1992, 29).

History likes to scoff at political scientists. Just as this dominant view unfolded in the 1990s, presidential impeachment became a common mechanism used to overcome executive-legislative crises while avoiding democratic breakdown. This emerging pattern posed an important challenge for the prevailing argument about the perils of presidentialism. The fact that impeachment replaced military coups as the standard procedure to oust presidents throughout the region suggested that executive-legislative conflict could lead to democratic breakdowns only under certain historical circumstances that had changed since the 1980s (Pérez-Liñán 2003b).

The proliferation of impeachments also challenged another leading assumption among students of Latin American presidentialism – the idea that presidents are too strong and that legislators are unable to hold them accountable. Presidential dominance over Congress was a distinctive historical trait of Latin American politics (Pierson and Gil 1957, 240; for important exceptions, see Stokes 1945), and it persisted after an extended period of democratization during the 1980s. The inability of Congress to check the president's corruption or abuse of power has been characteristic of, but not exclusive to, what Guillermo O'Donnell called "delegative democracies" (O'Donnell 1994). To different degrees and for different reasons, horizontal (i.e., interbranch) accountability was absent from democratic regimes like the Punto Fijo system in Venezuela (1958–99); from semidemocratic regimes like the first Perón administration in Argentina (1946–52); and, not surprisingly, from authoritarian presidential regimes like the Stronismo in Paraguay (1954–89), the Somozas' rule in Nicaragua (1936–79), and the Trujillo era in the Dominican Republic (1930–61). Congressional weakness did not result solely from a concentration of formal constitutional powers in the chief executive. In most cases, the concentration of substantive political resources – control over state revenues, mass support, and loyal security forces – in the hands of the president made it very difficult for Congress to exercise strong checks and often encouraged opposition legislators to ally themselves with rebel military leaders in order to check the executive by undemocratic means.

Defying this tradition, the political events at the turn of the century proved that legislators were becoming increasingly capable and willing to serve as agents of democratic accountability. The new trend came as a surprise in a region where impeachment – despite having been contemplated in the constitutions – was virtually unknown. In the four decades preceding the 1990s, only one episode – the trial of President José R. Guizado of Panama in 1955 – could be considered a true case of impeachment, and the reasons for that trial remain obscure (Romeu 2000; Zúñiga Guardia 1957). The sudden multiplication of cases since 1992 suggests that the pattern of congressional weakness traditionally manifested in the lack of presidential accountability was also changing rapidly.

A comparative analysis of impeachment is also critical for the study of presidentialism beyond Latin America. The American Congress has considered impeaching the president at least seven times since 1832, and a prominent dweller of the White House was impeached just as this book was being written (Perkins 2003). Over the last decade, the specter of impeachment has also threatened presidents in Madagascar (1996), Nigeria (2002), the Philippines (2000), Russia (1998–99), Taiwan (2000), South Korea (2004), and Lithuania (2004) (for discussions of some of these cases, see Allen 2003; Baumgartner 2003b; Kasuya 2003; Ohnesorge 2006). Yet scholars and policy makers lack a comparative framework to interpret such cases;[1] and because impeachment is a rare event, they have been unable to deploy their powerful statistical arsenal to address this research problem.

The last decade and a half in Latin America offers an interesting laboratory for the development of a comparative theory of impeachment. The concentration of several cases in a short period allows us to trace the political conditions that trigger an impeachment crisis while "holding constant" cultural and historical factors. If this explanation travels well in time and space, it may serve as the basis for a more general theory of presidential accountability (Hinojosa and Pérez-Liñán 2007).

Impeachment as an Institutional Outcome

In presidential systems, the term "impeachment" describes a particular trial of the president by which Congress (sometimes with the necessary agreement of the judiciary) is allowed to remove the president from office. In the United States, the first country to adopt a presidential constitution, the process is initiated by the House of Representatives and the trial is conducted by the Senate. An impeachment is intended to be not a criminal trial but a political procedure allowing the Senate to remove the president from office

---

[1] For a recent attempt to offer such comparative framework, see Baumgartner and Kada (2003).

in response to accusations of treason, bribery, or other "high crimes and misdemeanors." Although other presidential systems have often modified the details of the procedure (for instance, placing the trial in the hands of the Supreme Court rather than the Senate) and the range of impeachable offenses (for instance, allowing Congress to impeach the president on grounds of "misperformance in office"), presidential impeachments are always initiated by the legislature.

The latter point deserves careful consideration. When analyzed in comparative and historical perspective, presidential impeachment emerges as one among many tools used by legislators to prevail in their occasional confrontations with the executive branch. A major contention of this book is that impeachment is one of the many possible outcomes resulting from a presidential crisis.

I use the concept "presidential crisis" to refer to extreme instances of executive-legislative conflict in which one of the elected branches of government seeks the dissolution of the other. The term "crisis" is chosen to describe a pressing political situation marked by a sense of "immediacy and urgency" among powerful actors (Kiewe 1994, xvii). The adjective "presidential" simply identifies the constitutional framework in which such crises take place. In parliamentary regimes, this kind of confrontation can be resolved through ordinary procedures (the fall of the government following a vote of no confidence or the dissolution of the parliament followed by an election), but such procedures are prevented in most presidential regimes by rigid constitutional rules.

Operationally, this definition covers any situation in which the president attempts to disband Congress, Congress attempts to remove the president from office, or in which either of the elected branches supports a military or civilian uprising against the other (Pérez-Liñán 2003b). The common denominator in all of these cases is an attempt by some elected politicians to remove other elected officials from office, thus compromising the principle of fixed terms in office that characterizes presidential constitutions. As I show in Chapter 3, presidential crises may lead to the activation of constitutional mechanisms (such as impeachment), or they may unleash unconstitutional actions (e.g., a legislative coup against the president).

The analysis of presidential crises allows us to explore two critical questions: when and why Congress is able to hold the president accountable, and when and why executive-legislative conflict leads to the breakdown of democracy. Between 1950 and 2004, some fifty-eight presidential crises took place in Latin America, but only six of them involved a serious attempt

7

to impeach the president, and twenty-one of them involved a military coup.[2]

In order to address these questions, it is important to establish from the outset what presidential crises *are not*. From the definition outlined earlier, it is easy to infer that any presidential crisis constitutes an emergency situation for the president and his or her cabinet. The opposite, however, is not true. Presidential crises are defined here as a pattern of institutional conflict that affects the stability of the government (the executive *in relation to* the legislature) in the context of a presidential constitution. But not every major challenge demanding immediate action from the executive will fall into this category. Congress may not play a major role in some political crises, or it may cooperate with the president in the face of a national emergency.

This definition differs from one adopted in the literature on U.S. foreign policy. For authors like Windt (1973) and Kuypers (1997), crises are rhetorical constructs deployed by the president in order to frame the need for immediate policy action. Similarly, Kiewe (1994, xvii) describes them as characterized by the expectation of strong leadership qualities. This approach usually refers to policy crises rather than to institutional crises. As will become clear later in this work, policy challenges may lead to institutional turmoil, but this is not necessarily the case.

The previous discussion also suggests an important distinction between presidential crises as processes affecting the survival in office of particular elected officials and broader regime crises jeopardizing the stability of democracy. Government and regime crises may overlap, but they represent different analytical constructs in at least two ways. On the one hand, executive-legislative confrontation is not a necessary condition for regime instability. Quite often, the military have intervened against a ruling party controlling both the executive *and* the legislature. In fact, of forty-two military coups taking place in Latin America between 1950 and 2004, only twenty (48 percent) were related to a presidential crisis.[3] On the other

---

[2] I describe the procedure employed to identify and code presidential crises in Chapter 3.

[3] This figure includes only coups that took place in situations in which a presidential crisis was possible (i.e., when a president and a legislature coexisted at the time). I defined as a coup any episode in which the military successfully removed the president from office, closed Congress, or both. The cases are: Argentina (1955, 1962, 1966, 1976); Bolivia (1951, 1964, 1969, 1979, 1980); Brazil (1954 [an ambiguous case because President Vargas committed suicide in anticipation of the coup], 1955, 1964); Chile (1973); Colombia (1953); Cuba (1952); the Dominican Republic (1963); Ecuador (1961, 1963, 1970, 2000); El Salvador (1960, 1979); Guatemala (1954, 1957, 1963, 1982, 1993); Honduras (1954, 1957, 1963, 1972); Panama (1951, 1968, 1985, 1988); Paraguay (1954, 1989); Peru (1962, 1968, 1992);

hand, presidential crises are not sufficient for democratic instability. About half (45 percent) of the presidential crises taking place in Latin America during this period led to some sort of military intervention, and 36 percent ended with a full-blown military coup; but this book is inspired by the fact that a vast majority of presidential crises over the last decade and a half have not been related to any form of regime breakdown.

Episodes of impeachment are thus presented in this book as a subset of the universe of presidential crises, in turn an extremely hostile form of executive-legislative interaction. This perspective suggests that impeachment is not just a legal recourse to remove presidents who are proven guilty of high crimes; it is often an institutional weapon employed against presidents who confront a belligerent legislature. This may be true even in well-established democracies like the United States (Perkins 2003, 21). The question about the proper use of impeachment – that is, its use for the purpose of punishing actual misdemeanors rather than for merely partisan reasons – is often difficult to confront, both for the contemporary observer and for the analyst claiming the advantage of historical hindsight.

In spite of this approach, the reader should not be tempted to assume that the only relevant actors in the drama are the executive and the legislature. Impeachment crises often involve subtle negotiations to appease the military, media investigations, popular protests, and attempts to manipulate the judiciary (Whitehead 2002, 104). In fledgling democracies, the military may play a crucial role in shaping the outcome of a crisis – even when the survival of the regime is not threatened, for instance, generals may act as mediators. In well-established democracies, other institutions such as the press and the judiciary may play powerful roles in the confrontation. Executive-legislative conflicts may implicate various third parties according to the circumstances, but they usually involve a complex structure in which both institutions seek the support of a third party against the other branch (on the role of third party players in different contexts, see Caplow 1968).

Consider, for instance, the strategies adopted by legislators seeking to oust the president. In some cases, they investigate presidential misdeeds originally exposed by the press. The Watergate scandal in the United States and the Brazilian crisis of 1992 illustrate this situation. In other

Uruguay (1973); and Venezuela (1958). Twenty other coups taking place in countries without an operating legislature (e.g., Ecuador in 1972) were excluded from the count. These events were identified using *The New York Times Index* and other historical sources (Fossum 1967; Needler 1966).

circumstances, Congress confronts the executive in an attempt to contain a broader crisis triggered by the mobilization of the mass public. This was the case in Venezuela during 1993 and in Ecuador during 1997. Congress may even become a peripheral actor in a confrontation between the president and powerful groups, such as the military or social movements, acting simply to legalize the ousting of the president. In such cases, legislative action is a marginal event in a much larger shakedown of democracy. Here the role of Congress is typically reduced to swearing in the new president, preserving a minimum appearance of constitutionality. The crises of Ecuador in 2000, Argentina in 2001, and Bolivia in 2003 and 2005 (discussed in Chapter 7) represent this pattern.

I contend that the democratization process that took place in Latin America during the 1980s and early 1990s altered the relative weight of different political players. Military officers, once the arbiters of the political process, found themselves unable to remove civilian politicians from power. Media corporations, once vehicles of personal political ambitions or mouthpieces for the executive, claimed a new role as the guardians of public morality. Popular movements, once repressed or controlled by populist leaders, realized that politicians in competitive electoral systems could not ignore their grievances. These changes took place in parallel with major transformations in the model of economic development, as countries struggled to adopt neoliberal policies. The unexpected result of those realignments was a surprising erosion of presidential power.

About This Book

It has been more than forty years since Richard Neustadt distinguished between presidential "powers" (the legal or customary sources of presidential authority) and presidential *power* (the chief executive's actual influence in politics) (Neustadt [1960] 1990). Important as it was to understand the workings of the American presidency, the distinction is of even greater relevance in most Latin American countries, where the gap between formal (legal) powers and informal (de facto) power deserves serious consideration (for some examples, see Casar 2002; Corrales 2002a; Hartlyn 1998; Helmke 2002; Helmke and Levitsky 2004; Siavelis 2002).

Over the last decade, important works (Mainwaring and Shugart 1997b; Shugart and Carey 1992; Shugart and Haggard 2001) have emphasized that Latin American countries differ in their institutional configurations and that the accuracy of some stereotypes (like the excessive concentration of power in the executive or the supposed inability to overcome the deadlock created by the separation of powers) varies significantly from country to country. This book moves one step forward in that direction by arguing that informal political configurations vary from administration to administration even under the same constitutional arrangements. This is a well-established principle in the study of the American presidency, but it has been virtually ignored in studies of Latin American presidentialism – in which countries, rather than administrations, are typically the unit of analysis.

In the next chapter I reconstruct the history of six impeachment crises that took place in Brazil, Venezuela, Colombia, Ecuador, and twice in Paraguay between 1992 and 2004. This period defined the new pattern of political instability that currently dominates the region. I argue that in all six cases military intervention was hardly a viable option and that media coverage of presidential scandals was powerful. Where the president failed to command support in Congress, he was easily impeached. And where popular protests against the president were able to integrate multiple social sectors, the president was easily removed from office.

Chapter 3 traces the decline in military intervention as a component of presidential crises between 1950 and 2004. The analysis of fifty-eight crises suggests that there have been important changes in the ways in which executive-legislative confrontations are processed by the political system. This change has occurred not only at the level of political regimes (democracies are now less likely to break down under military pressure) but also at the level of governmental institutions (presidents are now less able to prevail in their confrontations with Congress than in the past). I view such changes as a consequence of deep transformations in the international context, political learning among the Latin American elites, and a greater legitimacy of democratic institutions in the late twentieth century (Fitch 1998).

In Chapter 4, I explore the conditions that have encouraged the multiplication of media scandals involving presidents, cabinet members, and their close relatives over the last two decades. Greater freedom of the press, deregulation of mass media markets, an expansion of television, and professionalization of the press corps have all fostered the emergence of more aggressive investigative journalism. Politicians throughout the region have noticed this change and adapted their strategies accordingly in order to navigate the politics of scandal.

Chapter 5 traces the impact of media scandals on the mass public. Using data on presidential approval for the six administrations discussed in Chapter 2, I show that both media scandals and economic performance drove the

11

emergence of popular outrage against the president. I also argue that the coverage of scandals may be endogenous to presidential approval: not only did presidential approval decline with media exposés, media outlets were also more likely to pursue new stories as presidents became less popular among their readers and audiences. This dynamic created a characteristic downward spiral leading to impeachment.

With media scandals hurting the administration and mounting public outrage against the president, even loyal legislators have found it difficult to resist public pressures for impeachment. Chapter 6 approaches this problem from a neo-institutional perspective. To what extent can constitutional rules facilitate or constrain the impeachment process? I argue that constitutional rules interact with the partisan configuration of Congress, the president's ability to form coalitions, and the political context (the nature of the scandals and the timing of the electoral calendar) to create a legislative shield to protect the president.

Chapter 7 documents an emerging pattern of political instability in Latin America. I contrast the episodes discussed in Chapter 2 with three alternative situations: presidential crises that forced the resignation of the president without an impeachment process, presidential crises that never led to the resignation of the president, and administrations that never faced a presidential crisis. I use the Argentine crisis of 2001 to illustrate a characteristic situation in which a political debacle outpaced the capacity of politicians to respond to events. These situations share some important commonalties with the core cases presented in Chapter 2, but they differ substantially in the outcome because the president resigned before an impeachment was feasible. A qualitative comparative analysis of these cases along with other presidential crises in which the president survived confirms the insight developed in earlier chapters: while scandals and legislative politics are key to explaining the impeachment process, mass mobilization constitutes the main factor driving the actual removal of presidents from office – irrespective of the specific procedure employed to achieve this goal. Further statistical analysis examining a large number of administrations that never faced a presidential crisis confirms this hypothesis, and shows that a distinctive form of political turmoil emerged in Latin America in the 1990s.

The last chapter explores the theoretical relevance of those findings for the study of presidential accountability and democracy in Latin America. A radical form of "social" accountability seems to be on the rise throughout the region (Smulovitz and Peruzzotti 2000). Impeachment may be the best institutional mechanism to channel the outbursts of public indignation, but it is often ineffective in preventing the episodes of corruption or abuse of power that create popular frustration in the first place.

One of the main lessons suggested by this book is that the same forces that sometimes grant Latin American presidents great power beyond their formal constitutional powers also create the conditions for their demise when they turn against the executive. Presidents may demand extraordinary authority to confront corruption, but they will be discredited if they are accused of being corrupt. They may present themselves as the only hope to fix an economy in shambles, but responsibility for a badly performing economy will be theirs alone. Presidents may confront or bypass other political institutions when riding a high wave of popularity, but they will be ferociously attacked when their approval ratings are low. These principles are not unknown in the White House; they just work in more extreme ways in many Latin American countries. The corollary is simple: presidential strength gained at the expense of other institutions' weaknesses is no guarantee of political survival in bad times.

In bad times, when people take to the streets to protest against the president, strategic politicians easily realize the need to abandon the president's boat and join the opposition camp. Public outrage may result from multiple factors: the imposition of unpopular economic policies, the poor performance of the administration in power, or the relentless coverage of government wrongdoing by the media. But expressions of public outrage do not necessarily result in a stronger system of checks and balances. The emerging pattern of governmental crises without regime breakdown is consistent with a model of spasmodic accountability in which institutional controls are activated only when an administration has fallen in disgrace. The paradoxical result has been Latin American legislatures with a proven capacity to punish presidential wrongdoing but with almost no capacity to prevent it.

2

Five Cases of Impeachment and a Presumed Madman

On the afternoon of October 2, 1992, Brazilian President Fernando Collor de Mello boarded the helicopter that regularly took him from Planalto, the presidential palace, to his nearby home in Brasília. It could have been a normal day, but it was not. Two days before, the Chamber of Deputies had suspended the president from office and initiated an impeachment process that would ultimately end his administration. The event certainly came as a surprise to many Brazilians accustomed to presidential dominance and political impunity, but the short helicopter ride sent shock waves throughout the rest of Latin America. Over the next decade, five other presidents would meet Collor's fate.

This chapter traces the political processes leading to five cases of impeachment and one declaration of presidential incapacity between 1992 and 2004.[1] This period constituted the foundational moment for a new pattern of instability in Latin America, and the experiences of Fernando Collor, Carlos Andrés Pérez, Ernesto Samper, Abdalá Bucaram, Raúl Cubas Grau, and Luis González Macchi epitomize such a pattern. Who were these presidents? Why did they face an impeachment process? Did they share some common characteristics that made them vulnerable and exposed their administrations to failure?

Comparison of the six episodes suggests some intriguing findings. These presidents had followed very different political careers before winning the presidential race. They were backed by different constituencies, operated in different institutional environments, presided over very different economies, and embraced somewhat different policies. However, they all faced a few similar challenges. The six presidents confronted important

---

[1] The discussion of the cases draws on Pérez-Liñán (2003a).

14

scandals involving corruption or abuse of power, and they operated in an international environment that discouraged military intervention against civilian leaders. In this context, impeachment became a feasible course of action for legislators in the opposition. The ruling parties were able to prevent an impeachment only when they controlled a large *and* disciplined bloc in Congress, and they were able to acquit the president only in the absence of a popular uprising calling for his resignation. In the following sections, I reconstruct the history of these episodes and their early scholarly interpretations. I close the chapter with a comparative exercise identifying the commonalties and differences across the cases and identifying their key characteristics.

Brazil, 1992

In 1989, after twenty-one years of military rule (1964–85) and a transitional government led by José Sarney (1985–89), Fernando Collor de Mello won the first direct presidential election that Brazil had seen in twenty-nine years. The governor of the poor state of Alagoas had campaigned against the political establishment, presenting himself as a political hero backed by a minuscule organization, the National Reconstruction Party (Partido da Reconstrução Nacional, PRN). Supported by the largest national TV network and perceived by many voters as the only alternative to Luiz Inácio Lula da Silva – the candidate of the leftist Worker's Party (Partido dos Trabalhadores, PT) – Collor obtained only 30 percent of the vote in the first round of the presidential election but ultimately prevailed with 53 percent in the runoff (de Lima 1993).

The presidential election was a spark of hope for a country in trouble. José Sarney left office haunted by an image of corruption and economic mismanagement, and the new president inherited an economy on the brink of hyperinflation – in March of 1990, the month Collor was sworn into office, the consumer price index rose by 84 percent. In an attempt to distance himself from the discredited Brazilian elite and in order to show his willingness to address the problems of the country, Collor formed a cabinet of unknown politicians and immediately launched his "Collor Plan."

The Collor Plan introduced a new currency and froze around 80 percent of the country's bank savings in order to drain liquidity (Bresser Pereira 1991, 18). But in spite of these extreme measures, government control of inflation proved elusive. Unable to produce a sustained decline in the consumer price index, the plan moved on to more orthodox policies in

May, giving way to the "Collor II" plan in January of 1991. Still lacking visible success, the minister of the economy resigned five months later. Chapter 5 will show to what extent the failure of Collor's economic policy bred popular dissatisfaction and weakened the position of the president in the following months.

While the government struggled to control inflation, the first signs of rent-seeking behavior began to surface. Scandals involving the Collor administration (although not the president personally) began to emerge in June of 1990 – just three months after the inauguration – when a decree allowed the Ministry of Infrastructure to hire contractors for a large highway maintenance project without public auction. Over the next two years, the administration suffered media scandals at a rate of one every two months. The accusations progressively involved high-ranking officials, members of the cabinet, some of the president's friends, the first lady – and finally Collor himself.

On May 13, 1992, the president's younger brother, Pedro, accused Collor's campaign manager, Paulo César (P. C.) Farias, of funneling corruption money into ghost offshore companies. Two weeks later, Pedro told the news magazine *Veja* that Farias managed a vast corruption network for the president (Collor de Mello 1993). Fernando Collor denied the accusations, and the police started to investigate Farias's business. In early June, sensing political opportunity, Congress created a bicameral committee to examine the accusations. With just 8 percent of the seats in the Chamber of Deputies and less than 4 percent of the seats in the Senate, Collor's party was unable to control the investigative process. Soon the committee discovered that Farias had routed six and a half million dollars into Collor's (and his cronies') bank accounts. In August, as public pressure against the administration mounted, the cabinet issued a public statement virtually withdrawing its support for the president.

By the end of August, the congressional committee had finished its report. Hundreds of thousands of demonstrators in São Paulo, Rio de Janeiro, Brasília, and other major cities marched calling for the resignation of the president. As mobilization escalated, various civic leaders formally requested Collor's impeachment. On September 29, the Chamber of Deputies approved – by a vote of 441–38 – the impeachment by the Senate and suspended Collor from office for a period of six months (Lins da Silva 1993b, 126). Three months later, the Senate voted 73–8 to oust Collor and authorized his prosecution on twenty-two charges of corruption. The president, anticipating the decision, presented his resignation.

Why was a president backed by thirty-five million votes so easily impeached? Many analysts of Brazilian politics were puzzled at the time, but their explanations mostly focused on the subtleties and nuances of the case. After holding several interviews with Brazilian politicians in the critical months of 1992, Flynn (1993) concluded that the Brazilian crisis was the result of three factors: unfortunate institutional arrangements, an electorate responsive to populism, and the explosive mixture of betrayal and inefficiency of the Collor administration. The Brazilian presidential constitution had allowed Collor's "imperial" style of government, while the electoral system had weakened political parties and campaign laws had failed to prevent corruption. The mostly young, mostly poor, and mostly illiterate Brazilian electorate – deeply disenchanted with politics and traditional politicians – had succumbed to Collor's anti-establishment rhetoric. But the Collor administration had been unable to govern because the PRN had never surpassed a meager 10 percent of the seats in the lower chamber, and Collor had been unable to forge a broad legislative coalition. He had therefore turned to *medidas provisórias* (temporary decrees) to implement public policies, but he had been unable to stop inflation, implement a broad privatization plan, or deliver the modernizing program he had promised. When charges of corruption surfaced, Collor was simply doomed.

A year later, Kurt Weyland (1993) argued that the very factors that had helped Collor become president were the ones that had ultimately sealed his fate. Collor had come to power as an anti-establishment politician with no commitment to any major political structure. Once in power, he had built an isolated command in order to preserve his autonomy vis-à-vis traditional interest groups and to centralize power in his personal office instead of building a stable, but costly, legislative coalition.

Weyland claimed that two consequences followed from this strategy. First, Collor and his team carved an exclusive niche for corruption. Political isolation made traditional lobbying channels ineffective. In order to influence policy making, corporations and interest groups were now forced to deal with Collor's personal operatives, headed by P. C. Farias. Second, isolation prevented the formation of a dominant center-right party, or even the emergence of a solid legislative coalition beyond the uncertain support of the Party of the Liberal Front (PFL). This failure deprived Collor of a strong political structure able to contain the collapse of his government once the scandal was triggered.

The effects of political isolation were joined with a changing political culture at the mass level. In contrast to previous decades, Brazilians had come to reject the idea that the president could be above the law. With the 1992 municipal elections approaching (and more than 15 percent of the deputies running for mayor), massive popular demonstrations against Collor convinced most legislators that the president should be removed from power (Weyland 1993, 20–25).

Venezuela, 1993

The "Collorgate" affair served as a model for the removal of Venezuelan President Carlos Andrés Pérez a few months later. But Pérez's personal trajectory and the institutional foundations of his administration differed substantially from the factors identified as the sources of the crisis in Collor's Brazil. Pérez won his second term in 1988 with a clear majority (53 percent of the vote). In contrast to Collor, he was the most seasoned leader of the largest party in the country, Democratic Action (Acción Democrática, AD). He had already been president of Venezuela in the 1970s, an age of prosperity, and was a mythical figure throughout Latin America when he was elected for the second time.

During Pérez's first term in office (1974–79), the oil boom had boosted living conditions in Venezuela and his administration had embraced "national-popular" policies, nationalizing the production of iron and oil, expanding the public sector, and denouncing multinational corporations and international financial institutions. Pérez's program for his second term, however, was radically different. The new administration inherited a critical situation from the Jaime Lusinchi government (1984–89), one that combined trade deficits, generalized price controls, scarcity of basic products, and unpaid international obligations.

Immediately after taking office in February of 1989, Pérez announced an economic reform package known as the Great Turnaround (El Gran Viraje). The program initially focused on price and interest rate liberalization and triggered an abrupt rise in inflation, from 7 percent in December of 1988 to 23 percent in March of 1989 (Corrales 2002a, 47). As a result, the presidential "honeymoon" soon ended: on February 27, 1989, riots against increases in public transportation fares and a scarcity of basic foodstuffs erupted in the city of Caracas and spread throughout the country. The ensuing action of the security forces caused more than 300 deaths (Kornblith 1998, Chapter 1; López Maya 1999; López Maya 2005, Chapter 3). The *Caracazo* and the human rights violations commited during those days left a deep wound in the Venezuelan political system. In May, the Venezuelan Labor Federation

(Confederación de Trabajadores de Venezuela, CTV), historically aligned with the ruling AD, launched its first general strike against a democractic president (Murillo 2001, Chapter 4). Protests and rioting against government policies continued throughout the term, initiating a protest cycle that would last into the 1990s, even after Pérez left office in 1993 (López Maya, Smilde, and Stephany 2002).

As in the case of Brazil, the administration's credibility and its capacity to control the economy were progessively compromised by media exposés. Scandals involving the administration began in April of 1990, when the governor of the state of Bolívar complained that the Ministry of Transportation charged a 10 percent "fee" on any project favoring his state. The minister resigned three months later, accused of demanding kickbacks from a French supplier of airport radar equipment. In the meantime, the director of the Office of Information (and spokesman for the president) was questioned for harassing adversarial journalists and allocating public advertisement to friendly media outlets. In June, an *Adeco* (member of the ruling AD) deputy charged the head of a public corporation with corruption in connivance with the ministers of health and agriculture. Scandals would eventually approach Pérez's inner circle in 1991, as his friend and future wife Cecilia Matos was accused of influence peddling and later implicated in a scandal involving military officers and foreign firms in the allocation of phony military contracts.

The golden days of the Punto Fijo regime, when corruption was hidden by a veil of prosperity, were gone. In August of 1990 some twenty-five celebrities, headed by the laureate writer and former minister (during the Medina Angarita dictatorship) Arturo Uslar Pietri, came together to demand deep transformations in the electoral system, political parties, government acquisitions procedures, and the judiciary. The press began to refer to this group as the *Notables*. Eventually, the president and opposition leaders agreed to sign a "Pact for Reform" with the *Notables* in a solemn ceremony that was soon to be forgotten.

Political malaise obscured the fact that 1991 was a year of economic recovery. The economy grew over 9 percent, inflation fell from 81 percent in 1989 to 31 percent, and privatization revenues allowed a government surplus of 1.3 percent of the gross domestic product (Naím 1993, Chapter 5). "President Pérez was truly euphoric," recalled his minister of planning, Miguel Rodríguez.[2] But dark clouds were rising on the political horizon.

[2] Interview with the author, July 28, 1998.

The *Notables* complained that the Pact for Reform had been ignored despite the "increasing moral and material decay of the country." The *Perecistas*, followers of Carlos A. Pérez within the ruling party, lost the internal elections of Democratic Action in September. The so-called orthodox faction, which opposed the administration's policies, retained control of the party's directorate (the powerful National Executive Committee, CEN). On October 7, two days after the election of the new CEN, AD's president, Humberto Celli, publicly demanded – the first sign of the battle to come – the resignation of the cabinet members in charge of the economy.

This was just the beginning. On February 4, 1992, a group of young army officers led by paratrooper Hugo Chávez Frías attempted a coup d'etat. After the situation was controlled, former president (and respected founder of the Copei Party) Rafael Caldera gave a speech in Congress condemning the military action but blaming Pérez for his unpopular policies. In the absence of a clear sign of rejection on the part of political elites, a second coup attempt was carried out by navy and air force officers in November of that year. The coup failed again, but the Pérez administration was now under siege. The *Notables* openly campaigned in favor of the resignation of the president, and although Pérez's AD controlled 48 percent of the seats in the lower chamber and in the Senate, partisan support for the president began to vanish as political leaders explored alternative ways to force an "institutional" exit of the chief executive (Rey 1993, 101–112; Rodríguez-Valdés 1993). In July, as part of a legislative debate on constitutional reform, the Chamber of Deputies contemplated the possibility of holding a recall election in order to shorten the presidential term. The topic moved to the Senate in late August, but the debate on constitutional reform was stalled after the second coup attempt (Kornblith 1998, 89–97).

In November of 1992, nineteen days before the coup attempt, the press began to publish stories about the unknown destiny of more than seventeen million dollars earmarked as "secret homeland security funds" for the Ministry of the Interior. According to the reports, the money (250 million bolívares) had been converted to dollars using the official Preferential Exchange Regime (*Régimen de Cambio Diferencial*, Recadi) and routed from Interior to the president's office. The Office of the President refused to provide any information on the issue, arguing that national security reasons prevented the disclosure, but the oversight committee (Comisión de Contraloría) of the Chamber of Deputies created a special subcommittee to investigate the trajectory of the funds (Chitty La Roche 1993). As the scandal grew, the prosecutor general (*Fiscal General*) asked the Supreme

Court to evaluate the merits of the case in order to prosecute the president. On May 20, the Court ruled that the case merited further investigation, giving anxious politicians the excuse they needed to act. The following day, the Senate unanimously suspended Pérez from office on a temporary basis and authorized the judiciary to prosecute the president. In late August, after President Pérez had been on "temporary leave" for three months, a joint session of Congress declared his leave "permanent," removing Pérez from office and appointing Ramón J. Velásquez to serve out the rest of the term (Kada 2003a, 126–127).

Observers trying to make sense of the Venezuelan crisis at the time focused on the collapse of the "petro-state" and the resulting decline in living standards during the 1980s as the underlying forces driving the dissolution of the system of elite conciliation that had been in place since 1958. For them, the ousting of Carlos Andrés Pérez was an indication – confirmed by later events – that the Punto Fijo regime was crumbling.[3] Shortly after the events, Juan Carlos Rey argued that the impeachment had resulted from a deeper "legitimacy crisis of the social and political order" (Rey 1993, 72; see also Crisp, Levine, and Rey 1995). In Rey's view, the decline of the Venezuelan economy had led voters to support Pérez in the 1988 election because he represented the good old times of prosperity. But the president had "betrayed" them by unilaterally imposing an economic adjustment program. The political parties (AD in particular) had failed not only to mobilize mass support for the president's program, but also to provide a viable alternative, "abdicating" their leadership roles. Military rebels had attempted to fill this vacuum in February and November of 1992, until corruption charges gave Congress an excuse to oust Pérez from office.

One year later, Michael Coppedge (1994a) presented a similar picture of economic decline, presidential isolation, and institutional failure. For Coppedge, the ousting of Pérez indicated the erosion of the Venezuelan governability formula. Since the 1960s, the regime had been structured as a *partyarchy*, a model that assigned a central role to the AD and Copei establishment and that operated through inclusive patterns of representation, strong party discipline, consensus policy making, and solid relationships between parties and interest groups (Coppedge 1994b). By the 1980s,

---

[3] The pact of Punto Fijo established the ground rules for the nascent Venezuelan democracy in 1958 (including power-sharing agreements that lasted until the late 1960s). On the pact, see Karl (1987). For a discussion of the rise and decline of the Venezuelan petro-state, see Karl (1997).

the House of Representatives voted 111–43 to acquit Samper of the charges. The possibility of an impeachment had been foreclosed. Although the debate around this issue would haunt the administration over the next two years (in July, the United States cancelled Samper's visa, and Colombia was "decertified" during 1996 and 1997), President Samper was able to complete his term in office.

Shortly after the congressional decision to acquit Samper was made, Juan Manuel López Caballero (1997) interpreted the crisis as the product of a deep confrontation between two social coalitions, one concerned with social justice and the other pushing for neoliberal reforms. The first group, aligned with the *Samperismo*, represented the "real" country. The second group was led by well-educated politicians, often trained in foreign universities, who defended neoliberal policies, disdained traditional parties as clientelistic and corrupt, and understood politics purely as a matter of spin control. According to López Caballero, the latter represented a neoliberally minded upper middle class, which sought to create a "New Colombia" at any cost. They had supported César Gaviria's economic policy and the constitutional reform of 1991, and they saw Samper as an obstacle to the consolidation of this transformation. Backed by the mainstream press and by the U.S. intelligence community, this group had used the campaign finance scandal to promote an impeachment, but the plan had failed owing to the lack of proof of the president's involvement.

John Dugas has correctly pointed out that much of "López Caballero's conspiracy theory lacks substance" (Dugas 2001, 168). But this interpretation is particularly important because it closely reflects the Samper administration's version of the events. To the extent that many Colombians perceived Ernesto Samper as a young Liberal president threatened by powerful elites and the U.S. government, they were less inclined to interpret the campaign finance scandal as a violation of the public trust and more willing to see it as a mere excuse invoked by his enemies to remove the president from office. In the absence of a strong public mobilization against the president, the Liberal Party ultimately closed ranks in support of Samper, and the Conservative opposition divided on the issue of impeachment.

Ecuador, 1997

A few weeks after Ernesto Samper was acquitted by the Colombian Congress, a new president was elected south of the border in Ecuador. In July of 1996, Abdalá Bucaram, leader of the Roldosista Party (Partido

Roldosista Ecuatoriano, PRE), won the runoff presidential election with 54.5 percent of the vote.[4] A few weeks earlier, the Social Christian candidate, Jaime Nebot (of the Partido Social Cristiano, PSC), had narrowly defeated Bucaram in the first round – with 27 percent of the vote against Bucaram's 25 percent. The PRE candidate reversed his luck thanks to a relentless campaigning style that combined entertainment (Bucaram sang and danced for his followers), vitriolic attacks against the "oligarchy" (the favorite target of Roldosista rhetoric), and the promise to achieve the presidency "in just one shot" (de la Torre 1996).[5]

As soon as he took office in August of 1996, Bucaram transferred his frantic campaigning style to the administration. He traveled between the capital city of Quito and his home town of Guayaquil, dispatching official businesses from the Carondelet palace as well as from his private home, and unexpectedly convening cabinet meetings in the towns he was visiting. He switched back and forth between the dignified attitude of a statesman and the flamboyant posture of a media entertainer. And for several weeks he played with the ambiguity of being both a proponent of neoliberal reform and a champion of popular causes.

Initially the strategy paid off, as the administration set the agenda for the press and constantly disoriented the opposition. But over the following six months, two problems became visible. First, in spite of its weak legislative contingent (the PRE held only 23 percent of the seats in the unicameral Congress), the administration showed a tendency to antagonize opposition politicians rather than to negotiate with them. This problem was compounded by increasing accusations of misbehavior (corruption, abuse of power, and just political rudeness) that compromised the public image of the president, his family, and key officials. Second, the administration delayed the announcement of its economic policy; by the time the plan was laid out, approval rates were low and it was too late to mobilize support for the program. This weakness encouraged the protests of trade unions in the public sector and of the indigenous movement that sought to veto Bucaram's "convertibility" program.

Beginning in the early days of the administration, the mainstream press complained about the president's behavior. Bucaram's personal style

---

[4] "Roldosista" refers to the followers of former President Jaime Roldós Aguilera (Bucaram's brother-in-law), who died in a plane crash in 1981.

[5] The campaign motto ("De un solo toque") was a soccer metaphor implying that the candidate would score a goal with just one shot. On the campaign, see de la Torre (1996) and Freidemberg (2003, Chapter 9).

was perceived by the Quito elite as too flamboyant, even rude – maybe appropriate for the coast but not for the capital. The Quito press had reservations about the new president from the outset and supported the administration only when major issues, like peace talks between Bucaram and Peruvian President Alberto Fujimori, were at stake. After mid-November, the press in Guayaquil – the PRE's stronghold – also began to criticize the government.

Criticism of the administration focused on three different themes. The first one was the "undignified" behavior of the chief executive. For instance, the president would shave his mustache on television in exchange for charity contributions, call former president Rodrigo Borja a "donkey," and mock his adversaries and critics. The Roldosistas still contend that much of that criticism was nothing but an elitist reaction against a president who felt quite comfortable among, and acting like, the Ecuadorian masses. A second theme was the administration's political stubbornness. Early in the term, Bucaram twisted some arms in Congress to obtain legislative approval for his unpopular nominee for comptroller general (see Chapter 6). Later on, he made a point of supporting ministers who were involved in scandals and were being investigated by the legislature – the minister of education, charged with plagiarizing her doctoral dissertation, and the minister of energy, accused of violent outbursts and of harassing union members. Last but not least, corruption became a major issue after Bucaram's third month in office. Public officials were said to collect a "party tax" from business people, and the customs service was depicted as highly corrupt. Even though investigative journalists had difficulties getting stories on the record – the sources were afraid to confront the government – the administration suffered, on average, a new scandal every two weeks. For the most part, Bucaram dismissed the accusations as upper-class hypocrisy and assumed that the scandals would not hurt his popularity.[6]

On the policy front, the administration was accused of producing a lot of controversy with few tangible results. Bucaram made several controversial proposals early in his term – the distribution of subsidized milk under the brand "Abdalact," the death penalty for anyone convicted of rape, and the creation of an "Ethnicity Ministry" against the will of the indigenous movement, among others. At the same time, however, he made an explicit effort to show an orthodox profile in terms of economic policy. Facing an economy in shambles and a country burdened by foreign debt (an estimated

---

[6] Interview with José Hernández, editor of *El Comercio*, December 1999.

45 percent of the budget was commited to servicing the debt in 1997), the administration insisted on pegging the Ecuadorian sucre to the U.S. dollar – a strategy modeled after the Argentine "convertibility" program of 1991. Indications of this new policy were clear from the outset, as Bucaram hired the former Argentine minister of the economy Domingo Cavallo. The blueprint of the program, however, was delayed for several months and only presented to the public on December 1, 1996, when presidential approval was already in decline (support was around 40 percent in Guayaquil and 20 percent in Quito) and opposition forces had prepared for the battle to come.

In response to the economic measures, which included an increase in the costs of transportation and natural gas, some demonstrators began to protest in early January. The Patriotic Front (Frente Patriótico), an alliance of trade unions and social movements, called a general strike for February 5, 1997. In the meantime, well-known politicians and former presidents like Rodrigo Borja and Osvaldo Hurtado began to call for the resignation of the president (Carrión 1997, 139). This climate of revolt significantly eroded the public standing of the president – survey data collected by *Informe Confidencial* suggest a fall of some 20 percentage points in both Quito and Guayaquil. With an increasing number of civic organizations announcing that they would join the strike, U.S. Ambassador Leslie Alexander denounced "rampant corruption" in the customs service on January 29, 1997. The declaration was read by many as a tacit support for the antigovernment movement.

Up to that point, the story of an unpopular president confronting mass protests was hardly a reason for headlines in Ecuador. The demonstrations of February 5, however, took both the government and the opposition by surprise. The streets of Quito – and, to a lesser extent, other cities in the country – displayed a colorful coalition of upper-middle-class protesters upset with Bucaram's style, indigenous demonstrators led by the Conaie (Confederation of Indigenous Nationalities of Ecuador), and trade unionists opposing the neoliberal reforms. Their only point of agreement was their contempt for the Bucaram administration.

To my knowledge, the mythical figure of two million protesters taking to the streets on February 5 and 6 has never been verified. But it is true that the massive attendance at the rally created both a challenge and an opportunity for Bucaram's adversaries in Congress. The protest leaders issued a "mandate" for Congress to remove the president from office. After some negotiations, the legislature called for an urgent session the following day. In a turbulent meeting, the opposition voted to declare Bucaram "mentally incapacitated" – a way of avoiding the supermajority required for a

27

normal impeachment procedure – and to appoint Speaker Fabián Alarcón as interim president. The Roldosistas, who controlled only a minority of the seats, found themselves unable to block the vote. In the confusing hours that followed, Bucaram rejected the decision as a coup, while Vice President Rosalía Arteaga claimed that she was the only legal successor in case of his removal. After the mediation of top military officers, Arteaga agreed to remain in power for two days and then resign to allow for the congressional appointment of Alarcón as interim president. Defeated, Bucaram fled to Panama.

The initial interpretations of the 1997 Ecuadorian crisis were framed in terms of the populist tradition of the country. Local scholars argued that Bucaram's populist style laid the groundwork for the political crisis in at least three ways. First, the new president was isolated from traditional elites. The Roldosista candidate entered the Carondelet Palace with a "vulgar" political style that terrorized Quito society (de la Torre 1996, 1997). To the extent that he had elite support, it came from an emergent coastal bourgeoisie that lacked social recognition among the aristocratic *patricios* and was viewed with suspicion by the "old wealth" (de la Torre 1996; Paredes 1997). Second, mass support for Bucaram proved to be volatile. Although he had prevailed with a majority of the vote in the 1996 runoff election, a significant share of those votes had come from middle- and lower-class sectors that turned out to vote *against* his elitist contender, Jaime Nebot (de la Torre 1996, 58–59, 72; Pachano 1997). This pattern of "negative" support was obscured by the majority-runoff electoral system that created an illusion of majoritarian support for Bucaram in the second round (Pachano 1997). Third, the isolation from elites and masses was compounded by a flamboyant and nepotistic style of government that alienated the middle class. According to Paz Ballivián and Cevallos, Bucaram's style overtly exposed the shameful aspects of Ecuadorian politics to a society that had become increasingly moralistic since the 1960s (Paz Ballivián and Cevallos 2001, 103–132).

In this view, the PRE's isolation from traditional elites, the masses, and the middle class ultimately led to the administration's fall. Despite Bucaram's neoliberal agenda, the *patricios* feared that the privatization program would advance only the interests of a new elite – the coastal parvenus represented by prosperous families of Lebanese origin (Paredes 1997; Pachano 1997). For most voters, on the other hand, the economic policy simply clashed with the populist promises of the campaign. The reduction of subsidies threatened to erode real income in the short run and alienated much popular support (Luna Tamayo 1997; Acosta 1997). In this context, the mobilization of early February emerged as a unique opportunity to terminate the discredited government. Elites and masses supported the demise of the administration, and both cheered as their legislators declared the president insane.

Abdalá Bucaram would not return to Ecuador for another eight years, and even then he would be allowed to stay in the country for less than a month. By then, the removal of elected presidents had become a chronic disease of Ecuadorian politics. The president elected in 1998, Jamil Mahuad, was ousted in early 2000 by the combined action of a military revolt led by Col. Lucio Gutiérrez and a mass mobilization organized by the indigenous movement. Lucio Gutiérrez in turn won the 2002 presidential election, only to confront protests against his unconstitutional dismissal of the Supreme Court – which allowed Bucaram's short-lived return to the country – in April of 2005. Challenged by popular mobilizations and a congressional action to remove him from office, Gutiérrez abandoned the country in late April (Pallares 2006). I will discuss the events that took place between 1998 and 2005 more systematically in Chapter 7. During that period, the wave of impeachments shifted toward the southern cone.

Paraguay, 1999

The Paraguayan crises of March 1999, September 2001, and December 2002 cannot be discussed without reference to the atomization of the Colorado Party (formally, the National Republican Association, ANR) that followed the fall of dictator Alfredo Stroessner in 1989. Gen. Stroessner took over in 1954 and ruled Paraguay for thirty-four years with the support of the ANR and the army. By the late 1980s, the question of succession was already in the air, and the attempt of the loyalist faction (the "Militantes") to gain control of the party and to place Stroessner's son in control of the armed forces ultimately ignited a military coup that triggered the transition to democracy in 1989. After displacing the dictator, Gen. Andrés Rodríguez charged a few politicians with corruption (Nickson 1997, 31–32), but Stroessner went into exile and his Militantes regrouped to support Luis María Argaña, a traditional Colorado politician and former chief justice of the Supreme Court.

Unable to seek reelection, Gen. Rodríguez left the country in 1993. Businessman Juan Carlos Wasmosy became the new Colorado president (1993–98), and Gen. Lino Oviedo, a close collaborator of Rodrígez in the

29

cavalry, became the strongman of the regime. The relations between Lino Oviedo and President Wasmosy were friendly at first, but increasing tensions between them led to a clash in April of 1996, when Wasmosy ordered Oviedo's retirement. The general initially resisted the decision, triggering a military crisis that for the first time endangered the Paraguayan transition to democracy. The Argañistas observed the showdown in silence and won the internal election for party officials a few days later, when an infuriated Oviedo ordered his followers to vote for Argaña's faction (Ayala Bogarín and Costa 1996, 121–122; interview with Angel Seifart, June 2002).

Removed from military command, Lino Oviedo devoted his energy to Colorado politics. In the following months, while his lawyers maneuvered to block a trial for military rebellion, the general organized his political machine. He campaigned to win the Colorado nomination and chose Raúl Cubas Grau, a businessman with little political experience, as his running mate for the presidential primary in September of 1997. Afraid of Oviedo's popularity among the ANR rank-and-file, President Wasmosy convened a military court to charge the general with sedition. Oviedo won the primary against Luis M. Argaña only to be sentenced to ten years in prison; he was arrested few weeks before the presidential race.

Since General Oviedo, now the official Colorado candidate, was barred from running, legal provisions mandated that his vice president, Raúl Cubas Grau, become the new presidential candidate and that Argaña, the runner-up in the primary, be his running mate. Oviedo's arrest thus united the two Colorado factions on the same ticket. In this overall climate of tension and legal chicanery, Cubas toured the country promising to pardon Oviedo were he elected. As insurance against this peril, five weeks after the May election the lame duck Congress passed a law restricting the president's pardon authority to convicts who had completed at least half of their prison terms.

The odd Cubas–Argaña ticket won the 1998 election with 55 percent of the vote (Turner 1999). Although the Colorado Party won 56 percent of the seats in the lower chamber and 53 percent of the Senate, the president's faction did not control a majority in Congress. With the exit of Wasmosy, the competition for power within the party now centered on the dispute between the Oviedo–Cubas faction (named the National Union of Ethical Colorados, Unace), controlling 34 percent of the seats in the lower chamber, and Argaña's Movement for Colorado Reconciliation (MRC), in control of the vice presidency and 19 percent of the seats.

Immediately after taking office in August of 1998, the president moved to free Gen. Oviedo by decree. Legally unable to *pardon* the general, Cubas *commuted* his prison term to a shorter sentence, allowing his immediate release and arousing the anger of the opposition parties and the Argañistas in Congress. After a seven-hour session, on August 20 Congress approved a resolution condemning Cubas's decision and requesting the Supreme Court to assess its constitutionality. The Court ruled against Cubas's decree and urged the president to recapture Oviedo. In the meantime, however, a military court had overturned the original sentence, allowing Cubas to claim that it was legally "impossible" for him to execute the Supreme Court's order.

Following a period of impasse, in January of 1999 Chief Justice Wildo Rienzi gave the executive seventy-two hours to arrest Oviedo, stating that the president could be impeached if he refused to comply with the Court's order. Rumors that Vice President Argaña was conspiring with the congressional opposition (the Liberals and the Partido Encuentro Nacional) to impeach Cubas and become the new head of the government were followed by rumors that Cubas and Oviedo were plotting a self-coup against Congress. Finally, in early March the Constitutional Affairs Committee of the Chamber of Deputies approved the initiation of impeachment proceedings by a vote of seven to one. The president was charged with violating the Supreme Court ruling in the Oviedo case.

In the morning of March 23, a squad of men dressed in military uniforms intercepted the vice president's car and shot Argaña and his bodyguard. Paraguayans were shocked. Argaña, the leader of the rebel Colorado faction, would have taken office had the impeachment been successful. In a public statement, the board of the Colorado Party openly accused the president "and the political movement behind him" of the crime. The following day, the Chamber of Deputies held a rushed early-morning session in which the impeachment of the president was unexpectedly authorized by a vote of 49–24 (with seven absent). The trial then moved to the Senate.

Outraged by Argaña's assassination, on the afternoon of March 23 the people began to take to the streets to demand the resignation of the president. A peasant demonstration demanding that public banks forgive agricultural debts evolved into a march for impeachment (Abente Brun 1999). After two days of tensions between pro- and antigovernment demonstrators, both of whom sought to occupy the public square in front of the Congress building, on March 26 the protests against the president turned deadly. Seven demonstrators were killed and some seven hundred were wounded when paramilitary snipers shot at the mob from a nearby building (Paredes 2001b, 156). Fearing an escalation of the conflict, members of the government, the opposition, the church, and foreign diplomats negotiated an "honorable solution" to the crisis. Anticipating a defeat in the Senate trial, President Cubas resigned two days later and sought refuge at the Brazilian embassy. Luis González Macchi, the speaker of the Senate and a member of the Argañista faction, took office and formed a cabinet of "national unity" with members of the Colorado Party (ANR), the Liberal Party (Partido Liberal Radical Auténtico, PLRA), and the National Encounter Party (Partido Encuentro Nacional, PEN). In the meantime, Gen. Oviedo abandoned the country.

In an early analysis of the events, Diego Abente Brun (1999), a political scientist and later a minister in the González Macchi administration, interpreted the crisis of March as the culmination of the Paraguayan transition to democracy. According to Abente, the politics of the transition since 1989 had remained under the control of the Colorado elite and had been marked by increasing factionalism within the party. Oviedo's popularity had grown because Paraguayan voters were tired of traditional politicians and poor economic performance, but it had quickly faded in the face of Argaña's assassination. A "strong citizenry," formerly unknown in Paraguayan politics, had unexpectedly taken to the streets to demand the impeachment of the president, and the mass media had provided live coverage of the events, igniting public outrage and encouraging mobilization. In this view, the events of March had shown that public opinion was becoming an important force in Paraguay, and that political outcomes would no longer be just the product of factional disputes.

Paraguay, 2002

In spite of the hopes created by the "Paraguayan March" (as the tragic events of 1999 eventually became known), the government of national unity was nothing but a short-lived experiment in consensus democracy (Pangrazio 2000, 324–325). The alliance formed by Colorados, Liberals, and *Encuentristas*, which initially comprised about two-thirds of the seats in the lower chamber, had few incentives to remain united. Although the Supreme Court confirmed González Macchi in office until the end of the Cubas term in 2003, the president's lack of electoral legitimacy and the effects of a five-year-long economic recession eroded his favorability ratings from 68 percent in April of 1999 to 33 percent one year later (data from Francisco Capli).

The erosion of the coalition was accelerated by a sequence of media exposés beginning in November of 1999. Among them was the accusation, in March of 2001, that the armored car used by the president had been stolen in Brazil and purchased by the Paraguayan government with the approval of the finance minister. Two months later, the executive was accused of transferring sixteen million dollars from the central bank to a private account in New York.

With a national vice presidential election scheduled for August of 2000, the coalition soon faced what David Altman has dubbed the "tyranny of the electoral calendar" (Altman 2000). The PLRA demanded 40 percent of all positions in the public administration and the nomination of a Liberal as the coalition's vice presidential candidate. When González Macchi refused to meet the demands, the Liberals quickly withdrew from the coalition and nominated their own candidate in early 2000.

In contrast to the PLRA, the middle-class National Encounter Party (PEN) remained in the cabinet. The decision created some disappointment in the ranks, particularly when PEN leaders backed the Colorado candidate for the vice presidency. In September of 2000, a group of dissidents broke with the party and formed a new organization called País Solidario (Solidary Country). In the end, the PEN preserved seven seats in the lower chamber and its splinter only two.

The electoral climate and the scandals combined with unpopular policies to accelerate public unrest. Overwhelmed by the fiscal deficit, the administration proposed privatizing telecommunications, water and sewerage, and the national railroads. In March of 2000, thousands of peasants marched to Asunción and joined forces with trade union workers against the proposal. In late June, the national union federation (Central Nacional de Trabajadores, CNT) called for a national strike. In October, the CNT marched to demand additional measures against unemployment.

The administration's weakness became evident on May 18, 2000, when cavalry officers linked to Gen. Oviedo attempted a coup d'état. The rebels surrounded the Congress building and occupied military barracks, the police headquarters, and a few TV and radio stations. The navy and air force refused to join them, and eventually the officers surrendered. But according to one analyst, "it became clear that the citizens were unwilling to raise one finger to sustain González Macchi in power" (Paredes 2001a, 178).

The vice presidential election of August showed a major realignment in Paraguayan politics. Oviedista bosses openly supported the PLRA candidate, "shattering the belief that it was impossible for a Colorado to vote for a Liberal" (Paredes 2001a, 185), while the middle-class PEN backed the Colorado candidate. In the end, the oppositional strategy of the PLRA paid off, and the Liberal candidate, Julio C. Franco, won the election with a narrow margin of less than ten thousand votes. This electoral defeat further undermined an administration in which the president had been appointed by Congress and the opposition vice president had been popularly elected. Liberal and Oviedista legislators soon discussed the possibility of impeaching the president on charges of bad macroeconomic management, a threat that locked the Argañistas in a dilemma. Protecting González Macchi could compromise their chances in the 2003 presidential race and hand more votes to Gen. Oviedo – who, from his exile in Brazil, had ordered the registration of Unace as an independent party. But failure to do so could open the way to an impeachment. The removal of the president would mean a takeover by the Liberal vice president and a loss of patronage positions critical to secure electoral support in 2003.

Even though a demonstration organized by the PLRA in March of 2001 failed to mobilize mass support for impeachment, the party demanded the trial on the grounds of "manifest incapacity and poor performance in office" (Paredes 2001b, 175). In August of 2001, following new protests against privatizations, the Catholic Church organized a round of national "dialogue." As part of the negotiations, the parties agreed to bring the impeachment rumors to a congressional close. On September 6, 2001, the charges were brought to the Chamber of Deputies and rejected in a 38–38 vote. The PLRA, the Oviedistas, País Solidario, and two Encuentro Nacional dissidents supported the impeachment. The Argañistas and a majority of the PEN opposed the trial.

The truce was brief. After the the illegal arrest and torture of two left-wing leaders in early 2002, new protests unfolded and the opposition proposed impeaching González Macchi on charges of "state terrorism." In April, with the human rights scandal still fresh, the media published new stories of corruption in the privatization process. Thousands of peasants marched to Asunción to protest against privatizations, and the CNT called a general strike. The Oviedista and Liberal legislators found a unique window of opportunity to bring the impeachment charges to the floor of the House. To prevent a crisis, on the afternoon of June 6 the Colorado legislators voted to suspend the sale of all public companies. President González

Macchi signed the bill immediately, averting an impeachment for the second time.

In October, Julio C. Franco resigned as vice president in order to run as a presidential candidate in the elections of April 2003. Although Congress was unable to agree on the appointment of a surrogate, Franco's resignation freed the dissident Colorados from the problem of voting a Liberal into office. Aware of this opportunity, the opposition tried to unseat the president for the third time. On December 5, while President González Macchi was attending an international meeting in Brazil, a Liberal deputy unexpectedly asked to bring the impeachment charges (this time based on the case of the sixteen million dollars, the stolen car, and the president's support for corrupt officials) to the floor of the House. The disoriented Argañistas found themselves unable to block the debate and unwilling to back the president in the midst of a presidential campaign. The impeachment was approved with fifty-two votes by the PLRA, Unace, the PEN, País Solidario, and some dissident Colorados against only eleven abstentions.

In mid-January, an electoral court banned the nomination of Gen. Oviedo for the April election, averting the possibility of a split in the Colorado electorate. Thus, when the Senate began the hearings in late January, President González Macchi ironically stated that the trial would be a "nice show." On February 11, after a ten-hour session, twenty-five senators voted in favor of removing the president from office, eighteen voted against, and one abstained. Unable to achieve a two-thirds majority, the trial failed. On April 27, the Colorado candidate, Nicanor Duarte, won the presidential race with 37 percent of the vote, and President González Macchi transferred power to his co-partisan four months later.

Fernando Collor's Specter

As the stories of Fernando Collor, Carlos Andrés Pérez, Ernesto Samper, Abdalá Bucaram, Raúl Cubas Grau, and Luis González Macchi document, a new specter is haunting Latin America – the specter of impeachment. These presidents pursued different policies, confronted different challenges, and embraced different leadership styles, but all of them faced the threat of being unseated by Congress – a novel experience in the Latin American presidential tradition.

Because of their focus on the historical dynamics of each country, case-specific interpretations provide limited insights into this regional trend. From a case-based perspective, the institutional setting explained the crisis in Brazil; the collapse of the petro-state was the source of the problem in Venezuela; the populist tradition was the underlying issue in Ecuador; the success of a reformist conspiracy was at stake in Colombia; and the atomization of the Colorado Party triggered repeated crises in Paraguay. These interpretations are in fact historically accurate, but they fail to explain why congressional action became a new standard procedure to oust presidents throughout the region.

A few commonalties shared by the cases shed light on this question. First and foremost, the use of congressional procedures to remove presidents from office indicated the unwillingness (or the incapacity) of the military to do the job. In some cases, as in Brazil and Colombia, civilian politicians refused to involve the military in the crisis. In others, as in Ecuador in 1997, the military refused to intervene except as mediators. In yet others, such as Venezuela in 1992 and Paraguay in 2000, the military attempted to take over but simply failed. In an international context that discouraged military intervention in politics, political elites were forced to find constitutional (or at least pseudo-constitutional) ways to solve their disputes. It is hard to overstate how much this factor has altered the dynamics of executive-legislative crises in recent years. The magnitude of this change will be documented in the following chapter.

The absence of military coups alone is not enough to explain why some presidents confronted the threat of impeachment and others did not – or why some presidents survived this threat while others were removed from office. The succinct case studies presented here suggest that a simple narrative of corruption and punishment usually does not suffice to account for an impeachment crisis. Beyond the merits of the legal case against the president, a complex configuration of social, partisan, and institutional forces has always determined the executive's fate.

First, there is the role of the press. In a context of increasing democratization in the 1990s, the mass media became more willing to unveil scandals about the president, the first family, and top public officials (Waisbord 2000). The exposés provided the ammunition that opposition legislators needed to initiate impeachment charges. Second, there is the president's ability to bring together a legislative coalition against impeachment. Presidents with the skills to build a strong legislative shield – Samper being the most visible example – were more likely to prevent the collapse of their administrations when scandals enveloped them (Hinojosa and Pérez-Liñán 2003). Last but not least, there is popular protest. Increasing freedom of expression and organization created the possibility of mass demonstrations against corruption and unpopular neoliberal reforms (Eckstein 2001; Smulovitz and Peruzzotti 2000; Zamosc 2006). Popular uprisings encouraged strategic politicians to act against the executive. Protest, however, was less effective when social movements failed to mobilize a broad social coalition (as in the case of Samper) or when they failed to coordinate their actions in a common front against the president (as in the case of González Macchi).

Table 2.1 compares the six historical configurations discussed in this chapter. In all the cases, scandals, public outrage, and legislative politics powerfully interacted to shape the dynamics of the crisis. The table suggests three conclusions. First, in the new historical context the military was not the main factor driving government instability. Second, presidents confronted an impeachment or declaration of incapacity not only because scandals offered a good reason – or excuse – for a congressional investigation, but also because the legislators lacked partisan incentives to protect the president. Third, even though scandals may have ignited popular outrage, in the end the magnitude of popular protests was the critical factor determining the sustainability of the administration in power. When popular protests unified multiple social sectors (peasants, the urban poor, the middle class) against the executive, the position of the government was virtually untenable. When protests were narrow or directed against specific policies rather than against the president, the legislature had less clout to remove the president from office.

Are those cases truly indicative of a new regional pattern? To what extent are the episodes discussed in this chapter representative of most Latin American presidents in the 1990s? Because the comparison deals only with presidents who confronted serious political crises, the conclusions of this comparative analysis could be misleading. For instance, many other presidents at the time may have confronted corruption scandals without facing a challenge to their power. These questions force us to consider the issue of selection bias in the previous comparative analysis.

"Selection bias" is the term used in comparative politics to refer to problems of causal inference created by the analysis of samples that contain episodes characterized by a single outcome – for instance, cases of impeachment.[7] The bias results from a research design that truncates the observed

---

[7] "Selection bias" is used with slightly different meanings in econometrics (e.g., in the discussion of Heckman selection models) and in the study of qualitative methods (Lustick 1996). For simplicity, I keep the discussion restricted to the standard problem of truncation in the dependent variable.

Table 2.1. *Impeachment crises in Latin America, 1992–2004*

Administration (Country, Year)	Military Intervention	Scandals	Legislative Support	Social Scope of Protests	Outcome
Collor de Mello (Brazil, 1992)	No	Yes	Small party	Broad	Impeachment (resigned)
Pérez (Venezuela, 1993)	Failed (1992)	Yes	Large party was distant	Broad	Impeachment (ousted)
Samper (Colombia, 1996)	No	Yes	Large party *and* coalition	Narrow	Avoided trial
Bucaram (Ecuador, 1997)	No	Yes	Small party	Broad	Declared mentally unfit
Cubas Grau (Paraguay, 1999)	No	Yes	Large party was divided	Broad	Impeachment (resigned)
González Macchi (Paraguay, 2002)	Failed (2000)	Yes	Large party was divided	Intermediate	Impeachment (survived)

distribution of the dependent variable, restricting the variance in the outcomes – for example, by ignoring instances of nonimpeachment (Collier and Mahoney 1996; Collier, Mahoney, and Seawright 2004; Geddes 2003). Two problems of causal inference can emerge from truncated samples of this sort. In statistical research, the most common problem is an underestimation of causal effects (for an illustration of this problem and its relevance for small-N designs, see Collier, Mahoney, and Seawright 2004). In historical comparative research, the most common problem is the opposite: analysts may assume that some causal factor plays a critical role simply because they fail to observe cases in which the same factor is present but the outcome of interest does not materialize (Geddes 2003, Chapter 3). In this situation, it is still possible to argue that a causal condition is *necessary* for the event to occur (if all episodes share this factor), but analysts are simply unable to assess whether the condition is causally sufficient (Dion 1998; Ragin 2000).

The perils of selection bias are attenuated in the current analysis by the actual range of variance observed in Table 2.1. Four presidents (Collor, Pérez, Cubas, and González Macchi) confronted an impeachment, but one (Samper) did not. (The case of Bucaram is ambiguous because while an impeachment did not take place, he faced a declaration of incapacity). On the other hand, four presidents were removed from office (Collor, Pérez, Cubas, and Bucaram), while two others (Samper and González Macchi) were not. Although the six cases represent instances of presidential crises, the outcomes of these crises varied from case to case.

Because presidential impeachment has resulted from the interaction of multiple factors, the following chapters will explore each of the component processes leading to the outcome of interest (Geddes 2003, Chapter 2). Chapters 3 through 6 will discuss how these explanatory variables (military intervention, media scandals, public outrage, and legislative support for the executive) evolved in Latin America during the post-1978 period, emphasizing the situation in the countries under study.

However, the analysis of a broader range of cases is necessary to test the hypotheses suggested by this comparative exercise. In particular, three types of presidents appear to be particularly relevant for this purpose: those who were ousted from power without an impeachment process, those who confronted a crisis but did not face an impeachment, and those who never confronted a presidential crisis. I will explore these ancillary cases in Chapter 7 and use them to identify the distinctive traits of the new pattern of political instability in Latin America.

3

Presidential Crises and the Decline of Military Intervention

What are the consequences of presidential crises for democratic stability? To what extent has the "third wave" of democratization reduced the risk of democratic breakdown and increased the likelihood of impeachments as a result of executive-legislative conflicts? This chapter places those questions in historical perspective by comparing fifty-eight presidential crises that took place in Latin America between 1950 and 2004.

In the first section of the chapter, I document the expansion of democracy and the related decline in military interventions that took place in Latin America after the late 1970s. Section two introduces the concept of presidential crisis – a situation in which one of the elected branches of government attempts to dissolve the other. In the following sections, I show that similar episodes of executive-legislative conflict have resulted in very different historical outcomes. I discuss presidential crises not only in terms of their consequences for the political regime (disruption, breakdown, or survival) but also in terms of their impact on checks and balances (whether one of the two branches asserts itself over the other). I map nine possible pathways from presidential crises and discuss historical instances of these ideal types.

The comparative analysis suggests that the incentives confronted by military officers in most Latin American countries changed significantly during the 1980s. As a result of those changes, the army withdrew from politics and civilian politicians found themselves unable to transform disputes over policy into broader disputes over the nature of the regime. Before the third wave of democratization, a vast majority of presidential crises had led to some form of military intervention; among the new democratic regimes, a vast majority did not. Only in this new context could presidential impeachment become the main mechanism regulating disputes between the executive and congress.

Democratization and the Decline of Military Intervention

The second half of the twentieth century was marked by a permanent struggle to build stable democratic institutions in Latin America. In the early 1950s, powerful presidents – whether populist leaders or neo-patrimonial rulers – dominated the politics of the region (Chehabi and Linz 1998; Lewis 2005). Although the executive branch was prevalent, those regimes typically allowed for an elected Congress, and executive-legislative confrontation was possible when opposition legislators dared to defy the president. Legislators alone were too weak to confront the executive, but they often recruited disgruntled military officers willing to lead an armed revolt. In the late 1950s, a brief "twilight of the tyrants" (Szulc 1959) was followed by a short wave of democratization: the number of democratic (or at least semidemocratic) regimes grew from five in 1955 to twelve by 1958. However, the fears ignited by the Cuban revolution (1959) and the conservative reaction that followed made this trend short-lived. In the 1960s and early 1970s, military officers displaced elected governments and took over in country after country. By 1977, only three nations (Colombia, Costa Rica, and Venezuela) could claim to be democratic.

Surprisingly, the trend was reversed in the late 1970s, when a new epidemic of democracy started in the Dominican Republic and Ecuador and spread to the rest of the region over the course of a decade. Following Huntington (1991), Hagopian and Mainwaring (2005) have described this surge as the "third wave" of democratization (the first one being the trend that affected a few Latin American countries in the early twentieth century, and the second one being the more extensive wave of the late 1950s). In the new democratic context of the 1980s and 1990s, presidents were regularly elected, legislatures were reopened, and the realities of executive-legislative conflict became part of day-to-day politics.

To illustrate the magnitude of this change, Figure 3.1 traces the number of democracies and semidemocracies in Latin America between 1950 and 2004. I have followed the classification of political regimes outlined by Mainwaring, Brinks, and Pérez-Liñán (2001; 2007), coding countries as democratic when four conditions were present: (1) the president

military rebellion (defined as any military action directed against the president or Congress) and by the percentage of successful coups (instances in which the military was able to force the exit of the president or the closure of the legislature).[2]

The return of military officers to the barracks in the 1980s is reflected in the decline in the number of insurrections. In the 1960s, 11 percent of all competitive regimes experienced a successful military coup, and 19 percent of them confronted some form of military rebellion. In the 1990s, the rates were 1 percent and 4 percent, respectively. For the historian concerned with the *long durée*, the last decade and a half may look like a brief flash of civilian stability in a long history of political turmoil. But for politicians operating in the 1990s, the new context represented a significant break with the past. How did this change affect the balance of power between the executive and legislative branches throughout the region? And more importantly, how did it alter the outcome of extreme interbranch confrontations?

Presidential Crises

In most presidential countries, executives and assemblies regularly confront each other on policy issues, bargain with each other, defy each other, and eventually agree on a common policy (or not). This is normal politics, and certainly not the focus of this book. I will focus on a particular type of situation labeled "presidential crisis" (Pérez Liñán 2003b). Presidential crises are episodes characterized by extreme levels of conflict and by the decision of one elected branch to dissolve the other in order to reshape its composition. This stance, which would be normal in a parliamentary system, unleashes the threat of constitutional breakdown in a presidential regime.

The operational definition of "presidential crisis" employed in this book includes any episode in which the chief executive threatens to dissolve Congress or supports a constitutional reform having that purpose, attempts a military coup against Congress, or "suspends" the term of the legislature (even if no decree proclaims its "dissolution") until the next election. It also

---

[2] Military interventions (particularly failed military coups) are not always easy to pinpoint. The events coded in Table 3.1 were identified using *The New York Times Index*, *Latin American Weekly Report*, and other historical sources (Fossum 1967; Needler 1966). I am indebted to Annabella España-Nájera and Scott Mainwaring for collecting and sharing important data on coups. Datasets and computer codes to generate the components of the table are available at ⟨http://www.pitt.edu/~asp27/Presidential/Impeachment.html⟩.

includes any situation in which congressional leaders announce a decision to impeach the president, to declare him or her incapacitated, or to force his or her resignation; in which at least one of the houses of Congress debates any of these alternatives; or in which Congress legitimizes a military or civilian uprising against the executive by accepting his "resignation" or by appointing a successor.[3]

Under this definition, some fifty-eight presidential crises took place in Latin America between 1950 and 2004. The identification of such crises can be a matter of debate, because information is often fragmentary and there is no single uncontested "historical record" (Lustick 1996). For the sake of consistency, I initially used *Keesing's Contemporary Archives* (1950–86) and *Keesing's Record of World Events* (1987–2004) to identify presidential crises in the nineteen countries under study. This information was supplemented by more than fifty articles and monographs. Short narratives were entered in a qualitative database, with the entries documenting the proximate causes of each crisis, the institutional context, the outcome, and the historical sources employed.[4] Table 3.2 lists those presidential crises, indicating the country, the year, and the nature of the political regime at the time of the event.

The table shows that strictly *democratic* rule is not a necessary condition for the occurrence of a presidential crisis. Crises may take place in any presidential regime in which the executive and the legislature are autonomous enough to display significant "separation of purpose" (Cox and McCubbins 2001). As the historical examples to be presented here will show, this situation has been common not only in contemporary presidential democracies but also in nineteenth-century competitive oligarchies (presidential regimes with civil liberties but limited participation) and in modern *democraduras* (regimes with separation of powers but restrictions on civil liberties).

Some of the episodes presented in Table 3.2 have already been covered in Chapter 2, and many others will be discussed in the pages that follow. It is important to note that the element of executive-legislative conflict was more visible in some crises than in others. The table includes a few episodes that arguably represent marginal instances of interbranch confrontation, like

---

[3] Note that this definition encompasses both situations in which constitutional mechanisms are activated and others in which nonconstitutional actions are unleashed. It is the willingness of one elected branch to reshape the composition of the other, not the outcome of the process, that defines a presidential crisis. This definition allows us to compare recent confrontations ending with impeachments to past crises leading to military coups.

[4] The qualitative database is available at ⟨http://www.pitt.edu/~asp27/Presidential/Impeachment.html⟩.

Table 3.2. *Presidential crises in Latin America, by type of regime, 1950–2004*

Competitive Regimes		Authoritarian Regimes
Democratic	Semidemocratic	
Argentina (1989)	Argentina (1962)	Brazil (1966)
Argentina (2001, twice)	Argentina (1976)	Brazil (1968)
Bolivia (1983)	Bolivia (1979)	Brazil (1977)
Bolivia (1985)	Brazil (1955, twice)	Guatemala (1957)
Bolivia (1990)	Colombia (1991)	Honduras (1954)
Bolivia (2003)	Colombia (1996)	Panama (1951)
Brazil (1954)	Ecuador (1963)	Panama (1955)
Brazil (1964)	Ecuador (1970)	Panama (1988)
Brazil (1992)	El Salvador (1987)	Paraguay (1954)
Chile (1954)	Guatemala (1993)	Paraguay (1959)
Chile (1973)	Guatemala (1994)	
Colombia (1977)	Honduras (1985)	
Dominican Republic (1994)	Nicaragua (1992)	
Ecuador (1961)	Panama (1968)	
Ecuador (1984)	Paraguay (1999)	
Ecuador (1987)	Paraguay (2001)	
Ecuador (1990)	Paraguay (2002)	
Ecuador (1997)	Peru (1991)	
Ecuador (2000)	Peru (1992)	
Ecuador (2004)	Peru (2000)	
Nicaragua (2004)		
Uruguay (1969)		
Uruguay (1971)		
Uruguay (1973)		
Venezuela (1993)		
Venezuela (1999)		
N 27	21	10

Source: Database on presidential crises, based on *Keesing's Contemporary Archives* (1950–86), *Keesing's Record of World Events* (1987–2000) (London: Longman), and country-specific sources.

the ousting of Presidents Fernando de la Rúa and Adolfo Rodríguez Saá in Argentina in 2001, or of Gonzalo Sánchez de Lozada in Bolivia in 2003 (see Mustapic 2005). I included those episodes in the analysis for the sake of consistency, but the element of executive-legislative conflict was peripheral to the turmoil that forced the exit of these presidents at the time.[5] I will return more systematically to this problem in Chapter 7.

---

[5] The degree of executive-legislative confrontation was also marginal in Colombia in 1977, in Bolivia in 1985, in Argentina in 1989, and in the Dominican Republic in 1994.

The Political Consequences of Presidential Crises

Presidential crises may lead to very different political outcomes depending on their effect on executive-legislative relations and their impact on the stability of the regime. Interbranch relations and regime stability constitute two related but analytically distinct levels of analysis. At the first level, one of the two branches may succeed in its attempt to dissolve the other. Thus, crises may lead to the removal of the president (via resignation, impeachment, or coup) or to the dissolution of Congress. It is also possible that no branch will succeed in this attempt (and thus that the elected president and legislators will coexist until the end of their terms) or that both branches will be dissolved by a military intervention, imposing a mutual defeat.

At a second level, a confrontation between the executive and the assembly often carries the potential to destabilize the presidential regime. A political crisis spills over onto the regime when political actors consider interbranch conflict as an indication of the weakness of the existing institutions, disregard the "rules of the game," and resort to praetorian politics. Under those circumstances, the military typically intervenes in the confrontation as the ultimate arbiter.

Once the crisis has spilled over onto the regime, two outcomes may follow: reequilibration or breakdown. Following Juan Linz, I employ the term "reequilibration" to denote "a political process that, after a crisis that has seriously threatened the continuity and stability of the basic political mechanisms, results in their continued existence" (Linz 1978, 87).[6] The term "breakdown" refers to the collapse of presidential regimes that, as discussed earlier, may or may not be fully democratic. Breakdowns in turn may have short-term or long-term consequences. In some cases (e.g., Argentina in 1962, Brazil in 1955, Ecuador in 2000), presidents or legislators supported a brief military disruption of the constitutional order and the reinstallation of the previous political formula shortly afterward. In others (e.g., Argentina in 1976, Brazil in 1964), the military intervened to replace the existing constitution with a lasting authoritarian arrangement.

---

[6] I use the term to refer to episodes of *early* reequilibration. "Early reequilibration" refers to the process by which breakdown is prevented without a major institutional disruption. By contrast, *late* reequilibration refers to situations in which an interruption of the existing regime occurs – as in the transition from the Fourth to the Fifth Republic in France – but where changes in the political order ultimately take place within the democratic framework. Linz (1978, 90) was aware of this distinction but never developed the idea.

These conditions create the nine alternative outcomes summarized in Figure 3.2 The figure provides a framework to classify the fifty-eight presidential crises introduced in the previous table. The episodes discussed in Chapter 2 basically fall into two categories: the removal of the president from office (Type VII) and political stabilization following a crisis (Type IX). The former category includes the removal of Presidents Guizado of Panama (1955), Collor of Brazil (1992), Pérez of Venezuela (1993), Bucaram of Ecuador (1997), and Cubas Grau of Paraguay (1999). It also captures cases in which Congress legalized the exit of an unpopular president, as happened in the resignations of Raúl Alfonsín (1989) and Fernando de la Rúa and Adolfo Rodríguez Saá (2001) in Argentina; Hernán Siles Zuazo (1985) and Gonzalo Sánchez de Lozada (2003) in Bolivia; and Alberto Fujimori in Peru (2000).[7] Notably, ten of the eleven cases of constitutional removal took place after 1978.

The category of stabilization with mutual survival (Type IX) includes the cases of President Ernesto Samper of Colombia and Luis González Macchi of Paraguay discussed in Chapter 2, plus nineteen other episodes that took place between 1950 and 2004. Against concerns with the "perils" of presidentialism, 36 percent of all crises (twenty-one of fifty-eight) did not lead to the ousting of any elected officials or to any form of regime breakdown. In the following sections, I discuss the nine ideal types presented in the figure and provide some historical illustrations of those outcomes. Based on this discussion, in the final section I will show how the consequences of presidential crises for democracy have changed over the last decade and a half.

Regime Disruptions and "Short-Term" Breakdowns

Presidential crises may disrupt the operation of the political regime if the constitution is suspended in order to resolve the stalemate. For example, a military rebellion supported by Congress may force the president to resign, allowing "normal politics" to resume afterward. Occasionally, this kind of military intervention may impose a suspension of the constitution for a longer interval. What I call a "short-term" breakdown is an authoritarian

---

[7] Fujimori resigned anticipating an impeachment, but executive-legislative conflict was less relevant in the other four cases. Siles Zuazo and Alfonsín negotiated with Congress an early exit from office, typical of what Mustapic (2005) has described as a "presidential" management of the crisis. In the Dominican Republic, Joaquín Balaguer (1994) also negotiated anticipated elections, but because of the time frame (two years), I have coded this case as an instance of stabilization.

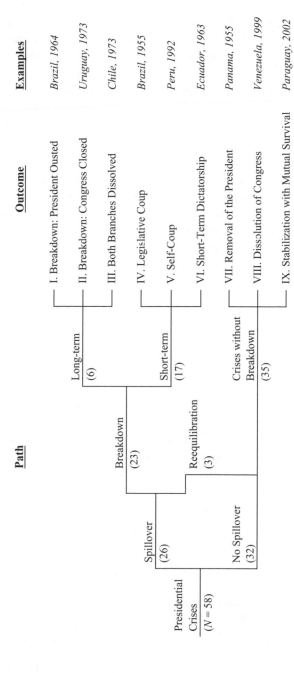

Figure 3.2 A typology of outcomes of presidential crises.

Path

Presidential
Crises
(N = 58)

Spillover
(26)

No Spillover
(32)

Breakdown
(23)

Reequilibration
(3)

Crises without
Breakdown
(35)

Long-term
(6)

Short-term
(17)

Outcome

I. Breakdown: President Ousted

II. Breakdown: Congress Closed

III. Both Branches Dissolved

IV. Legislative Coup

V. Self-Coup

VI. Short-Term Dictatorship

VII. Removal of the President

VIII. Dissolution of Congress

IX. Stabilization with Mutual Survival

Examples

Brazil, 1964

Uruguay, 1973

Chile, 1973

Brazil, 1955

Peru, 1992

Ecuador, 1963

Panama, 1955

Venezuela, 1999

Paraguay, 2002

49

interlude lasting up to three years. Although the three-year criterion is somewhat arbitrary – the duration of the authoritarian experience following a presidential crisis is a continuous rather than a discrete variable – this rule is intended to reflect the exceptional nature of the interim government (for a similar criterion, see Geddes 2003, 69–70). Short-term interventions (whether disruptions or temporary takeovers) are usually meant to "solve" a political crisis and to restore the nation's order (Stepan 1971, 63). For this reason, the military may not seek (and civilian politicians may not allow) the imposition of military rule except for a short transitional period.[8]

Short-term interventions may take three different forms, depending on the nature of civilian-military coalitions. The first one is what I call a "legislative coup," a joint action of the military and Congress to oust the president.[9] The second one corresponds to what is normally described as a "self-coup," an alliance between the executive and the army to dissolve Congress. The third pattern is one of short-term military takeover in which both the president and the legislators are ousted and a new civilian group is eventually allowed to take office.

Legislative Coups   Despite their name, legislative coups against the president are not always conducted by the legislators themselves. In most historical circumstances, the members of Congress have simply offered congressional support for a military conspiracy. This leads to an important distinction between proactive legislators, those who initiate and control the confrontation with the president, and reactive legislators, those who jump on the bandwagon of a confrontation driven by the military or by other social actors. As I will show later, this distinction is relevant for praetorian as well as for institutional outcomes, for past as well as for contemporary presidential crises.

The Brazilian coups of 1955 illustrate this point. After the suicide of Brazilian President Getúlio Vargas in August of 1954,[10] Juscelino

---

[8] The "exceptionality" of the military intervention can only be determined in historical perspective. In some instances (e.g., Argentina in 1930) military leaders intended to remain in power but were prevented from doing so, while in others (Chile in 1973) the apparent "short-term" intervention turned unexpectedly into a lasting military regime.

[9] This pattern roughly corresponds to what Alfred Stepan has called *moderating intervention*. "The military has played a crucial role in politics in Brazil, with . . . actual coups against the executive representing the *combined* efforts of both civilian and military groups" (Stepan 1971, 79).

[10] The suicide of President Vargas was itself the outcome of a previous crisis that had almost led to a legislative coup (see Saunders 1964).

Kubitschek won the ensuing presidential election with the support of the "Getulista" parties that had formed Vargas's coalition (the PSD and PTB) plus the ever-feared communists. Irate at this result, the sectors that had confronted Vargas in previous months encouraged a coup to prevent Kubitschek from taking office. As the situation put stress on his heart condition, Vice President João Café Filho requested medical leave in November of 1955 and was replaced by the speaker of the house, Carlos Coimbra da Luz. When Luz as acting president dismissed Café's minister of war, Gen. Henrique Teixeira Lott, the Getulistas feared that an anti-Kubitschek coup was in progress. On November 11, 1955, Gen. Lott launched a preemptive strike. Army tanks surrounded the presidential palace, and Luz sought refuge in a navy gunboat (Dulles 1970, 3–61; Stepan 1971, 118–119). The Getulistas in Congress declared Luz unable to govern and installed Nereu Ramos, the speaker of the Senate, as acting president by a vote of 185–72 in the Chamber of Deputies and 43–9 in the Senate (Dulles 1970, 48; *Diario do Congresso Nacional, Seção I*, November 11, 1955, 8372–8382).

In a desperate attempt to prevent Ramos from taking office, Café Filho claimed that he was fully recovered from his stroke. But fearing that he would obstruct Kubitschek's inauguration, army units surrounded the presidential palace, Café's home, the War Ministry, and the Chamber of Deputies. On November 22, Congress declared (by a vote of 179–94 in the lower house and 35–16 in the Senate) that Café was physically incapable of returning to office and confirmed Nereu Ramos as president. At the request of the army, Congress also declared a state of siege.

In contrast to the impeachment of Fernando Collor thirty-seven years later, in 1955 Brazilian legislators violated most procedural rules related to the declaration of presidential incapacity (not to speak of the impeachment process) in order to legitimize two coups in less than two weeks. The Getulista leaders acted in alliance with (and under heavy pressure from) the army. These two components, dubious congressional procedures and active military participation – even military *initiative* – are key components of any legislative coup. Similar elements were present in the ousting of Ecuadorian President José M. Velasco Ibarra in 1961 (Fitch 1977, 47–54) and in the "impeachment" of Panamanian President Eric Delvalle in 1988 (Velásquez 1993, 162).[11]

---

[11] The Panamanian "impeachment" was a praetorian outcome in the context of an already undemocratic presidential regime. I shall return to this connection between the nature of the regime and the pattern of crisis resolution later in this chapter.

Self-Coups The second form of short-term intervention is the presidential self-coup (in Spanish, *autogolpe*). According to Cameron, "the term *autogolpe* refers to a temporary suspension of constitutional guarantees and closure of Congress by the executive, which rules by decree and uses referenda and new legislative elections to ratify a regime with broader executive powers" (Cameron 1994, 146). Self-coups result from an alliance between the president and the military in order to dissolve Congress.

Although the Peruvian self-coup of 1992 is the example that immediately comes to mind (Cameron 1997; Conaghan 2005; Kenney 1996; 2004; McClintock 1993), *autogolpes* are not new in Latin American politics. Ecuadorian President José María Velasco Ibarra executed a self-coup in 1970, early in his fifth term in office (Fitch 1977, 174–176).[12] In December of 1954, when the Honduran Congress reached an impasse while attempting to elect the new president, outgoing President Julio Lozano dissolved the assembly and appointed himself the new chief executive. Facing a threat of impeachment, Colombian President Mariano Ospina closed Congress and declared a state of siege in November of 1949 (Hartlyn 1988, 40–41; 1994, 304). In Uruguay, President Gabriel Terra dissolved the legislature and the Council of Administration in March of 1933, and his successor, Alfredo Baldomir, in turn shut down the assembly by the end of his term in 1942.[13] In both cases, constitutional reform ensued (Taylor 1952; 1962, 23–32).

According to this definition, self-coups have taken place in democratic as well as in authoritarian regimes. President Alfredo Stroessner dissolved the Paraguayan Congress in May of 1959 after the Chamber of Deputies – fully controlled by his Colorado Party – condemned police repression of student demonstrations.[14] In Brazil, President Castello Branco dissolved Congress in late October of 1966 (until congressional elections took place a month later) when congressional leaders opposed the executive's removal

---

[12] In the end, Velasco's disruption of the regime led to a long-term breakdown, because the military later took over in order to prevent Assad Bucaram from winning the presidential election.

[13] The National Council of Administration was a nine-member independent branch of the executive in charge of domestic policy implementation. Authors concur in pointing out that it operated in practice as a "third chamber." On this topic, see Fizgibbon (1952).

[14] Although the 1940 constitution allowed the Paraguayan president to dissolve Congress, the repression and exile of party dissidents suggests that this was more than a mere constitutional procedure.

of six deputies by decree.[15] In fact, the first executive-legislative crisis of independent Latin America led to a self-coup when Agustín de Iturbide, hero of Mexican independence (and newly appointed emperor of Mexico), confronted Congress on the right to free speech (Bushnell and Macaulay 1994, 63–64).

The short life of the Mexican empire suggests that self-coups are a risky enterprise that easily turns on its head. In 1954, Chilean President Carlos Ibáñez flirted with the idea of a self-coup, but desisted when he realized that the risk was too high and that even part of his own cabinet openly opposed the plan (Bray 1961, 63–67). In May of 1951, facing a political and financial crisis, Panamanian President Arnulfo Arias abolished the 1946 constitution, dissolved Congress, dismissed the Supreme Court, and ousted several judges and officials. This self-coup quickly changed course when mass demonstrations called for the national police to back the constitutional order and political leaders agreed to impeach the president. Arias resisted the decision of the Assembly, and the police ousted the president after an armed confrontation that left three people dead and more than a hundred wounded (Pizzurno Gelós and Aráuz 1996, 369–373). In this case, as in the Guatemalan crisis of 1993 (discussed in Chapter 7), what began as an *autogolpe* concluded as a legislative coup.

For the sake of conceptual clarity, self-coups should be distinguished from two other related phenomena. As a form of short-term breakdown, *autogolpes* are different from presidential coups inaugurating an enduring authoritarian regime (the 1973 coup in Uruguay, to be discussed later, is a good example). On the other hand, presidents may lock up Congress in order to twist the arms of legislators, with no further intention of *dissolving* the assembly. In early 1908, for instance, Argentine President Figueroa Alcorta occupied Congress with police officers, prevented extraordinary sessions from being held, and reissued the 1907 budget by decree (Botana 1979, 228–229). In 1992, Nicaraguan President Violeta Chamorro similarly used military forces to prevail in her confrontation with Congress, but she did not close the legislature (McConnell 1993, 23; 1997, 49–50). Although unconstitutional, this type of move falls short of being a full-fledged *autogolpe*. Instead of resolving the presidential crisis through

---

[15] The ARENA party (pro-military) had been formed in late 1965 and already controlled 68 percent of the Brazilian Lower Chamber.

forced dissolution, this form of intervention typically represents a chapter in a longer conflict. Presidents' bold moves may result in reequilibration (as in Alcorta's Argentina or Chamorro's Nicaragua), or they may lead to a disastrous escalation of conflict, as in the Chilean civil war of 1891.

Short-term Dictatorship   The third pattern of short-term breakdown involves mutual defeat. In the context of a presidential crisis, the military may intervene to remove *both* the president and the legislators from office, impose an interim government, and reestablish a presidential regime after some months in office. This form of intervention is not necessarily neutral, because short-term breakdowns usually benefit the rise of certain political factions after civilian rule is restored. However, an intervention of this sort indicates that the armed forces consider the civilian elites incapable of solving the existing institutional crisis.

The Ecuadorian coup of 1963 illustrates this pattern. President Carlos Arosemena Monroy faced intense pressure, from left and right, on the issue of severing diplomatic relations with Fidel Castro's Cuba. Arosemena attempted to preserve a neutral stance, but when Conservatives and Social Christians left the ruling coalition in protest, the president was forced to end relations with Cuba and rebuild his cabinet with members of the Frente Democrático Nacional (Liberals and Socialists). In this context, Arosemena's drinking habits came to the fore as a highly controversial matter, and the Conservative leaders in Congress began to question the president's character. An early attempt to censure the president on charges of incapacity failed, and a second, formal motion of impeachment did not pass because Conservatives and Liberals could not agree on the succession. After an incident in December of 1962 – Arosemena was intoxicated when the Chilean president arrived on an official visit to Ecuador – the Conservatives called an urgent congressional session to discuss impeachment, but they were unable to collect the required number of signatures. Problems of collective action made the assembly unable to solve the crisis. At this point, noted Samuel Fitch, "the legalist mentality of the armed forces began to wane" (Fitch 1977, 59). Some military groups began to plot a coup in early 1963, in the midst of increasing public criticism of the government. After another diplomatic incident in which the president was drunk, the military took over on July 11, 1963, and imposed a military junta that ruled until April of 1966.

Long-Term Breakdown

In contemporary Latin America, the confrontations between the executive and Congress sometimes occurred in a context of broader social and political turmoil that ultimately led to the demise of the presidential regime (Bermeo 2003). The best example of this pattern is the establishment of what Guillermo O'Donnell has called Bureaucratic-Authoritarian (BA) regimes after the Brazilian coup of 1964, the Chilean and Uruguayan coups of 1973, and the Argentine coup in 1976 (Collier 1979; O'Donnell 1988).[16] Long-term breakdowns have produced three main outcomes: the ousting of the president and the establishment of a subservient assembly, the elimination of Congress and the installation of a puppet president, and the imposition of a military junta with a long time horizon.

President Ousted   In Brazil, President João Goulart (1961–64) attempted to mobilize mass support as he faced a mounting economic crisis and rising popular demands. In March of 1964, Goulart announced a program of land reform, nationalization of oil refineries, legalization of the Communist Party, and constitutional change. He threatened to bypass Congress by using a plebiscite to enforce changes in the status quo, and rumors of a self-coup unfolded (Bermeo 2003, 95; Menendez and Kerz 1993, 23–36; Stepan 1971, 191–192). In early April, the armed forces deposed Goulart and took over. The military requested extraordinary powers to control communist activities, but Congress refused. In response, the armed forces issued the first "Institutional Act" establishing, among other things, the indirect election of the president and the authority of the army to oust elected officials. Within a few days, the political rights of more than 150 leaders and the terms of 44 members of Congress – most of them from Goulart's PTB – had been terminated (Stepan 1971, 123; *Keesing's Contemporary Archives* 14, 1964). The reshuffled Congress ratified Gen. Castello Branco as the new president of Brazil, inaugurating twenty-one years of military rule.

Congress Closed   In Uruguay, the confrontation between parties (and their "fractions") interacted with the confrontation between politicians and military leaders. Since mid-1972, the Uruguayan armed forces had demanded

---

[16] The Argentine coup of 1966 also inaugurated a BA regime, but it was not preceded by a presidential crisis.

greater autonomy from civilian authorities, and in early 1973 they openly opposed the appointment of a new minister of defense. President Juan M. Bordaberry accepted greater military participation in government affairs through a National Security Council (Lerin and Torres 1987, 9–20; Weinstein 1988, 44–45). Congressional leaders from almost every quarter refused to back the government on this issue, expecting that President Bordaberry would be forced to resign (González and Gillespie 1994, 163). Bordaberry, however, turned to the military for help, and supported the officers when they demanded that Congress lift the immunity of a senator presumably linked to the Tupamaro guerrillas (Bermeo 2003, 128–130). The legislators not only refused to comply, but also warned the president that he could be impeached if the senator was arrested (Kaufman 1979, 114). Between April and June, the executive coalition in Congress collapsed. On June 27, the president dissolved the National Assembly and appointed a Council of State composed of civilians and military officers. The armed forces took control of state companies and the central bank, allowing Bordaberry to remain in office until 1976, when he was replaced by President Aparicio Méndez. Military rule lasted until 1984.

Military Takeover   In Chile, President Salvador Allende's socialist experiment (1970–73) increasingly faced social unrest and alienated political support from the center-right (Valenzuela 1994, 130–137). In early 1972, the Christian Democratic Party (DC) began to distance itself from the ruling Unidad Popular. Later that year, DC leaders openly began to ask for Allende's resignation (Kaufman 1988, 148–149), supported a critical truck owners' strike, and formed an electoral coalition with the rightist National Party for the midterm election of March 1973. The goal of the coalition was to gain control of two-thirds of the seats in Congress. According to Helios Prieto, the Christian Democrats sought to gain enough legislative leverage to blackmail the president, while the National Party intended to initiate an impeachment process (Prieto 1973, 17). The coalition, however, failed to capture a two-thirds majority in the midterm election. By August of 1973, the National Party was pressing for the use of article 43 of the constitution, which allowed Congress to declare the president unfit to rule (Sigmund 1977, 232). The Christian Democrats opposed this move but managed to pass (by an 81–47 vote) a resolution against the government. On September 11, 1973, the armed forces deposed the government and dissolved the two houses of Congress. The Christian Democrats expected the military to restore elections within "two or three years" (Kaufman 1988,

151), but the coup opened the way for seventeen years of military rule under the aegis of Gen. Augusto Pinochet (Bermeo 2003, Chapter 5).

The examples just presented suggest that long-term breakdowns solve presidential crises in a Hobbesian way, by expropriating power from the two conflicting branches in favor of a third player – the army or an individual dictator. Even when the president is kept in office, as in 1973 in Uruguay, or when Congress is not shut down, as in 1964 in Brazil, those institutions are progressively deprived of power because they have to perform new, diminished functions under the logic of bureaucratic authoritarianism.

Although bureaucratic authoritarianism represented the main pattern of long-term breakdowns during the period under study, presidential crises have opened the way for other forms of nondemocratic rule, such as state corporatism or neo-patrimonial rule. In 1937, President Getúlio Vargas of Brazil dissolved Congress to impose his *Estado Nôvo*, a corporatist regime. In 1954, the Paraguayan assembly accepted the resignation of President Federico Cháves when a military coup forced him out of office, opening the way for the ensuing election of Gen. Alfredo Stroessner as president (Seiferheld 1987). By 1954, the Paraguayan regime was hardly democratic (opposition to the Colorado Party had been banned since 1947), but it lacked the strong elements of personalism that Stroessner imposed on the new regime.

Presidential Crises without Breakdown

The cases discussed in Chapter 2 suggest that since the last decade of the twentieth century presidential crises have typically been resolved without compromising the stability of the existing regime. The concept of "crisis without breakdown" is drawn from Eugenio Kvaternik's study of military coups in Argentina (Kvaternik 1987).[17] In a crisis without breakdown, deadlock may place the system under stress, but (to recall Giuseppe Di Palma's expression) the regime will often "survive without governing" (Di Palma 1977). A presidential crisis without breakdown may end in the removal of

---

[17] In his study of the 1962 military coup in Argentina, Kvaternik identified four possible outcomes of a democractic crisis: breakdown, reequilibration, failed reequilibration, and no breakdown. The first two categories reflected Linz's thinking on the issue, while the other two were Kvaternik's own contributions. Failed reequilibration was at the core of Kvaternik's study; he related this type of failure to the moderating military interventions described by Stepan (1971) in the Brazilian context and to the 1962 coup in Argentina. The fourth category, crisis without breakdown, was not systematically explored.

(e.g., Presidents Andrew Johnson and Bill Clinton in the United States, or Luis González Macchi in Paraguay). In some cases, stabilization involves an additional component of regime reequilibration. For instance, to prevent Arnulfo Arias from winning the presidential election, in 1948 the Panamanian legislature passed a resolution "recovering" its status as Constitutional Assembly (a role exercised in 1945), dismissed President Enrique Jiménez, appointed the comptroller general as president for four years, and nullified the recent election. But the Supreme Court rejected the constitutionality of the resolution, and the national police backed President Jiménez. The president ignored the decision, the legislative coup folded, and the president and the legislators completed their terms (Pippin 1964, 20–28; Pizzurno Gelós and Aráuz 1996, 341–344).[21]

Presidential Crises and the New Politics of Impeachment

Table 3.3 compares the fifty-eight crises introduced in Table 3.2 according to the alternative outcomes presented in Figure 3.2 Because these categories represent ideal types, classification is not always straightforward. Some of these episodes were initially headed in one direction but ended in an unexpected outcome. In 1968, for instance, Panamanian legislators accused President Marco Aurelio Robles of using his powers to manipulate the electoral process and voted to remove him from office. In response, the National Guard surrounded the Assembly and preempted his removal. The Assembly was not dissolved, however, and Robles and the legislators finished their terms. This episode started as an attempt to remove the president, evolved into a potential self-coup, and ended as an instance of stabilization (the military nonetheless took over soon after the presidential crisis was over).

The table suggests that presidential crises are far from being the destabilizing force that the critics of presidentialism have assumed them to be. Sixty percent of the crises that took place during the period 1950–2004 had no disruptive effect at the level of the regime; more than half of them never posed a threat of spillover (see Figure 3.2); and over one-third were resolved without resorting to the dissolution of Congress or the ousting of the president. The likelihood of military intervention in those crises, however, has varied over time.

---

[21] Arias did not take office until 1951, however. The election results were rigged, and the *Liberal Doctrinario* candidate, Domingo Díaz, was proclaimed the victor.

Table 3.3. *Outcomes of presidential crises, 1950–2004*

Consequences for the Regime	Consequences for the Elected Branches		
	President Ousted	Congress Closed	Balanced Outcome
Breakdown	I. *President ousted* Brazil (1964) Paraguay (1954)[a]	II. *Congress closed* Ecuador (1970) Uruguay (1973)	III. *Takeover* Argentina (1976) Chile (1973)
Disruption	IV. *Legislative coup* Bolivia (1979) Brazil (1954) Brazil (1955, twice) Ecuador (1961) Ecuador (2000) Guatemala (1957)[a] Guatemala (1993) Panama (1951)[a] Panama (1988)[a]	V. *Self-coup* Argentina (1962) Brazil (1966)[a] Brazil (1968)[a] Honduras (1954)[a] Paraguay (1959)[a] Peru (1992)	VI. *Dictatorship* Ecuador (1963)
No Breakdown	VII. *Removal* Argentina (1989) Argentina (2001, twice) Bolivia (1985) Bolivia (2003) Brazil (1992) Ecuador (1997) Panama (1955)[a] Paraguay (1999) Peru (2000) Venezuela (1993)	VIII. *Dissolution* Colombia (1991) Guatemala (1994) Venezuela (1999)	IX. *Stabilization* Bolivia (1983) Bolivia (1990) Brazil (1977)[a] Chile (1954) Colombia (1977) Colombia (1996) Dominican Republic (1994) Ecuador (1984) Ecuador (1987) Ecuador (1990) Ecuador (2004) El Salvador (1987) Honduras (1985) Nicaragua (1992) Nicaragua (2004) Panama (1968) Paraguay (2001) Paraguay (2002) Peru (1991) Uruguay (1969) Uruguay (1971)

[a] Not a competitive regime at the time of the crisis.

Source: Table 3.2, Figure 3.2, and database on presidential crises ⟨www.pitt.edu/~asp27/ Presidential/Impeachment.html⟩.

4

Latin America in the Age of Scandal

In Chapter 2, I showed that political scandals have been a common denominator in all cases of impeachment. This is not surprising. Fernando Collor was accused by his own brother of managing a broad corruption network; Carlos Andrés Pérez was indicted for embezzlement; Ernesto Samper was charged with accepting campaign donations from the Cali drug cartel; and Raúl Cubas was blamed for defying the Supreme Court and tolerating the assassination of his vice president. Some leaders, like Samper and Cubas, confronted one single major issue throughout their terms. Others, like Collor, Pérez, Bucaram, and González Macchi, found their administrations surrounded by a permanent atmosphere of media scandals that enveloped members of the cabinet, the president's family, and ultimately the chief executive himself.

In fact, these presidents were not alone. This chapter documents a dramatic expansion of political scandals in Latin America in the 1980s and the 1990s, and traces the structural sources of this trend. I account for the growing number of scandals by analyzing the changes that the press was undergoing throughout the region. The combination of political democracy and the development of television networks, the emergence of corporate media groups, and the professionalization of the newsroom has created greater incentives for politicians to use scandal as a political weapon. The chapter illustrates these trends with two contrasting cases: Brazil, where such changes have been dramatic, and Venezuela, where they have been less noticeable but still significant. Further examples are borrowed from the experience of other Latin American countries and the United States to show that such trends are regional in nature. The concluding section discusses how the politics of scandal has been the kernel of recent impeachment crises in Latin America.

The Age of Scandal?

To what extent have political scandals proliferated in Latin America after the third wave of democratization? Comparative data on this subject is very scant, and an operational definition of "scandal" is often hard to achieve. Following Thompson, I understand scandals to be "actions or events involving certain kinds of transgressions which become known to others and are sufficiently serious to elicit a public response" (Thompson 2000, 13). For operational purposes, I will define "political scandals" as news events disclosing acts of corruption or abuse of power performed by politicians. Within this category, I emphasize news stories involving the president, his or her top cabinet members, the president's family, and the president's close friends – that is, the kind of scandals that might justify an impeachment.

In recent years, scandals have become part of everyday politics in Latin America. According to Silvio Waisbord, Argentine newspapers now feature regular articles on official wrongdoing, something that was rare years ago (Waisbord 1998, 53). Describing the situation during the Salinas administration in Mexico, Jorge Castañeda (1997, 134) observed that unprecedented levels of corruption were made public by journalistic coverage and promoted greater public sensitivity to the news. Catherine Conaghan also noticed that, after the 1992 Peruvian self-coup, the press played an important role by denouncing human rights violations, corruption, and abuse of power (Conaghan 1996, 7; see also 1998; 2005).

Assessing the recent proliferation of scandals is not easy, but the available evidence suggests that in most countries the number of exposés has grown since the early eighties (Waisbord 2000). To illustrate this regional trend, I rely on two indicators. The first one is based on news stories collected by the Foreign Broadcast Information Service (FBIS). FBIS monitored newspaper, broadcast, and news agency stories in virtually every country, clipped the major stories, and published English translations in its *Daily Reports*. Until 1996, news stories were classified according to the region of the world, the country, and the particular subject covered, and tabulated annually in the FBIS *Index* to the *Daily Reports*. Table 4.1 shows the number of news stories under the subject "Bribery and Corruption" for nineteen Latin American countries in 1983 and in 1993. In the early 1980s, revelations of corruption were scarce; ten years later, they were widespread. FBIS registered just 11 news stories on corruption in 1983 and 200 ten years later. This does not prove that corruption had become more extensive, but it does show that

Table 4.1. *Entries under "Bribery and Corruption," FBIS* Index, *1983 and 1993*

Country	Year		
	1983	1993	Difference
Argentina	2	5	3
Bolivia	1	14	13
Brazil	0	69	69
Chile	1	2	1
Colombia	1	16	15
Costa Rica	0	0	0
Cuba	0	1	1
Dominican Republic	0	1	1
Ecuador	0	1	1
El Salvador	0	0	0
Guatemala	1	6	5
Honduras	0	1	1
Mexico	2	3	1
Nicaragua	2	8	6
Panama	1	13	12
Paraguay	0	13	13
Peru	0	1	1
Uruguay	0	0	0
Venezuela	0	46	46
Average	0.6	10.5	+9.9
Total news items on corruption	11	200	+189
FBIS stories on Latin America	24,612	16,310	
Items as percentage of all stories	0.04	1.23	

Source: Index to FBIS *Daily Reports* (computer file) (New Canaan, CT: NewsBank/Readex).

media accusations had become more frequent.[1] Table 4.1 reflects to some extent the impact of the impeachment processes in Brazil and Venezuela – which made corruption a dominant topic during 1993 – but it also suggests that revelations were on the rise in most countries.

FBIS news stories under "Bribery and Corruption" reflect exposés that do not necessarily involve the president and his or her entourage. However, scandals are relevant for the unfolding of an impeachment process when

---

[1] The increase in the number of entries on bribery and corruption is not the result of an increase in the sheer number of news stories reported by FBIS. As shown in Table 4.1, the total number of stories on Latin America was smaller in 1993 than in 1983. Items on bribery and corruption represented only 0.08 percent of all news items on Latin America and the Caribbean indexed between 1980 and 1985, and 1.31 percent of those indexed between 1990 and 1995, a general pattern consistent with the two years selected as benchmarks.

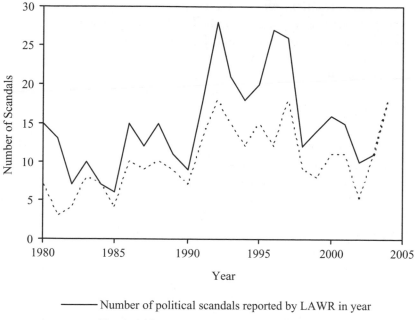

Figure 4.1 Political scandals, 1980–2004. *Source: Latin America Weekly Report* (LAWR).

they might compromise the inner circle of the administration. My second indicator captures all the scandals documented by the *Latin American Weekly Report* in eighteen countries (all countries included in the previous table except Cuba) between 1980 and 2004. Figure 4.1 shows the distribution of scandals over time. The newsletter identified 374 political scandals during this period. Of them, 254 involved the president of the country, the president's family, or cabinet members. Only 32 percent of all the scandals took place before 1991.

How shall we interpret this surge of scandals throughout the region? One explanation, advanced by Kurt Weyland, is that levels of corruption have risen in recent years. Kickbacks by public contractors in Brazil, for instance, used to be around 8–12 percent of the contract during the military regime, but rose to 15–20 percent under civilian rule (Weyland 1998a, 112). Weyland's hypothesis is hard to test because systematic data collection in this field is particularly difficult, but the author has provided valuable qualitative evidence in support of this claim.

Even if corruption were on the rise, however, this fact would not be enough to explain the surge in scandals. To a large extent, scandals may take place without corruption, and vice versa (Jiménez Sánchez 1994, 14). Given the definition presented here, in order for a scandal to take place, the mass media must *uncover* corrupt behavior. Therefore, the study of scandals must explain why malfeasance is exposed rather than the causes of corruption per se (Waisbord 1994, 21).

In fact, social scientists and media analysts have pointed out that the Latin American press has become increasingly willing to dig into dishonest politics. In the mid-1990s, a report by the Freedom Forum Media Studies Center noted "[w]hat has changed is the media's determination to uncover malfeasance and to hold government officials accountable to the public. The combat between the press and the political powers is intensifying in Latin America" (Vanden Heuvel and Dennis 1995, 14). Alves (1997) similarly documented the emergence of a "vanguard press" – a new generation of Latin American newspapers providing more aggressive coverage and displaying greater professionalism and independence.

If this is the key to understanding the rise of scandals, how can we explain this major transformation in the press? Over the last three decades, most Latin American countries have undergone four major changes that have enhanced the capacity of the media to publicize political wrongdoing and created incentives for politicians to disclose it. Political democratization has meant more freedom of the press throughout the region. Economic reforms have deprived governments of regulatory tools traditionally used to control the press and allowed for the emergence of a new and more powerful breed of media corporation. The growth of television has made news available to larger segments of the population and put pressure on newspapers to run investigative stories. Last but not least, over the last few decades journalists have become, in the words of a Brazilian journalist, "more professional and less emotional."[2] This trend has fostered new professional values and expectations regarding the role of the press in the new Latin American democracies (Waisbord 1996).

The new state of affairs in which the press has greater opportunities to investigate scandals has not been without pitfalls. Latin American journalists have many times pursued scandals for their own sake; the effects of deregulation on media markets are contested; the commitment of TV networks to quality news is, at best, doubtful; and investigative journalism has

---

[2] Interview with Carlos Chagas (TV Manchete), August of 1998.

often been confused with publishing unfounded accusations. Like the other major institutions in Latin America, the press still has important lessons to learn.

Political Factors: Democratization

The rapid expansion of democratic politics in Latin America since 1978 has created favorable conditions for the emergence of a more aggressive type of journalism (Waisbord 2000, 58–64). In 1977, only three countries in continental Latin America (Colombia, Costa Rica, and Venezuela) were democracies; twenty years later, twelve countries had democratic regimes, and six others could be considered at least semdemocratic (Mainwaring, Brinks, and Pérez-Liñán 2007).

The emergence of a more independent press during the process of democratization is part of what O'Donnell and Schmitter (1986, Chapter 5) called the resurrection of civil society. In Brazil, the military regime did not establish a formal censorship structure until 1968, although editors and reporters were imprisoned and left-wing newspapers harassed. In 1968, Institutional Act No. 5 imposed widespread censorship of the media, a situation that lasted until 1975 for the print media and 1978 for television. The process of liberalization initiated during the administration of Gen. Ernesto Geisel, however, allowed for more competitive elections and greater freedom of the press. By 1977, the press was already adopting a critical stand against the regime, denouncing the manipulation of gubernatorial elections and the existence of political prisoners. Later, in 1981, it took a central role in exposing the *Riocentro* affair – a bombing planned by hard-liners against a benefit concert for the opposition that accidentally failed. According to Dassin, "Riocentro was the most important test of press freedom since the *abertura* had begun. New techniques of investigative reporting were developed on the spot as the major media followed the story" (Dassin 1984, 396). The media had a "catalytic role" in the struggle for direct presidential elections in the early 1980s (Fox 1998, 32), and the new investigative techniques – eventually leading to the impeachment of Fernando Collor – would become an essential component of political coverage with the return to democracy in 1985.

The Chilean experience provides another good illustration of the correlation between democratization and the institutional development of the press. During the administration of Salvador Allende (1970–73), a political battle for the control of the mass media preceded the 1973 coup. And, as

Robert Buckman pointed out, "with the coup all communication media initially came under military censorship. Only four newspapers still appeared in the capital: the three Edwards newspapers – *El Mercurio*, *La Segunda*, and *Ultimas Noticias* – and Picó's *La Tercera*. All Marxist-oriented media were closed permanently, and many of their editors and writers were among those jailed, exiled, or disappeared" (Buckman 1996, 169). Overt censorship was soon replaced by self-censorship and by more selective forms of pressure, but the press remained largely controlled. During the 1980s, a slow process of liberalization allowed for the emergence of moderate opposition dailies like *La Epoca* and *Fortín Mapocho*; later in the decade, the mainstream press began to challenge the official spin on critical issues. Television news excluded the views of the opposition during the Pinochet regime, until the Concertación was granted limited airtime for the 1988 plebiscite (Hirmas 1993). With the return to democracy in 1990, the media gained greater independence (Sunkel 1997), although the Chilean mainstream press remains on average less aggressive than its Argentine and Brazilian counterparts, and the Chilean constitution inexplicably holds citizens liable "for crimes and abuses that may be committed in the exercise of [press] freedom" (article 19, section 12).

The protection of free expression and other civil rights is a necessary (but not sufficient) condition for the proliferation of political muckraking (Jiménez Sánchez 1994, 19–20). Although in a few countries, like Costa Rica and Venezuela, this precondition was already present by the late 1970s, in the rest of Latin America the third wave of democratization changed the conditions under which journalism was practiced. What military rulers could formerly hide from the public is nowadays easily exposed by the media (Weyland 1998a, 110).

The process of political liberalization fostered the creation of "vanguard" newspapers like *La Prensa* in Panama (founded in 1980, closed in 1988, and reopened in 1990), *El Norte* or *Reforma* (1993) in Mexico, *Siglo Veintiuno* (1990) in Guatemala, *Página/12* (1987) in Argentina, and the now-extinct *La Epoca* (1987) in Chile. By developing a more aggressive and professional brand of journalism, those newspapers changed the rules of the game in their countries and forced the mainstream newspapers (*El Universal* in Mexico, *Prensa Libre* in Guatemala, and *Clarín* in Argentina) to improve their own coverage (Alves 1997; Hughes 2006; Waisbord 1998, 54).

Free speech also allowed the press to play political roles that other institutions had left unattended. In democracies where reciprocal controls among political institutions are weak – where, in O'Donnell's terms, there is a lack of horizontal accountability (O'Donnell 1994) – the press often becomes the main watchdog of the executive (see Smulovitz and Peruzzotti 2000). Discussing the role of the press in Venezuela, Miguel Henrique Otero, publisher of *El Nacional* – one of the largest newspapers in the country – pointed out that "for a long time there was a great weakness in terms of social controls: there was no comptroller, no attorney general, no [independent] courts. . . . So the media played a major role in the trial against Pérez, in the trial against Lusinchi, in all that" (interview, July of 1998).

Economic Factors: Deregulating News

The market-oriented reforms that took place in many Latin American countries following the debt crisis of the 1980s had important consequences for the press as an institution. The reforms involved not only market deregulation and privatization of state enterprises, but also "a fundamental redrawing of the existing boundaries between politics and economics, and the public and the private" (Acuña and Smith 1994, 21). The dissolution of the state-centered matrix of state-society relations also affected the traditional patterns of interaction between the president's office and the press.

First, economic reforms deprived the executive of important tools traditionally used by the government to influence media coverage. In Mexico, the Salinas administration relinquished a monopoly over the production and importation of newsprint that had allowed its predecessors – especially the Echeverría administration – to put pressure on critical publications like *Proceso* and *El Norte* (Alves 1997; Sarmiento 1997, 34; Riva Palacio 1997, 25). As part of the "Great Turnaround," the Pérez administration dissolved the preferential exchange rate system (Recadi) in Venezuela. The preceding Lusinchi administration (1984–89) had used forign currency controls as an effective instrument to punish unfriendly newspapers, imposing bureaucratic delays in the allocation of quotas to import newsprint (Oviedo 1997, 60–61). In the words of a Copei congressman, "along with Recadi disappeared the extortion, and the media were left without dollars at 14.50 [bolívares per dollar], but free" (Chitty La Roche 1993, 230–231).

Second, privatization meant smaller advertising budgets in the hands of state-owned companies controlled by the government. Public advertising, one of the main instruments used to muzzle the critical press, declined rapidly with the state's participation in the economy (Alves 1997, 3), although Latin American governments still control significant advertising budgets (Waisbord 2000, 66).

71

This leads to a third mechanism: economic deregulation put competitive pressure on media conglomerates. There is a long tradition of large media corporations in some Latin American countries, a tradition best represented by Organizações Globo in Brazil, Televisa in Mexico, and the Cisneros group in Venezuela. These corporations often anchor their core business in national TV networks and extend into print journalism, book publishing, radio, and cable (plus mobile communications, satellite, and internet services in recent years). They have a dominant position in their local markets and powerful transnational partners abroad. Because of their financial strength, these conglomerates are in a privileged position to confront the government and to pursue investigative stories. Traditionally, however, they have refrained from doing so because they have grown with the support of powerful political allies. Televisa's legendary CEO, the late Emilio Azcárraga, openly acknowledged in 1991 that "Televisa considers itself part of the government system and, as such, supports the campaign of PRI candidates.... The President of the Republic, Carlos Salinas de Gortari, is our maximum leader and we are happy about that" (quoted in Miller and Darling 1997, 65).

In the 1990s, economic deregulation allowed for tougher competition, creating stronger incentives for media corporations to take an independent stand and to distance themselves from the president's office. The Salinas administration privatized the public TV network Imevisión – then renamed Televisión Azteca – creating a competitive front for Azcárraga's Televisa (Lopez 1997, 92; Orme 1997, 8; but see Belejack 1997, 55; Castañeda 1997; and Hughes 2006). In Argentina, the Menem administration not only privatized all commercial TV stations after 1989, but also allowed cross-ownership of print and broadcast media. In addition, a 1994 investment treaty with the United States virtually lifted the ban on foreign investment in the media industry (Galperín 2002). One year before the Pérez administration adopted a comprehensive neoliberal policy, the Lusinchi government – for reasons that remain unclear – opened the TV market and granted eight new licenses (Mayobre 2002, 181). In Brazil, the dominance of Globo has not vanished, but regulatory reforms have allowed the entrance of foreign capital in cable and telecommunications, and there are several major players in the communications industry (de Lima 1998).

Silvio Waisbord has claimed that financial independence, more than market competition per se, constitutes the main explanation for the investigative leanings of large media groups. After 1989, according to Waisbord, media executives and politicians in Argentina came to believe that in a "market now populated by a handful of media groups, the name of the game [had become] getting and printing fast-breaking, and even sensationalistic, news" (Waisbord 1994, 27). But competition was less relevant for muckraking than market strength, because only media corporations in a solid position could "take a jab at governments without fearing potential financial damages" (Waisbord 2000, 73).

Financial strength gives media conglomerates the capacity to confront the government, while the dynamics of democratization and market competition may give them the incentive to do so. Democratization creates uncertainty about the permanence of any particular group in power, discouraging media corporations from developing open, long-term commitments to particular parties or factions. In contrast to Televisa's Azcárraga, corporate officers heading media groups in competitive party systems are reluctant to adopt partisan views and usually prefer middle-of-the-road positions that protect their strategic independence. Only when the rules of the game become uncertain and the economic stakes are too high, as in Hugo Chávez's Venezuela after 1999, may media owners abandon any pretense of journalistic independence and embrace an overtly militant position.

On the other hand, market competition gives large media corporations three incentives to become autonomous from the government. First, there is an increasing competition for readers and audiences. In the words of Alvaro Saieh, head of the Copesa group in Chile, "You cannot use the newspapers to sell your personal ideas; you will lose your clientele" (quoted by Buckman 1996, 177). In democracies with weak horizontal accountability, keeping an aggressive posture against the government usually builds prestige and recognition among readers and audiences and helps to establish a journalistic brand name (see Waisbord 1998, 53–54; but see also Waisbord 2000, 69–71). Second, there is competition for talent. Large media outlets are complex organizations, and it is difficult for their managers to control the production of news stories on a regular basis. If professional journalists have incentives to pursue investigative stories (and I will argue later that they do), an intrusive administration of the newsroom may prevent the recruitment of the more capable journalists trained in the values of independence and professional autonomy.

Paradoxically, the third reason to maintain an aggressive posture toward the government is the competition for political favors. In a monopolistic news market, the government and the dominant news organization may develop a long-term cooperative relationship. But in a competitive news market, media corporations need to secure their share of official perks. The power to unleash scandal – the power to put investigative stories on hold or to defect in favor of full disclosure if agreements between media owners and public officials are not honored – is one of the main strengths that media corporations bring to their negotiations with governments. For reasons of credibility (in the game-theoretic sense of players being capable of enforcing their threats), the practice of investigative journalism may be the best strategy for media corporations willing to negotiate with government officials.

Technological Factors: The Expansion of Television

The rapid expansion of television between the 1970s and the 1990s was relevant for the politics of scandal. TV networks made the news available to broader segments of the population and forced newspapers to diversify their editorial offerings (and thus to invest in investigative journalism, among other, more trivial marketing strategies). Television broadcasts began in most of Latin America during the 1950s, but access to TV sets was limited in many countries until the 1980s. Hirmas's description of the Chilean experience is illustrative: from 1962 to 1973, few people owned TV sets. Television had a limited audience, and its political impact was negligible. When democracy was reestablished in the early 1990s, more than 90 percent of Chilean homes had a television set, and TV news was a more common source of information than radio (Hirmas 1993, 83).

Television gains critical relevance for national politics when it becomes a powerful medium able to reach a majority of the households in the country. In gross operational terms, this means a penetration rate above one hundred TV sets per thousand inhabitants (PTI). The United States reached this threshold in the early 1950s, and the average Latin American country did so in the mid-1980s. In 1975, the average Latin American country had just 60 TV sets PTI, and only two countries in the region had crossed the 100 mark. By 1990, in contrast, the average country had 149 TV sets PTI, and 11 countries had crossed this threshold.

Consider, for instance, the case of Venezuela. Public television began in Caracas in late 1952, and within few months the first private networks began to broadcast. During the late 1950s and early 1960s, regional networks emerged in Maracaibo and Valencia, and by the late sixties Venezuela already had five private networks in addition to public television (D'Amico 1992; J. Walter Thompson 1970). In 1970, however, the penetration of television was still limited to 44 percent of Venezuelan households, with wide disparities across regions. In the northern region (including Caracas, Valencia, and Maracay), 75 percent of the homes had access to television; in Zulia, the wealthy, oil-producing state, 48 percent of the homes did. But in Los Llanos – the second-largest region in terms of population – less than 6 percent of the households had access to TV sets. In 1968, television absorbed 34 percent of the total advertising budget, while newspapers still controlled 36 percent (J. Walter Thompson 1970, 25–29).

This situation changed dramatically over the next two decades. From 950,000 TV sets in 1970, Venezuela reached 1.7 million in 1980 and 3.1 million in 1990. The penetration rate grew from 89 TV sets per thousand inhabitants in 1970 to over 160 in the early 1990s and later stabilized (UNESCO 1996, Table 9.11; World Bank 2005). In 1973, investment in TV advertising barely matched newspaper advertising, but in 1983 TV stations absorbed 60 percent of the total advertising revenue, and ten years later they controlled 72 percent of the business (Díaz Rangel 1994, 130).

This trend has been even more dramatic in Brazil. According to Dassin (1984), when television began in 1950, there were just two hundred TV sets in the country. By 1958, there were 78,000 sets, concentrated in Rio and São Paulo, and television continued to be a luxury item. In the 1960s, however, the Brazilian government encouraged the development of a national television network, which was seen by the military as a key instrument for modernization and national integration. By 1980, the Globo network dominated the Brazilian TV industry, and there were an estimated twenty million TV sets all over the country.

Figure 4.2 compares the increasing penetration of television in Venezuela and Brazil to the trend in the average Latin American country.[3] Although television developed earlier in Brazil and Venezuela than in most Latin American countries, the expansive trend has been similar throughout the region.

The expansion of television had two important consequences for the political role of the press in the region. First, the development and increasing sophistication of TV newscasts put pressure on old-fashioned newspapers. Television became equally able to break news and a more entertaining source of information. A Venezuelan producer recalled that in the 1960s "newscasts stopped being mere summaries of cold and lifeless news to forge public opinion – allowing us to take part in the toughest dramas" (Mata

[3] The regional average includes all countries in Table 4.1.

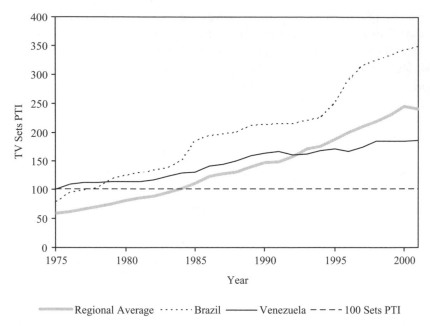

Figure 4.2 Television sets per thousand inhabitants, 1975–2001. *Source:* International Telecommunication Union – World Development Indicators (World Bank 2005). Average based on nineteen Latin American countries.

1992, 14). Progressively, print journalism was challenged to abandon traditional forms of "institutional" reporting anchored in official sources for the sake of sharper analytical coverage. The rise of TV newscasts created incentives not only for the development of newspapers' special interest sections – lifestyle pages and magazines – but also for the practice of investigative journalism.

According to the Brazilian anchor Carlos Chagas, the expansion of television news represented a "cataclysm" for the newspaper industry. Until the 1970s, newspapers had set the agenda for TV newscasts. But in the seventies, evening news began to anticipate in prime time what readers would find in newspapers the following morning.

With satellite, with microwaves, with a more agile television, now the evening newscasts set the agenda for next-day newspapers. . . . It is of course true that the print press also sets the agenda for us many times – sometimes it breaks news, stories that we have not offered the night before. But on average, television shows the night before, with color and movement, what newspapers will offer the following day.

Thus, the role of newspapers had to be recycled; they had to offer *something else* to their readers, something different from whatever newscasts had offered the night before. This was a contest in which the winner was the reader, the viewer.... After freedom returned with the end of the dictatorship, that *something else* in Brazil happened to be scandal, the frantic chase of thieves.... But after a while, that stopped. Nowadays that *something else* that newspapers provide is better information with greater analysis. (interview with Carlos Chagas, August 7, 1998)

This process was less marked in other countries such as Argentina and Venezuela, where newspapers and morning radio still set most of the journalistic agenda (Zuleta Puceiro 1993, 74), but in every country newspaper editors felt pressures to modernize and to provide "something else" in order to give their products an edge.

Second, broadcast radio and television allowed larger segments of the population access to daily news, particularly in countries where illiteracy had precluded massive consumption of print journalism (Pérez-Liñán 2002a). In Brazil, for instance, 18.3 percent of the population over the age of fourteen was illiterate in 1990 (ECLAC 1997, 41). In practice, this meant that one-third of the electorate was illiterate and that two-thirds had not finished grade school (*Folha de São Paulo*, August 4, 1998, I-2). UNESCO estimated that in 1990 illiteracy affected 45 percent of the population age fifteen and over in Guatemala, 27 percent in El Salvador and Honduras, and 21 percent in Bolivia. Figures were lower but still alarming in Mexico (13 percent) and Venezuela (10 percent), and fell under 4 percent in countries like Argentina and Uruguay (see ECLAC 1997, 41). These figures suggest that the expansion of the broadcast media was more critical for the diffusion of news in some countries than in others.

Because of its entertaining power, television has become a widespread medium and a focus of attention for many people.[4] Miller and Darling, for instance, noted that in the late 1990s Mexico had three times more television sets than telephones (1997, 61). In countries with low newspaper readership, television has a unique power to multiply the political impact of scandals, because accusations and investigative stories that would have limited diffusion through the pages of newspapers may reach every home in the country once they are exposed on national television. When newscast producers are interested in scandals – and I have argued that in a context of democratization and growing market competition they increasingly

---

[4] In Venezuela, evening news became late night news, with newscasts placed in the 11 P.M. slot. In the 1990s, prime time was mostly devoted to soap operas and news magazines.

are – television compounds the impact of scandals on public opinion by giving spin to the accusations.

A study of TV coverage during Collor's impeachment concluded that television legitimized the framing of news stories and the investigative roles played by the other media though positive cross-references (Fausto Neto 1995). This "cross-referencing power," as Antônio Fausto Neto called it, is particularly relevant because it facilitates the mobilization of public opinion against the president – a critical factor shaping the outcome of the presidential crises to be discussed in the following chapters.

Professional Factors: Careers in Journalism

A key factor deserving consideration is the ongoing transformation in the professional mindset of journalists. Over the last three decades, Latin American journalists have become more professional and inclined toward investigative work (Hughes 2006; Waisbord 1994; 1996). According to Guido Grooscors, the top communications officer during the Betancourt, the Leoni, and the first Pérez administrations in Venezuela, journalists in the 1990s were "more aggressive and professional, more investigative" than their colleagues in the 1970s.[5] After describing the culture of collusion that linked the Mexican press with the PRI (Partido Revolucionario Institucional) for years, Riva Palacio (1997, 29) noted with hope that younger, better-educated journalists began exerting pressure for change within newsrooms in the 1990s (see also Hughes 2006).

Available figures for Brazil and Venezuela suggest that careers in journalism are on the rise. According to data gathered by the Venezuelan University Council (Consejo Nacional de Universidades) in 1974, the year the Watergate scandal came to an end, Venezuela had 2,148 college students majoring in social communication. By 1993, the year of the trial of President Pérez, the number had increased to 5,300. In the late nineties, social communication had already become the major in greatest demand in Venezuela, and private universities were opening new courses to attract students who had failed to gain admission to the more traditional programs (*El Nacional*, June 26, 2000, C1). In Brazil, this trend has been even more striking: in 1974,

---

[5] Interview, July of 1998. Grooscors was *Director Nacional de Información* under Betancourt, director of the Oficina Central de Información under Leoni, and founding minister of the OCI (Oficina Central de Información) in the first Pérez administration. He later pursued a diplomatic career.

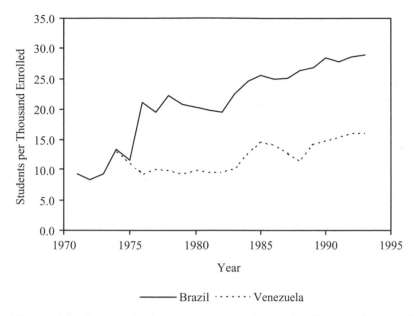

Figure 4.3 Communication students per thousand college students, 1971–1993. *Sources:* Consejo Nacional de Universidades (Venezuela) and Ministerio da Educação (Brazil). (Nationwide figures. Data for Brazil are based on all students classified as *ensino superior.*)

Brazilian institutions of higher education reported 12,554 students in social communication programs. By 1993, this figure had risen to 46,239. Virtue and Heise (1996, 200) reported that in 1993 the enrollment in the School of Social Communication at the Universidad de Guayaquil in Ecuador was 1,600 – a figure larger than the total number of journalists employed all over Ecuador at the time.

The number of communication students has increased not only in absolute, but also in relative terms.[6] Figure 4.3 displays the number of social communication enrollments for every thousand college students. In 1974, there were thirteen communication students for every thousand college students in Brazil. In 1993, this figure was twenty-nine per thousand. Venezuela departed from a similar point (thirteen students per thousand in 1974). Here the growth was slower (to sixteen per thousand by 1993) but still significant.

[6] Programs in "social communication" in Latin American universities can be broader than training in journalism. Some graduates pursue academic careers, public relations positions, or advertising jobs.

Table 4.2. *Students of communication and documentation (C&D) per thousand university students, 1980–ca. 1990*

	1980		ca. 1990		Ratio		
Country	C&D	Total	C&D	Total	1980s	1990s	Change
Argentina	1,788	491.5	n.d.	n.d.	3.6	n.d.	n.d.
Bolivia (1991)	86	52.9	3,017	109.5	1.6	27.6	25.9
Brazil (1991)	34,486	1,409.2	48,756	1,565.1	24.5	31.2	6.7
Chile (1991)	2,825	145.5	1,774	287.0	19.4	6.2	−13.2
Colombia (1991)	n.d.	271.6	n.d.	510.6	n.d.	n.d.	n.d.
Costa Rica (1991)	636	50.8	2,193	80.4	12.5	27.3	14.7
Ecuador (1991)	1,377	269.8	6,779	206.5	5.1	32.8	27.7
El Salvador (1990)	n.d.	16.8	2,698	78.2	n.d.	34.5	n.d.
Guatemala	n.d.	n.d.	n.d.	n.d.	n.d.	n.d.	n.d.
Honduras (1990)	147	25.8	1,081	39.3	5.7	27.5	21.8
Mexico (1990)	13,188	897.7	41,535	1,252.0	14.7	33.2	18.5
Nicaragua (1991)	346	35.3	435	31.5	9.8	13.8	4.0
Panama (1991)	968	31.3	2,319	58.0	30.9	40.0	9.0
Paraguay (1990)	n.d.	n.d.	142	32.9	n.d.	4.3	n.d.
Peru (1991)	5,670	306.4	7,277	475.7	18.5	15.3	−3.2
Uruguay (1990)	156	36.3	1,195	71.6	4.3	16.7	12.4
Venezuela (1989)	3,667	307.1	5,879	500.3	11.9	11.8	−0.1

Key: n.d. = no data available; C&D = students in communication and documentation programs (all levels); Total = total number of third-level students (all levels, in thousands); Ratio = communication/documentation students for every thousand university students.
Sources: UNESCO *Statistical Yearbooks* (1992; 1994; 1997, Table 3.13).

The number of students in social communication has grown faster than the total number of students in higher education, indicating the rising social status of the profession.

This trend is not restricted to Brazil and Venezuela. Table 4.2 compares the evolution of communication careers in seventeen Latin American countries between the 1980s and the 1990s. Although UNESCO aggregated into a single category students in social communication and in documentation majors, most of these students were in journalism programs. The figures do not allow a clear distinction between graduate and undergraduate programs, but most students were enrolled at the undergraduate level. Among the twelve countries with comparable data, eleven showed absolute increases in the number of students in communication programs over the decade, and nine displayed significant increases relative to the total enrollment. Only three countries appeared to suffer some relative decline. One of them was Venezuela, but the decline was not significant (p = .26, one-tailed z-test), and the series from the Consejo Nacional de Universidades displayed earlier suggest a sharp increase until the mideighties, then some decline, followed by a recovery in the 1990s. The only two countries with a decline in journalism careers were Peru and, most visibly, Chile. Although the UNESCO figures should be read with some caution, they suggest that there is a trend toward a more professional press corps in most countries throughout the region.

This rising number of journalism majors was exposed to teachers for whom the Watergate scandal in the United States had been a distant but crucial experience in their own youth. According to the Brazilian journalist Ricardo Noblat, "After Watergate, the dream of every journalist somehow became: *I will bring my president down if I am capable enough.*" Noblat recalled that during the Collor affair, the image of Watergate was "hanging as a ghost" over Brazilian journalists, and that many of his colleagues felt proud when the president was ousted (interview, August of 1998).

Many teachers of this generation had also been trained in the idea that journalism should confront power. Waisbord (1996, 346) has described a Latin American tradition that deemed "journalists as partisans equipped with typewriters." Resistance against censorship and coercion was a formative experience for this generation. In countries like Argentina, Brazil, and Chile, many journalists had fought against – and suffered the repression of – military regimes in the 1970s. In Venezuela, where civilian governments ruled, the press corps had viewed with horror a long advertising boycott (1961–63) against *El Nacional*, when American and local corporations condemned the newspaper for being too sympathetic to Fidel Castro and forced publisher Miguel Otero Silva to leave his own newspaper (Díaz Rangel 1994, 96–99; interview with Gloria Cuenca, July 21, 1998). The militant tradition among Latin American journalists was passed to the younger generations in the form of a "muckraking ethos" (Waisbord 1994, 29). Miguel H. Otero, publisher of *El Nacional*, pointed out that "thirty years ago, our journalists were on the left, so they had a philosophy [of contesting power]. Journalists nowadays are trained in that culture at journalism schools" (interview, July of 1998).

In this new context, journalists viewed the exposure of politicians' misdeeds as part of their professional role. Investigation became a professional value and the disclosure of scandals the path to a successful career. This professional culture brought greater incentives for journalists to investigate the president and his or her collaborators, strengthening the watchdog role of the press but also creating important institutional problems.

The New Press in Perspective

Even though the four processes just described have transformed the nature of presidential accountability in Latin America, it is important to avoid a naïve interpretation of the position of the press in this new environment. The new press has played a critical role in making governments more accountable (Smulovitz and Peruzzotti 2000), but it is far from being a transparent institution. Nobody is more aware of its institutional vices than the journalists themselves.

According to the Venezuelan journalist and university teacher Gloria Cuenca, three challenges compromise the quality of journalism in Latin America. The first one is cynicism: many journalists adopt a skeptical view of anything related to politics (see Patterson 1994 for a similar claim in the U.S. context). The second one is corruption: some journalists receive bribes in exchange for favorable coverage – a practice Venezuelans call *palangrismo*. Coppedge (1994b, 36) also noted this problem in the Venezuelan context; Lavieri (1996, 187–189) identified a similar pattern in Argentina; and Orme (1997, 8) and Keenan (1997) did so for Mexico. The third problem is reliability: professional ambition encourages many journalists to seek "accusations for their own sake" (interview with Gloria Cuenca, July of 1998). Discussing this issue, Sarmiento noted that in Mexico greater press freedom did not always inspire a more professional press (Sarmiento 1997, 33). The Brazilian news anchor Carlos Chagas described this third problem as the result of a "pendulum effect":

The [Brazilian] press of the late eighties was too irritated, too exaggerated. That [behavior] was natural after twenty-one years of military rule. With freedom recovered, the press overstated a little: *every* politician was a thief, *every* official was corrupt. They wanted to denounce *every* irregularity, because that used to be forbidden.... Therefore, well, the press exaggerated. (interview, August, 1998)

The new investigative drive has not always been backed by proper professional skills, and resources. Waisbord (1996, 351) reported that the investigative teams created by Peruvian newspapers failed to produce many remarkable stories. A journalist who shall remain anonymous complained about the Venezuelan press lacking a real investigative tradition, and claimed that most scandal stories are not investigated in depth: "Issues are born and die within few days.... This is a servile press, a press for hire, a, a ... *very strange* press" (interview, July of 1998). Professional values were eventually set back to nineteenth-century standards in the early 2000s, when the Venezuelan mainstream press vehemently embraced the task of confronting the populist President Hugo Chávez instead of reporting the facts in a balanced way (on this issue see Francia 2002; Petkoff 2002; Tanner Hawkins 2003).[7]

The press has also been unable to pursue stories because of the restricted access to public information in many Latin American countries. According to the journalist Daniel Santoro, "investigative journalism is no easy task in Argentina because journalists lack the legal resources to enable automatic access to public records" (quoted by Lavieri 1996, 195).

To some extent, this gap between the capacity to produce good investigative reporting and the professional (and political) impulse to disclose cases of corruption has been resolved through "declarative journalism." Several journalists interviewed for this project described a style of reporting that emphasizes politicians' statements more than any other form of evidence, one that seeks to report accusations voiced by traditional sources rather than documenting the actual misdeeds. Sometimes, explained the publisher of *El Nacional*, declarative journalism falls on the verge of manipulation:

In the 1980s the editorial line combined with a *more interactive* [sic] relationship with politicians.... The editor had information about corruption, so he collected statements by politicians who pointed in that direction. The lack of depth in the investigation – because there was no way of finding documents – was compensated by statements, by other means.... The ones in charge [of the newsroom] had the intuition that someone was corrupt and produced declarations of politicians saying so.... Here [at *El Nacional*] they used to say: "Minister So and So is corrupt. Let's get that guy who is his enemy to tell us so." They would interview the guy, run the story, and then the whole thing relied on the statement from a guy who was the minister's enemy saying that the minister was corrupt. They used to do that in good faith, because they had information but lacked the proof. But we can make mistakes that way.... (interview, July of 1998)

According to Otero, the solution to this problem is to hire more journalists, to create more investigative teams, and to rely less on politicians' declarations. Ricardo Noblat, the editor of the newspaper *Correio Braziliense*, confirmed this diagnosis in the Brazilian setting:

I would not say that this is a malformation of all Brazilian journalism, but we do have in Brazil too much *journalism of declaration*.... Declarative journalism is [practiced] in Brazil not only to avoid investigating accusations – although we investigate less

[7] The other side of the coin was Chávez's ambiguous position regarding free speech, his administration's hostile reaction to any form of press criticism, and its politicizacion of state-owned media (see Tanner Hawkins 2003).

than we could and should do. I think that this is more of a collective state of laziness. It is easier for a journalist to go to Congress and come back with some statements than to go after the facts.

According to Noblat, other factors also account for the practice of declarative journalism: a professional culture that has a fascination with statements and with the spoken word, and the need to have people on record to back up news stories (interview, August of 1998).

Waisbord (2000, 103–110) called this practice *denuncismo* ("quick and easy reporting" based on few sources) and portrayed it as a common problem in South America (see also Palermo 2002, 307). Describing the situation of the press in Mexico, Riva Palacio (1997, 29) also noted that "most publishers and editors were trained in the old school of journalism, in which statements weight more heavily than actions, and rhetoric is more important than information. Newspapers are full of speeches, statements and press releases." Declarative journalism is not unique to Latin America; it is also well known in American newsrooms. Patterson (1994, 245) called this style of reporting "attack journalism," and Boorstin (1987, 24–26) noted that professional pressures had made this practice common long before Watergate.

Media Incentives and the Politics of Scandal

How did the trends discussed in this chapter – democratization, deregulation, the expansion of television, and increasing professionalism – contribute to the emergence of impeachment crises in the 1990s? Understood in broad terms, the press is a set of formal and informal institutions (news organizations' procedures, media markets, technical standards, and professional values) that regulates the way in which most politicians have daily access to mass audiences. By defining what is newsworthy, media institutions operate as gatekeepers, preventing some politicians from achieving visibility and exposing the behavior of others when they would like to remain hidden from the public eye.[8] Therefore, after the third wave of democratization, political careers became highly dependent on access to the mass

---

[8] I do not imply that journalists unilaterally control the agenda. The press relies on government officials to set the agenda (Oviedo 1997), and a complex set of formal and informal rules typically regulates the interaction between politicians and the press corps (e.g., see Keenan 1997; Riva Palacio 1997).

media. In the classic words of Thomas Patterson, "the road to nomination now runs through the newsrooms" (Patterson 1994, 33).

The transformation of the Latin American media shaped the politics of impeachment in two ways. On the one hand, technological changes allowed presidents to gain greater independence from their party structures while creating new incentives to build corruption networks. According to Kurt Weyland (1998a), neopopulist politicians (like Fernando Collor in Brazil, Carlos Menem in Argentina, Alberto Fujimori in Peru, and even Carlos A. Pérez in Venezuela) were able to reach independent voters, including urban informal workers and the rural poor, via television. Television made them less dependent on party bosses and conventional mobilization structures and thus more willing to confront traditional elites. At the same time, reliance on public opinion polls and television advertising made their operations very expensive. The lack of horizontal accountability, combined with the increasing need for resources, created incentives to build comprehensive corruption schemes.

On the other hand, greater press freedom and a new professional ethos among journalists created the right environment for the politics of scandal (see Ginsberg and Shefter 1990; Jiménez Sánchez 1994; Waisbord 2000, 110–118). Quite often, politicians and other elite members advance their own policy goals and careers by hurting their adversaries, and media scandals became increasingly effective for this purpose. Insiders of party politics leaked contentious information to the press hoping that public outrage would wipe their competitors (inside or outside the party) from the electoral arena. Corporations leaked stories of corruption when public officials pushed requests for kickbacks beyond customary practice. These sources hardly controlled the consequences of scandals once they had spoken, but they learned to use disclosure as a powerful political weapon.[9] Professional conventions for speaking "off the record" or remaining "in the background"

---

[9] Most of the journalists interviewed for this project agreed that sources – in politics, just as in show business – use disclosure as a weapon against their rivals. Francisco Figueroa (EFE, Caracas) summarized this view: "No one has ever unveiled a scandal unless there was a rivalry involved. [Scandals serve] to attack your enemy, to knock off your rivals in a public contract, in an election, or in other situations." Miguel Otero (*El Nacional*, Caracas) pointed out that "sources speak due to the struggle for power: internal factions seek to destroy others; someone was left out of the loop; someone wants to take over and needs to bring down the guy at the top." Carlos Chagas (TV Manchete, Brasília): "Sources generally speak in pursuit of their interests – interests, revenge, *vendetta*.... If the guy was betrayed [he threatens]: *I am going to implicate you all.* But, well, some of them speak with good intentions, too...."

guaranteed that the information would be published without exposing the source, minimizing the risk for those insiders who could unleash accusations from a relatively safe position (Waisbord 2000, 95–100).

In this context, scandals became a powerful political weapon. Some presidents rejoiced when media scandals weakened the popularity of their predecessors and adversaries: Carlos Andrés Pérez seemed to benefit when accusations against Jaime Lusinchi erupted in Venezuela, and Alberto Fujimori took advantage of a well-publicized trial against Alan García in Peru. But their enemies increasingly turned this weapon against them when presidential approval ratings started to wane. In turn, other officials (judges, prosecutors, comptrollers, and solicitors general) advanced their own careers by investigating such accusations and publicizing their findings in the media.

Any interpretation emphasizing the strategic use of scandals by ambitious politicians opens the question of similar strategic behavior on the part of the media. If professional politicians "prey on the weak" by disclosing sensitive information when the president's popularity is in decline, it is possible that editors and producers behave in a similar way, pursuing more investigative stories when their readers and audiences are dissatisfied with the administration and the president's office is in a weak position to retaliate. Thus, the distribution of scandals during the life cycle of an administration may not only reflect the evolution of wrongdoing; it may also signal the changing perceptions of presidential strength of the sources disclosing information and the media outlets disseminating news stories. I will return to this issue in the following chapter.

To the extent that the political, economic, technological, and professional changes discussed in this chapter explain the proliferation of scandals in the 1990s, they cannot explain their political consequences. According to Natahan Yanai (1990), not every scandal becomes a true political *affair* – scandals refer to particular invidicuals, while affairs involve the polity as a whole (Yanai 1990, 185). In the cases discussed in Chapter 2, accusations only became true "affairs" when particular scandals combined with public outrage to breed an impeachment crisis.

5

Scandals and the Political Economy of
Popular Outrage

To what extent are scandals capable of compromising public support for the president? Although the six presidents discussed in Chapter 2 took office with the support of significant majorities, they suffered considerable losses in public approval throughout the process leading to the impeachment crisis. The average president in this group started his term with an approval rating of 64 percent but left office with a rating of just 23 percent. An overall declining trend in approval ratings is not uncommon among presidents in office, but these cases are notable for the level of deterioration and for the ultimate consequences of the process. The escalation of public discontent fueled mass protests that ultimately encouraged impeachment proceedings against the president.

Although impeachment charges in each case resulted from specific accusations against the president – with the exception of Bucaram, who was declared mentally unfit after a long series of exposés – the conventional wisdom suggests that unpopular economic reforms and poor economic performance were important factors explaining the emergence of public unrest in those countries. On the one hand, the historical narratives presented in the second chapter suggest that at least in three cases (Bucaram, González Macchi, and Pérez) popular protest was in part a direct reaction to the administration's attempts to impose neoliberal reforms. On the other hand, students of advanced industrial democracies have consistently shown that macroeconomic performance is one of the best predictors of public support for the government. This argument is particularly relevant for Latin America during this period: Kurt Weyland has convincingly argued that the impeachments of Fernando Collor and Carlos Andrés Pérez resulted not only from political isolation but also from their incapacity to "stop further economic deterioration" (Weyland 2002, 158).

It is therefore essential to determine whether the public standing of these six administrations was hurt by media scandals, by the adoption of unpopular policies, by poor macroeconomic outcomes, or by all of these factors simultaneously. If, on the one hand, public outrage is explained solely by unpopular policies or by negative macroeconomic conditions, impeachment can be a highly unreliable procedure: corrupt or abusive politicians in new democracies will be immune to scandal when the economy is performing well, and honest politicians will be exposed to popular calls for their removal if they adopt controversial programs (see Kada 2003a).[1] If, on the other hand, public outrage is the product of media accusations, it is important to determine what factors drive the production of exposés in the first place. The previous chapter suggested that the press and its sources often follow strategic considerations, and this could mean that low approval ratings encourage the publication of scandals as much as they result from them.

In the first section of this chapter, I document the decline in presidential approval in the six cases under study and explore three conventional explanations for this drop. In the following section, I trace the process of declining approval in Brazil (1990–92), Venezuela (1989–93), Colombia (1994–98), Ecuador (1996–97), and Paraguay (1998–2002). I revisit the historical narratives presented in Chapter 2 in order to identify the timing and sequence of events (scandals, policy decisions, and economic trends) that presumably undermined presidential approval. In the third section, I test alternative explanations for the emergence of public outrage using time-series cross-section models. Although limited, the available evidence suggests that both policy issues and media accusations drove the decline of public support for these presidents. Moreover, the results support the hypothesis regarding strategic behavior on the part of the media.

Scandals and the Economics of Presidential Approval

The six presidents who confronted impeachment crises initially enjoyed respectable approval ratings ranging from 81 percent in the case of Ernesto Samper to 53 percent in the case of Raúl Cubas Grau. But over their terms,

---

[1] Unfortunately, the reelection of Presidents Carlos Menem of Argentina (1995) and Alberto Fujimori of Perú (1995) lends credibility to these doubts. On the problem of type I and type II errors in the impeachment process, see Kada (2003a).

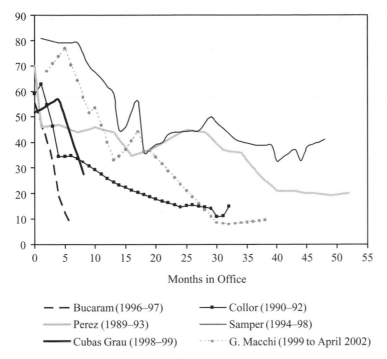

Figure 5.1 presidential approval lines chart showing Months in Office (x-axis 0–55) versus approval (y-axis 0–90).

Legend:
- — — Bucaram (1996–97)
- ——•— Collor (1990–92)
- ——— Perez (1989–93)
- ——— Samper (1994–98)
- ——— Cubas Grau (1998–99)
- ····•··· G. Macchi (1999 to April 2002)

Figure 5.1 Presidential approval in six impeachment crises. *Sources:* Datafolha and IBOPE (Brazil), Napoleón Franco y Asociados (Colombia), Market (Ecuador), First (Paraguay), and Consultores 21 (Venezuela).

popular support fell significantly. Luis González Macchi lost the support of 58 percent of the population; Carlos Andrés Pérez, of 50 percent; Fernando Collor, of 48 percent; Ernesto Samper, of 40 percent; and Raúl Cubas Grau, of 26 percent. Abdalá Bucaram's approval rating declined between 17 and 46 percent points, depending on whether polls were conducted in his stronghold, the city of Guayaquil, or in the Ecuadorian highlands. Those figures suggest that the politics of scandal discussed in the previous chapter may have weakened those presidents significantly.

Figure 5.1 traces the erosion of approval ratings for the six presidents over the course of their terms. On average, they lost between one and one and a half points of popularity every month. The exceptions were Abdalá Bucaram and Raúl Cubas, who lost ground at a much faster pace – about five and three points per month, respectively. Not surprisingly, Bucaram and Cubas were not able to finish their first year in office.

89

How can we interpret the different patterns of decline in presidential approval? I explore three possible explanations. The first one, particularly relevant for Latin America in the 1990s, refers to the imposition of unpopular neoliberal reforms. The second one, based on the well-known literature on sociotropic voting, emphasizes dismal macroeconomic performance. The third interpretation refers to the impact of political scandals. These three explanations are not contradictory but rather complementary. The key question, however, is how much of the popular outrage unleashed against these administrations can be imputed to each of these factors.

Economic Reforms

Throughout the 1990s, several Latin American presidents adopted (or attempted to adopt) harsh economic reforms. In spite of their campaign promises, presidents told voters that their bank savings would be frozen; that gas rates, electricity rates, and bus fares would be raised; that subsidies for the poor would be cut; and that public employees would be laid off (Stokes 2001; Weyland 2002). A quick look at the data suggests that these announcements had significant political costs. Fernando Collor's approval rating (71 percent in March of 1990) fell to 36 percent by June, after all bank accounts were frozen for eighteen months. Carlos Andrés Pérez's approval rating (70 percent in January of 1989) dropped to 46 percent by March, after increases in bus fares triggered violent riots. Confirming this perception, one of his ministers noted that "Pérez displayed an unusual willingness to incur the political costs that inevitably accompany major reforms" (Naím 1993, 46).

Multivariate analyses tend to support the "political cost" hypothesis. Buendía (1996) showed that basic price increases led to declining presidential approval in Mexico, and Weyland (1998b) documented a link between support for economic reforms and presidential approval in Venezuela. However, the relationship between economic adjustment and presidential approval deserves a more careful examination. On the one hand, because presidents typically launch economic reforms early in their terms (when they are stronger, but when their approval rates are volatile), it is unclear how much of the subsequent drop in public support is the result of their policies and how much is explained by the end of the "honeymoon" period (Gronke and Brehm 2002). On the other hand, voters may support reformist governments despite the costs of adjustment, either in the hope that ensuing economic recovery will compensate for the losses (Stokes 1996a) or to overcome a hyperinflationary crisis (Gervasoni 1998; Stokes 1996b; Weyland 1999; Weyland 2002).

Macroeconomic Performance

Studies of presidential approval and voting behavior in industrial democracies have consistently shown that economic performance is a major predictor of public support for the government (Beck 1991; Lewis-Beck and Paldam 2000; Lewis-Beck and Stegmaier 2000). Although there is general agreement that people hold the president accountable for economic performance, the literature has shown some disagreement on the specifics. It has been argued that the electorate is more sensitive to economic downturns than to prosperity (Bloom and Price 1975), that voters react more strongly to trends in the national economy than to their individual (pocketbook) situation (Kinder and Kiewiet 1981), that their evaluations of the economy are prospective rather than retrospective (Chappell and Keech 1985; MacKuen, Erikson, and Stimson 1992), and that the impact of retrospective evaluations is greater when an incumbent is running for reelection (Nadeau and Lewis-Beck 2001).

Given the need to achieve comparability across cases and the existing limitations of information, I will bypass some of these debates and concentrate instead on the more general question of how macroeconomic performance (inflation and unemployment) shaped the decline in public support for the six administrations under study. Susan Stokes (2001) has shown that during this period Latin American voters based their judgment of incumbent governments on actual macroeconomic results rather than on the ideological content of the policies implemented. In turn, Weyland (1998b) showed that pocketbook expectations of the economy dominated the evaluations of Carlos Andrés Pérez and his economic program between 1989 and 1993. There is also clear evidence of economic voting in new democracies outside Latin America (e.g., Hesli and Bashkirova 2001).

Scandals, Voter Subjectivity, and the Feeding Frenzy

Students of political behavior have long considered the presence of scandals as an important control variable in models of presidential approval. Norpoth (1996) claimed that the impact of economic expectations on presidential approval is extremely sensitive to scandals and other political factors. After looking at the Clinton–Lewinsky affair in the United States, Shah and colleagues (2002) concluded that the framing of media scandals may have a significant impact on presidential approval even when the president's popularity appears to be impregnable to the accusations. In a comparative study of public opinion trends during the Colombian and Venezuelan crises, Jaime Bermúdez (1999) similarly showed that media coverage was an important predictor of Samper's and Pérez's approval ratings.

Unfortunately, the effects of media scandals on presidential approval may be hard to pinpoint. For instance, in a study of the Lewinsky episode, Fischle (2000) found that the impact of subjective considerations (e.g., the importance given to the allegations) on individual reactions to the scandal was conditional on the respondent's prior support for President Clinton. Stokes (2001, 135–136, 149) claimed that in the case of Carlos A. Pérez, poor economic performance encouraged citizens to believe that government corruption was to blame.[2] These findings suggest that the effect of scandals on aggregate approval rates at time t may be mediated by the president's political capital at time $t - 1$.

At the same time, the previous chapter suggested that strategic politicians, editors, and publishers may be more likely to engage in the politics of scandal when the president is weak and when the public already distrusts the chief executive. Like the general public, journalists may lend little credence to the first accusations reaching the newsrooms, but they may actively pursue exposés if prior scandals have enveloped the executive. A Brazilian journalist discussing the Collor case recalled that "[w]e heard the first corruption story, then the second, then the third.... In the end we realized that the country was ruled by the Mob" (Carlos Chagas, interview August 1998). The news media may therefore be reluctant to investigate a popular president, but they may easily join the "feeding frenzy" once the executive is discredited (Sabato 1993). If this hypothesis is correct, scandals and presidential approval may have a reciprocal causal relationship.[3]

In the following section, I reconstruct the interactions among neoliberal reforms, economic performance, media scandals, and presidential approval in the countries under study. Approval data (presented in Figure 5.1) is confronted with data on inflation and unemployment for Brazil (sources: IBGE

---

[2] Similarly, Elimar Pinheiro claimed that in Brazil "for corruption to be identified, investigated, and made public ... it was necessary to make the President symbolically responsible for the situation of economic difficulty that most people were suffering" (Pinheiro 1992, 32).

[3] I am indebted to Susan Stokes for her comments on this issue.

and SPES), Colombia (DANE), Ecuador (INEC), Venezuela (BCV and OCEI), and Paraguay (Departamento de Cuentas Nacionales, DGEEC).

I chose to measure the incidence of media scandals using a simple indicator: the ratio of total exposés to the administration's time in office in months. This index of exposure to scandals is defined as $S_t = (N_t/t) \times 100$, where S_t is the value of the index for the president's t-th month in office; N_t is the total number of scandals involving the president, his close collaborators (ministers, personal advisors, etc.), and his family since the administration's inauguration; and t is the number of time units (months in office) elapsed. Scandals are defined as news events disclosing episodes of corruption or abuse of power; they were coded using local news sources and some secondary sources (for a complete list of scandals for each administration, see the appendix table to this chapter).[4] This simple measure has two major advantages. First, it captures the incidence of scandals as opposed to general positive or negative coverage (e.g., news stories related to the economy). Second, it is relatively easy to compute, to compare across countries, and to replicate using alternative sources. The index provides a summary measure of how much an administration is subject to accusations at any given point in time. In the following pages, I discuss the values of this index in the historical context of each administration.

Case Studies

Table 5.1 summarizes the situation of the six administrations under study. The top panel compares the administrations in terms of their adoption of neoliberal reforms and the average monthly and yearly levels of inflation and unemployment. As a reference point, I have also included performance indicators for the administrations that immediately preceded them.[5] It is not clear that those administrations performed much worse than their predecessors (although some deterioration seemed to occur under Collor and Pérez regarding inflation and under Samper and Bucaram regarding unemployment), but they were clearly unable to implement successful policies.

---

[4] Sources used to identify scandals included the following newspapers and magazines: *Folha de São Paulo* (Brazil), *El Nacional* (Venezuela), *El Comercio* (Ecuador), *Ultima Hora* (Paraguay), *Semana* (Colombia), and *Latin American Weekly Report* (for several countries). For the sequence of events in the Samper case, I also relied on Betancourt Pulecio (1996).

[5] The administrations of José Sarney in Brazil, César Gaviria in Colombia, Sixto Durán Ballén in Ecuador, Juan Carlos Wasmosy in Paraguay, and Jaime Lusinchi in Venezuela.

Table 5.1. *Summary of the six administrations*

Administration's Average Performance	Collor	Pérez	Samper	Bucaram		Cubas	González Macchi
Economy							
Adjustment policy	Yes	Yes	No	Yes		No	Yes?
Monthly inflation (1)	21.3	3.4	1.5	2.7		0.5	0.9
Annual inflation (2)	1690.3	47.7	20.9	24.4		11.5	8.4
(Prior administration)	532.3	18.4	27.3	37.4		13.8	11.5
Unemployment (1)	5.4	9.0	11.1	10.1		12.7	9.5
Unemployment (2)	3.7	9.4	10.1	10.4		5.4	6.8
(Prior administration)	3.2	10.7	9.3	7.8		5.3	5.4
Scandals							
Scandal index	43	33	31	256		48	16
President involved?	Yes	Yes	Yes	No		Yes?	No?
Approval (3)				Quito	Coast		
Maximum approval	63	70	81	53	54	57	77
Minimum approval	11	19	33	4	11	27	8
Average rate of change	−1.4	−2.8	−0.9	−2.8	0.3	−3.1	−1.6
Protest coalition	Broad	Broad	Narrow	Broad	Medium	Broad	Medium
Months in office	32	54	49	7		8	38

Sources: Economy: (1) Average monthly (or quarterly) rates compiled from IBGE and SPES (Brazil), DANE (Colombia), INEC (Ecuador), Departamento de Cuentas Nacionales and DGEEC (Paraguay), BCV and OCEI (Venezuela). These figures are used in the pooled time-series models to be discussed later. (2) Yearly rates reported by the World Development Indicators (World Bank, 2005). Comparisons to previous administrations are based on yearly figures.

Scandals: *Folha de São Paulo* (Brazil), *El Comercio* (Ecuador), Betancourt Pulecio (1996) and *Semana* (Colombia), *Ultima Hora* (Paraguay), *El Nacional* (Venezuela), and *Latin American Weekly Report* (for several countries). See the appendix table to this chapter for a complete list of scandals.

Approval: Datafolha and IBOPE (Brazil), Napoleón Franco (Colombia), Informe Confidencial (Ecuador), First (Paraguay), and Consultores 21 (Venezuela). (3) Surveys in Ecuador were conducted separately in Quito and Guayaquil by Informe Confidencial.

The table also presents monthly averages for the scandal index introduced in the previous section, and indicates whether the president was directly affected by the accusations. Episodes of direct involvement include Pedro Collor's accusations against his brother Fernando, the investigation of the 250 Million case in Venezuela, and the accusations against Ernesto Samper by Santiago Medina and Fernando Botero. No such accusations were ever explicitly made against Abdalá Bucaram, and the evidence is mixed regarding Paraguayan Presidents Raúl Cubas and Luis González Macchi. Cubas was accused of being in contempt of the Supreme Court, but his reluctance to imprison Oviedo (as requested by the Court) was never a secret. By contrast, it was always assumed that González Macchi was personally involved in several corruption scandals, but the opposition failed to create a high-profile investigation linking the president to the cases.

The bottom panel summarizes the reaction of the mass public to each administration's performance. In addition to the rate of change in presidential approval ratings, I included a qualitative assessment of the scope of the social movements calling for the resignation of the president. This assessment is based on historical analysis of the cases to be presented later.

Table 5.1 suggests that the combination of scandals and (failed) economic reforms can erode presidential popularity and encourage multiclass protests against the president. There are, however, partial exceptions to this pattern. In Guayaquil, where Bucaram's party preserved historical patronage networks among the popular sectors, the combined effects of scandals and economic reforms were less harmful for the administration. In another case, the willingness of the González Macchi administration to compromise on policy issues hindered the formation of a multiclass coalition in favor of impeachment. As I will show, Paraguayan peasants mobilized against specific policies, but the administration was able to deactivate peasant protests and prevented a mass movement in favor of impeachment.

The evidence presented in the table fails to establish an indisputable causal pattern, suggesting instead that these factors can provide only partial explanations for the emergence of public unrest. In order to address this problem, I follow two opposite but complementary strategies. In the following sections, I engage in process tracing to establish the precise sequence of events leading to the impeachment crises. In contrast to my approach in Chapter 2, these narratives emphasize the evolution of the key variables presented in Table 5.1 (see George and Bennett 2005, Chapter 10). Building on the insights of these case studies, in the final part of the chapter I conduct a quantitative analysis of the interrelationships among neoliberal policies, economic performance, media scandals, and public outrage.

Angry Left, Perplexed Right

By the time Fernando Collor took office, the Brazilian economy was in disarray. The failure of three heterodox economic plans during the Sarney administration had left the country on the brink of hyperinflation. As consumer prices increased by 1,322 percent in 1989, candidate Collor promised to "kill the tiger of inflation with a stroke of my sword."

Confronted with a loss of credibility and political support, Collor reshuffled his cabinet in April of 1992. The plan would not fly. A few weeks later, his younger brother, Pedro Collor, told *Veja* magazine that the president was involved with his former campaign manager, Paulo César (P. C.) Farias, in a vast corruption scheme. Sensing Collor's weakness, the Brazilian Congress responded by creating a joint committee (Comissão Parlamentar de Inquerito, CPI) to investigate the case (Kada 2003a, 121–123). During July and August, the CPI exposed important parts of the scheme, igniting mass demonstrations in favor of the impeachment process. Presidential approval ratings dropped further, from 15 percent in May to 11 percent in August. The scandal index reached an all-time high of 71 points in September of 1992, dropping slightly to 69 points (or one scandal every six weeks) in October.

Popular protests in support of Collor's impeachment represented the largest mobilization since Brazilians had taken to the streets to demand direct presidential elections at the end of the military dictatorship in 1984 (during the *direitas já* campaign). Hundreds of thousands joined the protests in several cities. When Collor denounced a conspiracy and asked voters to dress in the colors of the national flag to signal their support for the president, demonstrators dressed in black to denote mourning and painted their hostile faces green and yellow. The mainstream media multiplied those images. A public opinion survey conducted in the city of São Paulo by *Datafolha* in late August indicated that, although the street coalition against Collor was mainly formed by large contingents of lower-class voters, participation by the upper middle class was proportionally greater: while 7 percent of the respondents with an income below five minimum salaries had participated in the protests, 10 percent of the respondents between five and ten minimum salaries, and 17 percent of the respondents in the bracket above ten minimum salaries, had joined the movement.

In 1990, Fernando Collor had promised that his policies would "infuriate the Left and leave the Right perplexed." His promise was certainly honored. Thirty-two months after taking office, Collor's political capital had shrunk by 48 percentage points, owing to the combined effects of harsh economic adjustment, poor economic performance, and corruption scandals. At the time, Margaret Keck argued that Collor's impeachment was not just about corruption. It was, she claimed, "about repeatedly raised expectations and about repeated failure and disappointment.... Not only was the government incompetent; it lacked dignity, and people cared" (Keck 1992, 7).

The Political Economy of Popular Outrage

Pérez's Great Turnaround

"Collor's ousting is a warning for President Pérez," declared Rafael Caldera, founder of the Venezuelan Christian Democratic party (Copei), who was looking for a second presidential term to crown his political career. Caldera's moralizing rhetoric in September of 1992 was cheap but timely. After barely surviving a failed military coup in February, the Pérez administration was on the ropes. Within two months, a new military uprising would take place.

By the time Collor's impeachment began, the Pérez administration had been in power for more than three and a half years. When Carlos Andrés Pérez took office for the second time in February of 1989, Venezuela was far from being the prosperous economy he had presided over in the 1970s. Oil exports – which had reached a ceiling of $32.5 billion in 1980 – had fallen to $10.5 billion by 1988 (figures in 1995 U.S. dollars; World Bank 2005). Throughout the 1980s, Venezuela had implemented no major economic transformations, and inflation, poverty, and income inequality were on the rise (Crisp and Kelly 1999). The Lusinchi administration (1984–89) had transferred an explosive situation to the incoming government. According to Moisés Naím, the minister of industry,

Venezuelans seemed astonished when the new government disclosed in early 1989 that foreign currency reserves were severely depleted, that the fiscal deficit for 1988 exceeded 9 percent of the GDP, that the current account had registered its largest deficit in history, and that all prices, from interest rates to eggs, from medicine to bus fares, were artificially low and impossible to sustain. (Naím 1993, 28)

But President Pérez still had his charisma: he was a living myth among Latin American politicians, and 70 percent of the voters had a favorable image of him in January of 1989, right after the election. He decided to invest this political capital in a bold gamble: economic recovery would require a "great turnaround" of the oil-dependent, import-substitution model. In February of 1989, the administration announced an economic program that included price deregulation, liberalization of exchange and interest rates, and adjustments in public sector prices (gasoline; public transportation; water, telephone, and electricity rates; and other public services). The long-term components of the reform involved plans for the adoption of a value-added tax (a shocking novelty for Venezuelans), trade liberalization, and privatizations (Naím 1993; Stokes 2001; Weyland 2002; interview with Miguel Rodríguez, July of 1998).

As an immediate consequence of the measures, the bolívar suffered a sharp devaluation (170 percent); interest rates climbed by 30 percent; and

bodyguards. Teodoro Petkoff, a leader of the left-wing MAS (Movimiento al Socialismo), who years later would become a key minister of the second Caldera administration, backed Uslar's story: the bodyguards were presumably trained at a private ranch in the state of Falcón. The human rights advocate Enrique Ochoa Antich announced that some fifty agents of the Disip (the political police) had been deployed in New York to protect the president's mistress, Cecilia Matos, during her vacation.

In mid-August, a leader of the Causa R Party demanded a congressional investigation of the "intimate entourage" (*entorno íntimo*) of President Pérez – a coded reference to Cecilia Matos. Members of AD asked the party's disciplinary tribunal to conduct an investigation of Matos's assets and the use of official bodyguards to protect her. Meanwhile, a court ordered the arrest of one of Pérez's close collaborators, a Navy officer linked to a 1988 case in which military communication equipment had been bought without public auction and related equipment worth six million dollars had been reported lost. By September of 1992, as the political crisis unfolded in Brazil, Pérez's exposure to scandals held steady at forty-eight points – roughly one new exposé every two months – and his approval rating had stabilized at around 20 percent.

In this context, voters took to the streets to demand Pérez's resignation by beating pots and pans – a form of middle-class protest that would survive into the Hugo Chávez era. As in the case of Collor, the available evidence suggests the presence of a multiclass protest coalition. In March of 1992, the research firm Consultores 21 asked a national sample of respondents about their participation in recent pan beatings. Seventeen percent of the people classified as members of "marginal" and "popular" sectors admitted their participation in the protests, while 27 percent of the "middle" and 46 percent of the "upper" sectors did so.

The Brazilian crisis was seen by the disoriented Venezuelan elite as a sign of the times. In September, a MAS politician asked the prosecutor general to initiate charges against the president for embezzlement, participation by his collaborators in fraud against the armed forces, and violations of human rights during the *Caracazo* and afterward. Meanwhile, Rafael Caldera preached that the ousting of Collor should send a warning to Pérez. On Sunday, November 8, José Vicente Rangel (future vice president in the Hugo Chávez administration) exposed the story of the secret funds during his TV show: 250 million bolívares had been taken from a secret account of the interior ministry and converted to $17.2 million at the preferential exchange rate. By Thursday, the story was on the front page of all major newspapers. Rangel openly wondered: "if Brazilian democracy was able to conduct an investigation [of the president] and was strengthened by its results, couldn't Venezuelan democracy do the same?"

On November 17, the oversight committee of the Chamber of Deputies formed an ad hoc subcommittee to study the case. In the following months, lower-level officials began to involve higher-ranking politicians in testimony during the hearings. In January of 1993, former solicitor general (*procurador general*) Nelson Socorro linked President Pérez to the story, followed a few weeks later by a former minister of interior, Alejandro Izaguirre, who admitted that the president had commanded the operation (Chitty La Roche 1993). Prosecutor General Jorge Escovar-Salom, who was conducting his own investigation, then asked the Supreme Court to assess the legal merits of the case in order to initiate a trial against the president. When the Court cleared the case, President Pérez took to the airwaves to express his farewell to the Venezuelan people, and the Senate unanimously suspended him from office.

Stokes and Baughman noted that "[i]n 1988 Venezuelans were worried about the economy; by 1989 they were worried about the economy and stability; and in 1993 they were still worried about the economy and stability, but they were also worried about corruption" (Stokes and Baughman 1999, 9). In March of 1989, when the scandal score for the Pérez administration was still at zero, only 2 percent of poll respondents mentioned corruption as one of their main concerns. By July of 1993, after twenty-four uninterrupted months with scandal scores over forty-five points, 20 percent referred to corruption as the main problem, placing this concern in second place after the cost of living.

The Pérez debacle resembles the Brazilian experience because the particular accusations that triggered the impeachment process arrived at a time when presidential approval was already low. In many ways the emergence of public outrage *preceded* the specific accusations that justified the president's removal from office – outrage was grounded, among other things, in a previous sequence of exposés. This situation was quite evident in the Pérez case: both demonstrations calling for the president's resignation and the legislative debate on how to replace the chief executive began long before the 250 Million scandal was even considered (see Chapter 2, this volume; Kornblith 1998, Chapter 3). It was not until Collor was suspended from office in September of 1992 that Venezuelan politicians realized that a trial was the constitutional course of action to solve the crisis – at least in the short run.

Surviving without Governing

Politicians in other countries were learning, too. When charges that his campaign had been financed by the Cali drug cartel surfaced two months before he was to be sworn into office, President Ernesto Samper understood that he would start his term under gloomy conditions. But in contrast to Fernando Collor and Carlos Andrés Pérez, both of whom initiated an era of economic reform in his country, President Ernesto Samper intended to moderate the pace of neoliberal reform imposed by César Gaviria (1990–94). Gaviria's program, popularly called "the shake-up" (*el Revolcón*), involved monetary policies targeted against inflation, trade liberalization (reduction of tariffs, abolition of import licenses and quotas), fiscal and financial reforms to encourage investment, a new foreign exchange regime that reduced controls and deregulated foreign investment, and a moderate deregulation of labor markets (see Hommes 1992). The 1991 constitutional reform also facilitated the creation of an independent central bank and a social security reform.

Samper took office in 1994 with a yearly inflation rate of 23 percent, and inflation continued at this level throughout his term: 19 percent in 1995, 22 percent in 1996, and 18 percent in 1997 (Banco de la República 1997). Unemployment, however, became a growing problem. Labor market analysts concluded that "the urban unemployment rate, in decline since 1986, increased from 9% in 1995 (June) to...15.8% in 1998, growing by more than 2 percent a year" (ILO 1998, 7). In addition, the administration was unable to implement effective negotiations with the guerrillas, and political violence kept rising. In 1996, almost 27,000 people were killed, more than 3,000 of them for political reasons (Chernick 1997, 20). Although the police were able to arrest important leaders of the Cali cartel in 1995 (reducing, to some extent, the credibility of the accusations against the president), the U.S. Congress decertified Colombia two years in a row (1996 and 1997).

Thus, although Samper presented himself as the alternative to his predecessor's neoliberalism, he could not present his administration as a model of policy success. According to John Dugas, the administration's focus on survival prevented the development of more ambitious initiatives of social and political reform. Political violence by both guerrillas and paramilitaries remained steady, and the economy entered a period of stagnation – the most severe recession since the Great Depression (Dugas 2001, 173).

In contrast to the cases of Collor, Pérez, and Bucaram (to be discussed later), the Samper administration was hurt not by a permanent background noise of multiple revelations, but by one recurrent issue: the use of drug-related funds during the presidential campaign. This complicates the use of my measure of scandals because it is hard to decide when one exposé ended and a new one began. For simplicity, I consider each phase of the Samper saga – that is, each episode disclosing new information and involving new people – as a separate scandal.

Although Samper never enjoyed a presidential honeymoon – scandals began immediately after he won the runoff election – the accusations initially faded because little new information was uncovered during his first months in office. By the end of 1994, Samper's approval rating remained at 79 percent, and the index of exposure to scandals was at twenty points (signaling some danger for a president in his fourth month in office) but declining. However, in early 1995 the investigative press published additional information that compromised several Liberal leaders in Congress as well as the comptroller general. In July, the treasurer of the campaign was arrested and confessed that he had received funds from the Cali cartel. The scandal score rose to thirty-eight points by August, when *Semana* magazine published the transcript of a cozy telephone conversation between President Samper and a woman related to the drug-dealing circuits. The president's approval rating fell to 45 percent by September.

In January, former campaign manager and minister of defense Fernando Botero (arrested in August) declared in a TV interview that President Samper was fully aware of the campaign-finance scheme. This cataclysmic episode kept the scandal index above the thirty-point mark for the rest of the year, as the investigation continued and Liberal legislators were charged and arrested (for a chronology of the scandal, see Betancourt 1996, 197–208; and Escallón and Ferreira 1996). Samper's approval rating fell to 36 percent in January following Botero's accusations, but recovered slightly afterward, reaching 44 percent by the time impeachment charges took shape in June.

This periodization is consistent with other interpretations of the process. Luis Alberto Restrepo, for instance, identified three phases of the scandal:

The first accusations against Samper came [in June of 1994] from the defeated presidential candidate, Andrés Pastrana, from the newspaper owned by his family, *La Prensa*, and from other public figures like candidate Enrique Parejo. Many

Colombians took them as an expression of resentment and almost as a betrayal to the country in front of the international community. After Medina's declarations [in July of 1995], criticism expanded to a well-known group of journalists, pundits, political leaders, and presidential candidates. Only at the beginning of 1996, after Botero's declarations and U.S. decertification, the critical voice of trade unions, the Catholic hierarchy, some NGOs, and small student and women caucuses in Bogotá was heard. (Restrepo 1996, 52)

Restrepo's analysis suggests that public outrage emerged only after 1995 and was concentrated in the Colombian middle and upper classes, as well as in some organized sectors of civil society (see Bermúdez 1999, 110–115). Describing the demonstrations in favor of Samper's impeachment, Cepeda Ulloa also noted that the "demonstrations of students and ladies[8] never acquired a popular flavor, reinforcing the unpalatable class overtones that characterized the most boisterous and notorious confrontation with a president [ever]" (Cepeda Ulloa 1996, 80).

After the Chamber of Representatives dismissed the impeachment charges in mid-1996, the incidence of scandals declined. In a futile attempt to convey its own verdict against Samper, the Clinton administration cancelled the Colombian president's visa. But it was not until early 1997 that new accusations against specific ministers surfaced. In March, the minister of defense resigned after being linked to a drug-related scandal. In May, the minister of transportation was accused of allowing Liberal politicians to use a public helicopter for campaign purposes. Three months later, the ministers of energy and communications resigned after *Semana* revealed that they had granted FM radio frequencies to political friends and split the benefits "half-and-half." By then, the measure of exposure to scandals was around thirty points – a pace of one exposé every three months – and any possibility of impeachment had been forestalled. The president's approval rating remained above the 30 percent mark until the end of the term, while the unemployment rate rose to 15 percent. The Samper administration had become a case of surviving without governing.

In Just One Shot

Maybe no other president included in this study has projected a more negative image than Abdalá Bucaram. Paradoxically, his administration was

---

[8] The translation is mine. Cepeda employs the term "señoras" (ladies) with an overt class connotation to refer to the upper-class women leading some demonstrations.

never enveloped by a high-profile, deeply investigated, Watergate-like scandal. Nor was Bucaram personally involved in any major investigation, as were Presidents Collor and Samper. But measured by the crude indicator adopted in this chapter, the exposure of Bucaram's administration to scandal was astonishing: some sixteen episodes of corruption or abuse of power were exposed over a six-month period in office, yielding a score of 267 points – or one scandal every ten days – by the time Bucaram was removed from office.

Bucaram's initial approval ratings were modest but solid: in August of 1996, 45 percent of respondents in the coastal city of Guayaquil and 53 percent of respondents in the Andean city of Quito supported the president. In contrast to Fernando Collor and Carlos Andrés Pérez, who took advantage of their honeymoon approval ratings to launch ambitious economic reforms, the Bucaram administration delayed the unpopular decisions for several months. As shown in Chapter 2, it was not until December 1, 1996 – almost four months after taking office – that Bucaram presented his economic program to the public.

While the administration failed to adopt a clear policy, the multiplication of scandals involving Bucaram's family and members of the cabinet quickly eroded its image. Shortly after he took office in August, the press accused the president of nepotism when he appointed his brother Adolfo and his brother-in-law Pablo Concha as members of the cabinet. At the same time, Congress complained that the president sought to impose a PRE politician for the nonpartisan position of comptroller general (this episode will be described in greater detail in Chapter 6). In September, the minister of energy, Alfredo Adum, was accused of physically assaulting the oil union leader Marcelo Román during a meeting. Two months into office, the administration already had a score of 200 points in the scandal index. In Guayaquil, the president's bailiwick, the levels of approval remained between 40 and 50 percent until early November. But in Quito, where voters viewed with great distaste the "coastal" style of Bucaram and his entourage, support quickly dropped to 29 percent by late October.

In mid-October, Bucaram unexpectedly flew to Miami in the presidential airplane with his son, Jacobo, without even transferring power to the vice president. Speculation about the reasons for the trip triggered a wave of mutual accusations between Bucaram and opposition legislators. Rumors about a substance abuse treatment for Jacobo infuriated the Bucaram family, but nobody, in the government or in the opposition, ever provided a clear explanation for the journey. In the meantime, the press disclosed that

Minister of Education Sandra Correa had plagiarized her doctoral dissertation. As the rather comical Correa affair unfolded in November, Alfredo Adum was again charged with attacking a female employee. The administration reached a scandal score of 300 points – an accusation every nine days – in November, when Bucaram's son was accused of meddling in government affairs and opposition politicians announced that PRE officials were charging public contractors a "party tax" on all government disbursements.

In early December, with approval ratings down to 37 percent in the coastal areas and 25 percent in the highlands, the administration finally presented its economic blueprint. The anchor of the program was the so-called convertibility plan: beginning in July of 1997, the new Ecuadorian currency (*nuevo sucre*) would be pegged to the dollar at a 4:1 ratio. The rest of the program was standard Washington consensus: the government would open the oil industry to foreign investment, privatize the electric company (Inecel), reform social security to allow for the creation of private retirement funds, reduce subsidies and government expenditures to eliminate the fiscal deficit, and "flexibilize" labor markets while providing new social programs for the unemployed.

Despite the announcement, the program never saw the light of day. The implementation of the package required important legal reforms in the areas of taxation, financial institutions, oil production, mining, and tariffs.[9] The Quito press estimated that implementing the whole program would require twenty-eight legal reforms, twenty new laws, and twenty-four constitutional amendments (*El Comercio*, August 12, 1996, A7). Although Congress ultimately resisted those measures (see Chapter 6), the initial adjustment of prices in preparation for the program sparked an escalation of inflation. The average monthly increase in the consumer price index had been around 2 percent during the first four months of the Bucaram administration. Following the announcements, inflation escalated to 8 percent on the coast and 6 percent in the highlands during January.

In the meantime, the administration was criticized for interfering in a private lawsuit involving the millionaire heirs of the Noboa family in order to favor the president of the Monetary Board. The minister of public works threatened a journalist after the EFE news service released a story reporting that somebody had stolen his underwear during his stay at a Quito hotel.

---

[9] The *Roldosistas* sensed the opportunity to introduce important political reforms as well. They dreamed of a constitutional reform that would allow presidential reelection, establish a five-tear term, and schedule legislative elections concurrent with the presidential runoff.

Later in December, Bucaram hosted a special Christmas TV program (the *"Teletón"*) in which he raised money for Ecuadorian children. After the show, the *Roldosistas* were charged with mishandling the donations. In January, accusations about the *Teletón* funds escalated; Sandra Correa resigned as Congress prepared to impeach her (presumably on charges of plagiarism); and Bucaram entered a bitter verbal fight with Social Christian leader Jaime Nebot. Most important, accusations about corruption in the customs service began to surface, triggering open criticism by the U.S. ambassador.

By January, approval ratings had collapsed to 11 percent on the coast and 6 percent in Quito. Confronted with increases in the prices of electricity, domestic gas, public transportation, and telephone service, people began to mobilize against the economic plan. Demonstrations took place in Quito, Guayaquil, Cuenca, and other cities. On January 11, a group of major trade unions and social movements formed the Frente Patriótico against the economic program and called for a general strike on February 5. The middle class in the highlands supported the strike as a way of protesting against the large number of scandals. On February 5, when a heterogeneous street coalition of Indian leaders, union workers, middle-class voters, and respectable upper-class *Quiteños* joined the "civic strike," an adversarial Congress seized the opportunity to declare the president insane (Ribadeneira 1997, 17; Ribadeneira, Hernández, and Aráuz 1997, 227). A poll conducted by *Informe Confidencial* in the cities of Quito and Guayaquil ten days later indicated that, just as in Brazil and Venezuela, respondents in the "upper" social stratum had participated in the protest proportionately more than members of the "popular" sectors (at rates of 43 percent in Quito and 30 percent in Guayaquil, versus 37 percent in Quito and 9 percent in Guayaquil for the popular sectors).

The Paraguayan Saga

The cases of Presidents Raúl Cubas Grau and Luis González Macchi present an interesting contrast. As explained in Chapter 2, the two administrations were shaken as a result of the ongoing conflict within the Colorado Party. In both cases, the Liberal Party sided with the administration's challengers in an attempt to weaken the Colorado hegemony. However, the life of the Cubas administration was, to borrow a Hobbesian metaphor, "nasty, brutish, and short," while the González Macchi administration suffered a slow, never-ending agony. During the Cubas era, one single issue – abuse of power – dominated the accusations against the executive. By contrast,

González Macchi, his family, and his collaborators confronted a myriad of more banal exposés over a longer period. Probably against his own will, Raul Cubas adopted a confrontational all-or-nothing stance, while Luis González Macchi was willing to bargain on virtually every front to avoid an impeachment.

Shortly after taking office with an approval rating of 53 percent, President Cubas issued a decree reducing Gen. Lino Oviedo's prison term and allowing for his immediate release. As explained in Chapter 2, Congress responded by framing this decision as a violation of the law. This interpretation gained currency early in December of 1998, when the Supreme Court ruled against the decree and urged the president to recapture Oviedo. Arguing that a military court had already overruled the original sentence against the general, Cubas responded that he had no legal ground to enforce the Court's order. The opposition then framed this reluctant position as a major threat to the rule of law in the country. By December of 1998 accusations of abuse of power were building up, and Cubas's scandal index was at forty points, but his approval ratings remained solidly around 50 percent.

Maybe it was this perception of strong popular support (Gen. Oviedo's own popularity remained at 44 percent in November of 1998) that encouraged the *Oviedista* camp to mobilize. On December 10, at a meeting of Oviedo's faction, Unace (National Union of Ethical Colorados), more than seven thousand demonstrators called for the resignation of the Supreme Court. The aggressive stand of the Unace forces – mobilizations multiplied throughout December – reinforced the media's framing of the issue in terms of abuse of power. The president was unable to counteract this narrative because General Oviedo appeared to be increasingly in control. In January of 1999, Chief Justice Wildo Rienzi responded by ruling that Cubas had "violated the rule of law" and ordered the executive branch to arrest Oviedo within three days.

The assassination of Vice President Luis M. Argaña on the morning of March 23 confirmed the worst fears of many Paraguayans. A lengthy investigation by the media, Congress, or the judiciary was considered unnecessary. Congressional leaders of all blocs – with the exception of the *Oviedista* faction – released a communiqué that blamed "President Raúl Cubas, in conspiracy with the runaway Lino Oviedo," for the "terrorist plan." The opposition warned that "the National Congress will adopt all necessary measures to reestablish the rule of law" (*ABC Color*, March 24, 1999).

The public's intimate conviction that Gen. Oviedo had organized the slaughter of the vice president triggered mass protests and drove the general's popularity down to 15 percent in April. President Cubas, responsible for Oviedo's freedom, also saw his approval rating drop to 20 percent. In spite of the sharp decline, those figures indicate the presence of a hardcore group of Unace voters willing to back the Oviedo–Cubas team under any circumstances. As mass protests unfolded, pro- and anti-impeachment demonstrators fought to gain control of the square in front of the Congress building. The first group was composed mostly of middle-class students, outraged at the slaughter of Argaña, and peasant unions, mobilized to demand policies for agricultural debt relief. The second group was made up of Unace militants. The debacle of the administration took place after March 26, when paramilitary snipers shot the anti-Oviedo demonstrators in the plaza. Confronting an impeachment in the Senate and major international pressures, and unwilling to see himself associated with the outbreak of violence, President Cubas boarded an airplane to Brazil two days later.

As explained in previous chapters, the Paraguayan elite responded to the crisis by forming a coalition government headed by the little-known speaker of the senate, Luis González Macchi. Initially, the collegial political style of González Macchi constituted an asset. Although not a popularly elected president, González Macchi started his term with a 68 percent approval rating, reaching 77 percent by July of 1999. However, public support began to fade afterward, and the coalition quickly broke up. One year later, in July of 2000, the president's approval rating was already at 44 percent. Two years later, in July of 2001, his popularity had plummeted to 10 percent. By then, Gen. Oviedo, bête noire in exile, had rebuilt his popularity to levels ranging around 40 percent.

The context of the decline in González Macchi's popular support was one of dismal economic performance. Unemployment, already at 13 percent during the Cubas period, reached 16 percent in 2000. The average growth rate between 1996 and 2000 was −1.9 percent (World Bank 2005). Confronted with mounting deficits, the administration embarked on a program to privatize telecommunication services, water and sewerage, and the national railroads. The policy met with suspicion among orthodox Colorados and was overtly opposed by the trade unions and the peasant movement. In March of 2000, fifteen thousand peasants marched to Asunción and joined forces with the trade unions against privatizations. In June, the National Workers Confederation (Central Nacional de

Trabajadores, CNT) called for a national strike. Even though many Liberals agreed with the privatization program, electoral incentives – the vice presidential election was scheduled for August – drove them away from supporting the administration's policies.

The decline in approval ratings was also encouraged by a sequence of media exposés beginning in November of 1999, when the comptroller general was accused of embezzlement, money laundering, and corruption. As the case received ample coverage in February and March of 2000, the media disclosed additional stories about irregular contracts in the Social Security Institute (IPS). The scandal index rose from zero in October of 1999 to seventeen points in February of 2000 – a scandal every six months – and approval ratings declined from 51 percent in November of 1999 to 33 percent following the peasant protests in March of 2000.

Some military officers saw this drop in public support as an opportunity and attempted to seize power in May of 2000, fourteen months after González Macchi had taken office. The wave of accusations receded for a few months in the aftermath of this failed coup, but resurged later in 2000 when the Ministry of Public Works was charged with diverting funds collected at toll roads for purposes other than road maintenance. In February of 2001, the press published stories revealing that the president had instructed the Social Security Institute to invest almost half of its reserves to rescue a public bank. Around that time, a Japanese development bank accused Minister of Public Works Walter Bower of manipulating the rules for the allocation of road maintenance contracts.

In March, press investigations confirmed ongoing stories that the BMW regularly used by President González Macchi had been stolen in Brazil, and that the Finance Ministry had authorized the purchase of the stolen car. Two months later, the executive was accused of transferring $16 million from the coffers of two banks intervened by the Central Bank to a private account in New York. The head of the central bank was forced to resign, and an opposition front of Liberals and *Oviedistas* in Congress called for the impeachment of the president.

Thirty thousand peasants again marched to Asunción to demand access to credit and better conditions for cotton production in March of 2001. Following new protests against privatizations in August, the Catholic Church organized a round table of national dialogue. By then, presidential approval ratings were around 8 percent and the scandal index had reached twenty-six points – or a scandal every four months. Although the opposition talked about impeaching the president, it failed to develop a high-profile congressional investigation. The negotiations sponsored by the church deactivated the threats of impeachment in early September of 2001.

The truce did not last. In January of 2002, live television showed the dramatic release of two leaders of a left-wing movement (prime suspects in a woman's kidnapping) who had been held by security forces in a clandestine prison for thirteen days. After this incident, the prosecutor general was indicted for human rights abuses, the minister of the interior resigned, and the president was accused of "state terrorism." On February 21, a thousand people marched against human rights abuses, calling for the impeachment of the prosecutor general and the president.

In April, with the human rights scandal still fresh, the media published a new corruption story. The government had paid more than a half-million dollars to a private notary to register the transfer of assets from the old public telephone company to the new corporation to be privatized – but according to Paraguayan public law, a state notary should have registered the transfer at no cost. This episode, which involved the president's brother and sister, shook the already weak political foundations of the privatization process. Two months later, thousands of peasants marched for the third time to Asunción to protest against privatizations, and the CNT called a general strike for June 14, 2002. This would be the only moment during the González Macchi administration when mass mobilizations seemed to converge with the goal of *Oviedista* and Liberal legislators of impeaching the president.

Worried about the situation, Colorado leaders publicly requested the suspension of the privatization process. On June 4, a commission of members of Congress negotiated with union and peasant leaders the repeal of the program in exchange for the deactivation of the protests. Without popular mobilization, the opposition in Congress lost momentum. On the afternoon of June 6, 2002, Congress suspended the sale of all public companies, and the administration had averted an impeachment crisis for the second time.

The success of the antiprivatization movement encouraged a new round of protests. In mid-July, thousands of peasants blocked roads in Asunción and in five other departments, including key cities and bridges on the borders with Brazil and Argentina. The government declared a national emergency for two days, and police repression led to the deaths of two demonstrators and hundreds of arrests. Two months later, the police disbanded thousands of *Oviedista* and Liberal demonstrators who demanded the resignation of the president in downtown Asunción. Even at this point, and in contrast to March of 1999, the peasant movement remained centered on specific policy goals and did not serve as the fulcrum for a broad multiclass movement demanding the removal of the president. The middle class despised the president but remained divided – since mobilizing against González Macchi implicitly meant supporting Gen. Oviedo.

By late 2002, when the opposition attempted to unleash an impeachment process for the last time, the González Macchi administration had become another example of surviving without governing. Its main policies had been vetoed, the unemployment rate remained above 10 percent, and the president had dismal approval ratings and little control over the Colorado Party. Unwilling either to back the unpopular president or to unseat him right before the 2003 election, Colorado members of Congress allowed the impeachment to move to the Senate and then closed the case in a 25–18 vote. Eighteen votes sufficed to prevent the two-thirds majority needed to convict González Macchi.[10]

Understanding Public Outrage

To what extent can the emergence of public outrage be blamed on unpopular policies, poor government performance, or media scandals? The case studies presented in the preceding pages provide a few insights. The Bucaram story indicates that the decline in presidential approval that often followed the adoption of neoliberal policies was independent of any honeymoon effects. In contrast to Collor and Pérez, Bucaram did not launch his reform package during his first hundred days in office, and his popularity still suffered after the announcements. Although good economic performance (for instance, control of hyperinflation) could have offset the political costs of economic reforms (see Stokes 1996a; Weyland 2002), none of the administrations under study was able to display an uncontested success on the economic front.

At the same time, the experiences of Fernando Collor and Carlos A. Pérez indicate that recurrent media exposés may erode the credibility of an

---

[10] Luis González Macchi was charged with instigating the illegal transfer of $16 million from the Central Bank to a private account and sentenced to six years in prison by a Paraguayan court in June of 2006. In December, he was sentenced to eight years in prison for embezzlement. At the time of this writing the former president was appealing the sentences.

administration long before the president is personally involved in any scandal. Moreover, given the dynamics of investigative journalism described in Chapter 4, this progressive loss of credibility may ultimately encourage public officials and other news sources to implicate the president, thereby giving the media enough confidence to publish such stories. Finally (and I will return to this issue in Chapter 7), the survival of Samper and González Macchi suggests that the scope of the social mobilization against the president may have tipped the balance in each case. Where the middle class converged with popular sectors to confront the president (often participating at a proportionately higher rate, but supplying smaller numbers of protestors than popular movements in absolute terms), a comprehensive popular uprising took place and the administration was severely destabilized. By contrast, where the upper middle class acted alone or failed to coordinate its efforts with the popular sectors, the administration remained in a better position to maneuver.

Multivariate Analysis

The key question, of course, is how to disentangle the simultaneous effects of those causal factors. In order to address this problem, I developed a multivariate model of presidential approval pooling the data for the six administrations. The dependent variable is the percentage of respondents supporting the president at any point in time (month). The independent variables reflect, on a monthly basis, the evolution of the key factors presented in Table 5.1. The introduction of neoliberal economic reforms was captured by an intervention variable that adopts a value of zero before the policy was launched and of one afterward. Macroeconomic conditions were measured using monthly changes in the consumer price index and the rate of unemployment. The incidence of scandals was captured using the scandal index presented early in the chapter (the number of media exposés over the elapsed months in office). I also introduced two intervention variables to reflect the "honeymoon" (the first three months in office) and any period when presidents were directly implicated by the investigations.[11]

---

[11] Collor was considered "directly involved" in the accusations between May and September of 1992; Pérez between November 1992 and June 1993; Samper between July 1995 and June 1996; and Cubas Grau between December 1998 and March 1999. No explicit charges were ever made against Bucaram or González Macchi (accusations in these latter cases remained diffuse, compromising the president through the deeds of collaborators and family members).

Data Comparative data on presidential approval in Latin America are very scant, particularly before the late 1990s. As noted earlier, I compiled approval series from multiple sources, including Datafolha and IBOPE (Brazil), Consultores 21 (Venezuela), Napoleón Franco y Asociados (Colombia), Informe Confidencial (Ecuador), and First (Paraguay). Several factors suggest a cautious interpretation of pooled time-series results in this context. First, although the indicator of approval (the percentage of respondents supporting the president) is generally comparable across the cases, "approval rates" were measured using somewhat different questions in different countries.[12] Second, sample designs were not fully equivalent for all surveys – even when conducted by the same pollster in the same country.[13]

Third, and most important, the frequency of surveys was irregular, both within and across countries. I strived to solve this problem while imposing as few assumptions on the original data as possible. When surveys were conducted frequently but at irregular intervals (Datafolha and IBOPE in Brazil, Napoleón Franco in Colombia, First in Paraguay), I reconstructed monthly series by interpolating values (assuming a linear trend) for the few missing observations. In the case of Venezuela, where Consultores 21 conducted regular surveys on a quarterly basis, I did not interpolate monthly values in order to avoid a 2:1 imputation ratio, but instead accepted the reality of having observations every three months (the sample imbalance was corrected in model 5.2.4 by weighting these observations by three). Ecuador presented the opposite problem: Informe Confidencial conducted regular

---

[12] With a few recent exceptions (Cima 1998) there are no comparative surveys of presidential approval in Latin America. The survey instruments used by Consultores 21, Napoleón Franco y Asociados, Informe Confidencial, and First captured presidential *favorability* (i.e., the percentage of respondents with a positive image of the president), while Datafolha and IBOPE measured presidential *job approval* (i.e., the percentage of respondents ranking the president's performance as excellent or good).

[13] In Brazil, Datafolha and IBOPE's surveys (N ≈ 5,000) were typically conducted in all "major cities" (usually defined as São Paulo, Rio de Janeiro, Belo Horizonte, Curitiba, Porto Alegre, Salvador, Recife, Fortaleza, Belem, and Brasília or Goiania), although in one case the sample covered only São Paulo. Consultores 21 (Venezuela) used national samples for urban areas covering approximately 77 percent of the adult population (N ≈ 1,500). Napoleón Franco y Asociados (Colombia) developed national polls for the Samper administration covering thirty-six urban and rural municipalities (N ≈ 1,500), as well as surveys in the four major cities only (Bogotá, Barranquilla, Cali, Medellín; N ≈ 850). Informe Confidencial (Ecuador) measured favorability in the two largest cities, Quito and Guayaquil (N ≈ 400 for each city).

Table 5.2. *Fixed-effects models of presidential approval*

Model	5.2.1 Base	5.2.2 Log-odds	5.2.3 PCSE	5.2.4 Weighted	5.2.5 Tobit
Scandal index	−0.11*	−0.01*	−0.11*	−0.17*	−0.11*
	(0.05)	(0.00)	(0.05)	(0.06)	(0.05)
President involved	−9.70*	−0.49*	−9.70*	−10.10*	−9.70*
	(3.08)	(0.16)	(2.45)	(3.40)	(2.96)
Honeymoon	17.37*	0.82*	17.37*	18.38*	17.37*
	(3.36)	(0.17)	(4.00)	(3.90)	(3.22)
Inflation	0.05	0.00	0.05	−0.06	0.05
	(0.16)	(0.01)	(0.10)	(0.18)	(0.16)
Unemployment	−1.82*	−0.07	−1.81*	−0.85	−1.82*
	(0.69)	(0.04)	(0.63)	(0.88)	(0.67)
Adjustment policy	−15.76*	−0.90*	−15.76*	−7.53	−15.76*
	(3.09)	(0.16)	(3.73)	(4.52)	(2.97)
Constant	66.69*	0.71	60.75*	47.45*	60.75*
	(8.35)	(0.43)	(7.17)	(9.99)	(7.24)
R^2	.46	.46	.61	.54	.11
N = 165					

Note: Entries are regression coefficients (standard errors). All models include fixed effects; each administration was treated as a unit except in the case of Bucaram (Guayaquil and Quito). Unit effects are not reported in order to save space. Models with inflation logged (measured as $\ln[1 + i]$ if $i \geq 0$, $-\ln[1 + |i|]$ if $i < 0$) generated equivalent results.

Key:
* Coefficient is significant at the .05 level.
Base: Standard fixed-effects model (demeaned estimator).
Log odds: Approval (percent A_{it}) was "linearized" using the formula $Y_{it} = \ln(A_{it}/(100 - A_{it}))$.
PCSE: Panel-corrected standard errors (pairwise covariance matrix).
Weighted: Observations were weighted to account for the frequency of surveys (weight equals the number of months between data points).
Tobit: Tobit model (lower truncation at 0%, upper truncation at 100%).
R^2: Corresponds to "within" R^2 in models 5.2.1 and 5.2.2; to standard R^2 in models 5.2.3 and 5.2.4; and to pseudo- R^2 in model 5.2.5.

surveys in two cities (Quito and Guayaquil), on a biweekly basis. Because the Bucaram administration lasted only seven months in office, I preserved the biweekly observations, but weighted them accordingly (w = 0.5) in the corrected model. It turned out that models with weighted and unweighted observations generated very similar results (see Table 5.2), suggesting that the uneven frequency of surveys may not be very problematic, but the unavoidable gaps in the monthly sequence prevented the use of standard corrections for autocorrelation.

Analysis Given the limitations of the data, the most conservative strategy was to perform the analysis using fixed-effects regression models.[14] This approach was able to accommodate the irregular structure of the dataset while at the same time offering a rigorous way to deal with unit effects (to capture, for instance, the overall level of support commanded by each president, or the unique nature of the instrument employed by each pollster). This approach does not assume that unit effects are uncorrelated with other independent variables or that they follow any particular distribution. Each administration was treated as a unit, with the exception of the Bucaram case, in which parallel surveys were conducted in Quito and Guayaquil independently.

Table 5.2 presents the results of the analysis. In addition to the standard fixed-effects estimator (5.2.1), I verified the results in several ways: the dependent variable (a percentage naturally bounded between 0 and 100) was "linearized" by taking the natural logarithm of the odds of approval (5.2.2); standard errors were corrected to allow for the possibility of different residual variance and residual covariance across panels (5.2.3); observations were weighted (as discussed earlier) to correct for the irregular frequency of surveys (5.2.4); and estimates were obtained using a Tobit model (5.2.5). The results in four of the five models suggest that the adoption of neoliberal policies hurt public support for these presidents by sixteen points on average, even after controlling for the honeymoon period. Rising unemployment may also have eroded presidential approval (an increase from, say, 5 to 10 percent unemployment predicted, on average, a nine-point decline in approval ratings).

Although the effects of inflation are not significant, this result must be interpreted with caution. In this sample, inflation data are biased because of the extreme values during the first months of the Collor administration (prices rose by 82 percent in March of 1990). Attempts to correct for this problem by using a log transformation of inflation still yielded insignificant coefficients for this variable. This finding is consistent with Kurt Weyland's claim that extreme inflation may in fact boost public

---

[14] The alternative to pooling was treating each administration separately, conducting individual time-series analyses. Unfortunately, this strategy generated inconclusive results because some administrations lasted in office for very short periods, because some important predictors vary across administrations more than within them, and because some variables turned out to be significant for one case but not for others (see Pérez-Liñán 2001, Chapter 6). Moreover, the problems of endogeneity addressed later in this chapter would be virtually intractable if dealing with the series individually.

118

support for presidents who are perceived as brave risk takers confronting a crisis (Weyland 2002). Lourdes Sola similarly argued that the legitimacy provided by Collor's direct election and the gravity of the economic crisis explained "the surprising responses of public opinion to the reforms, such as the responses of workers and employees in state-owned enterprises, many of whom became supporters of privatization" (Sola 1994, 158).

The results also show that media scandals were a significant force behind the erosion of presidential approval. Given the coefficients in Table 5.2, we would expect that a president confronting a scandal every two months (that is, with an average score of fifty points in the index) would see his or her approval rates decline between six and eight percentage points. A president directly implicated by those investigations of wrongdoing would suffer, on average, an additional loss of ten percentage points.

Feeding Frenzy?

The previous models assume that media scandals take place independent of presidential approval. However, the earlier discussion suggests that media informants, editors, and publishers do not operate in isolation from the broader political context. Editors may be more willing to risk the publication of controversial stories when the president is weak and when their audience is avid for criticism. Journalists may be encouraged to pursue scandals when newsroom managers want to make headlines with them. And politicians may be tempted to leak sensitive information about the president when they are dealing with a receptive press corps.

This idea suggests that the emergence of media scandals may not be random or solely determined by the level of corruption in the executive branch. In fact, there are good reasons to suspect that presidential approval and executive performance at any given time t may in part drive the production of scandals at time $t + 1$. If this is the case, the analysis presented in Table 5.2 may violate some fundamental assumptions of regression analysis: to the extent that the scandal index is sensitive to prior levels of presidential approval, any omitted exogenous factor driving up approval at time t could indirectly reduce the likelihood of scandals at time $t + 1$. This pattern of reverse causation would make the error term covary with two independent variables, the scandal index and the involvement of the president's image in the investigations, and therefore could bias the estimates in models 5.2.1 through 5.2.5.

In order to address this problem, I employed an instrumental variable approach (two-stage least squares, or 2SLS). This approach requires the analyst to perform three tasks: (1) find an exogenous variable that is uncorrelated with the dependent variable (approval) but is a reasonable predictor of the endogenous independent variable (scandals); (2) as a first stage in the analysis, use this exogenous variable (plus any other exogenous variables in the original model) to estimate a proxy for the endogenous independent variable (by construction, this proxy represents expected values of the endogenous predictor once it is purged of the reciprocal effects of the dependent variable); and (3) at the second stage, estimate the dependent variable using the proxy rather than the original measure of the predictor. The second stage therefore produces estimates unbiased by endogeneity (Berry 1984).

A major challenge to this approach frequently lies in the preliminary step: it is often hard to find an exogenous variable that is a reasonable predictor of the endogenous factor (in this case, scandals) and yet is not correlated with the outcome (presidential approval). In the present example, any variable with such characteristics (e.g., undisclosed levels of corruption, the investigative skill of journalists) would be extremely difficult to measure for the five countries on a monthly basis. Rather than searching for such an ideal variable, I relied on the theoretical understanding of the causal process to identify the model. The first two columns of Table 5.3 present this strategy. Given that the scandal index is presumably affected by prior levels of presidential approval, I estimated an OLS model with scandals as the dependent variable and the prior level of approval as an independent variable. (The model also includes a time trend, since the number of months in office is by definition part of the scandal index and is also likely to be correlated with presidential approval.) The residual of this regression was saved to play the role of "exogenous" instrument for the scandal index; by construction, it is correlated with the frequency of scandals ($r = .84$) but not with presidential approval ($r = -.03$). A similar strategy was followed to model the direct involvement of the president in the accusations. Because involvement is a dichotomous variable, I employed a logistic regression including past levels of approval, months in office, and the scandal index as predictors. The scandal index was included in the equation because, as noted at the beginning of this section, there are reasons to believe that a high frequency of exposés involving ministers, close friends, or the president's family may erode the president's credibility and ultimately encourage the disclosure of information compromising the chief executive personally.

120

Table 5.3. *Instrumental variable model of presidential approval*

	OLS	Logit	Fixed-Effects 2SLS		
Model	5.3.1	5.3.2	5.3.3	5.3.4	5.3.5
Dependent Variable (DV)	Scandal	Involved	Scandal	Involved	Approval
Stage	*Instrument*	*Instrument*	*First*	*First*	*Second*
Instrumented					
Scandal[a]		0.00			−0.24*
		(0.00)			(0.07)
President involved					−7.51*
					(3.13)
Instruments					
Honeymoon			−13.91*	0.00	13.18*
			(3.37)	(0.01)	(3.82)
Inflation			−0.20	0.00	0.04
			(0.16)	(0.00)	(0.17)
Unemployment			−3.56*	0.00*	−1.94*
			(0.69)	(0.00)	(0.71)
Adjustment policy			13.43*	0.00	−15.54*
			(3.24)	(0.00)	(3.13)
Instrument for scandal			0.49*	0.00*	
(Residual in 5.3.1)			(0.04)	(0.00)	
Instrument for involved			2.18	0.40*	
(Residual in 5.3.2)			(1.24)	(0.00)	
Approval ($t − 1$)	−1.94*	0.00			
	(0.31)	(0.02)			
Months in office	−3.34*	0.01			
	(0.42)	(0.02)			
Constant	197.79*	−1.83	90.70*	0.18*	75.86*
	(18.12)	(1.02)	(6.83)	(0.01)	(9.41)
R^2	.30	.02	.67	.99	.44
Correlation of DV with:					
Instrument for scandal			.84	−.05	−.03
Instrument for involved			−.01	.99	−.03
N	166	166	164	164	164

Note: Entries are regression coefficients (standard errors).

[a] Scandal not instrumented in 5.3.2. R^2 corresponds to R^2 in OLS; to pseudo-R^2 in logistic regression; and to "within" R^2 in fixed-effects models.

* Coefficient is significant at the .05 level.

(If this is the case, a new problem of endogeneity would arise, which needs to be corrected at this stage). Although none of the variables proved to be statistically significant, the residuals of the logistic model were also saved as a "purged" instrument; they are highly correlated with the involvement dummy, but not with the scandal index ($r = -.01$) or with presidential approval ($r = -.03$).

Using those instruments, I conducted the two-stage least-square analysis. The first stage is reflected in Models 5.3.3 and 5.3.4, which estimate the proxies for the scandal index and the presidential involvement variable. Scandals are less frequent during the honeymoon period and more frequent when presidents adopt unpopular policies, but there is no evidence that scandals are more likely when the economy is doing poorly. In turn, presidents are more likely to be directly affected by the accusations when recurrent scandals have eroded their credibility and when unemployment is high. (I have limited the number of decimal points in the table for reasons of space, but the bold entries indicate that the coefficients, albeit small, are significant at the .05 level.)[15] Taken together, these models suggest that there is some evidence in favor of the argument about strategic behavior on the part of the press, although further research needs to be conducted on this issue.

The second stage (5.3.5) replicates the general model of presidential approval (5.2.1) using the instrumental variables instead of the original indicators (standard errors are estimated based on the variance of the original predictors). Both variables have significant coefficients, suggesting that – irrespective of whether exposés are in fact driven by the strategic calculations of the media – presidential approval is hurt both by the frequency of scandals and by their proximity to the chief executive. The coefficient for the scandal index is stronger in this estimation: a president with a scandal score of fifty points would see his or her popularity decline twelve points on average (about twenty points if he or she is directly involved in the accusations).

---

[15] The coefficient for unemployment in 5.3.4 was .004 (s.e. $= .001$), indicating that a 10 percent increase in unemployment would yield a small increase of 4 percent in the probability of scandals directly involving the president. The coefficient for the scandal index was .00019 (s.e. $= .00005$), indicating that a president facing a scandal every month ($S = 100$) would see the risk of being personally involved grow by just 2 percent. Note that 5.3.4 relies on a crude linear probability assumption, which may partly explain the small size of the coefficients. The results should therefore be taken as merely indicative of underlying effects.

Conclusions

Were calls for impeachment a legitimate response to corruption scandals, the product of media manipulation, or just an indication of policy failure in the context of weakly institutionalized democracies? Maybe the answer is: all of the above. The combination of case studies and quantitative analysis has presented a complex picture of the sources of popular discontent. High levels of unemployment, the imposition of neoliberal reforms, and media scandals (particularly when they involved the president directly) eroded presidential popularity and encouraged popular uprisings against these administrations.

The analysis also suggests three conclusions. First, it seems that any single scandal in isolation is unlikely to result in a public opinion crisis. In most of the cases discussed here, media exposés accumulated over time, eroding the president's reputation and making every new accusation more credible than the previous one. Second, the timing and frequency of scandals is not a product of chance. Although limited by problems of comparability, the quantitative evidence indicates that scandals are likely to multiply when an administration is weak. The results of the two-stage least-squares analysis suggest a very distinctive form of feeding frenzy: if an exogenous factor hurts the popularity of an administration, weakness may encourage subsequent leaks and investigations, which will further erode the public standing of the president and in turn encourage new exposés. Mass support for the president may discourage the production of media scandals, while political weakness may initiate a downward spiral of accusations and declining public trust.

Shall we conclude from this finding that the fourth estate is just an opportunistic actor? The answer to this question will vary from case to case, but a more general point has been advanced in Chapter 4: members of the press should be considered strategic players, just as members of other institutions (courts and legislatures, for instance) are treated in this way by contemporary political science. Paradoxically, a modern press corps with autonomous career goals and advanced investigative skills is more likely to engage in this sort of strategic behavior than a traditional press reliant on official sources or driven by partisan goals.

Third, the decline in presidential approval is likely to force the removal of the president only if it translates into significant public mobilization (Hochstetler 2006). But not every form of mobilization constitutes a serious challenge to presidential survival. Protests can be destructive when they constitute what I have called a "popular uprising" against the president – a broad multiclass coalition united by a common desire to oust the chief executive – but they may have a modest impact when they reflect narrow interests or when they fail to incorporate important sectors, for example, those who refuse to throw their support behind an alternative that seems to be worse than the president they despise.

Appendix Table to Chapter 5. *Main scandals involving the president, close collaborators, or the first family*

Date	Episode	Involved
	Fernando Collor de Mello	
June 1990	Road maintenance contracts for $500 million allocated without public bidding.	Marcelo Ribeiro (secretary of transportation), Ozires Silva (minister of infrastructure)
July 1990	Two advertising agencies that supported Collor in the campaign received contracts (Giovanni and Setembro).	Cláudio H. Rosa e Silva (spokesman), Claudio Vieira (Collor's secretary)
Oct. 1990	President of Petrobras, Luiz da Motta Veiga, resigned and reported that P. C. Farias lobbied for loan to VASP.	P. C. Farias (Collor's operative), Marcos Coimbra (Planalto's chief of staff)
Feb. 1991	Social policy agency LBA suspected of overpayments in São Paulo and Amazonas.	Rosane Collor (first lady), indirectly
March 1991	Economic advisor accused of leaking information about coffee export policy.	Ricardo Mesquita (advisor to Minister Zelia Cardoso)
April 1991	Minister of labor receiving two salaries (one from Eletropaulo).	Antônio R. Magri (minister of labor)
April 1991	Minister of economy accused secretary of regional development of manipulating policy of Manaus free trade zone to benefit his brother. She resigns in early May.	Egberto Baptista (secretary for regional development), indirectly Fernando Collor
June 1991	Banco do Brasil paid part of the foreign debt of the Alagoan sugar producers.	Officials of BB, indirectly Zelia Cardoso and F. Collor
July 1991	First lady celebrated friend's birthday in president's house. Party paid for with public funds.	Rosane Collor (first lady)
Aug. 1991	Relatives of first lady accused of irregularities in the use of LBA funds. First lady resigned from LBA. Collor stopped wearing wedding ring in public for a while.	Rosane (first lady) and Fernando Collor
Nov. 1991	Ministry of Health accused of purchases without public bids and overpayments.	Alceni Guerra (minister of health)
Feb. 1992	Air force minister accused of remodeling his house with public funds.	Socrates Monteiro (minister of aeronautics)
March 1992	Minister of welfare received Jet-Ski and campaign funds from contractors.	Ricardo Fiuza (minister of social action)

(continued)

125

Appendix Table to Chapter 5 *(continued)*

Date	Episode	Involved
March 1992	Secretary of strategic affairs accused of brokering kickbacks for Petrobras.	Pedro P. Leoni Ramos (Secretary of Asuntos Estrategicos)
May 1992	President's brother accused P. C. Farias of working for Collor.	P. C. Farias, Fernando Collor
June 1992	Congressional investigative committee: businessman denounces Farias operation.	P. C. Farias, Fernando Collor
June 1992	CPI: driver E. França reports money transfers through checking accounts.	P. C. Farias, Fernando Collor
July 1992	CPI investigates Collor's secretary's bank accounts.	P. C. Farias, Fernando Collor, Ana Acioli (secretary)
Aug. 1992	CPI: Farias fabricates Uruguayan loan to cover up funds.	P. C. Farias, Fernando Collor
Aug. 1992	CPI: car in Collor's house purchased using ghost account.	P. C. Farias, Fernando Collor, first family
Aug. 1992	CPI: Collor's secretary and Farias avoided freezing of bank accounts in 1990.	P. C. Farias, Fernando Collor, first family
Sep. 1992	Rosane Collor investigated for LBA affairs.	Rosane Collor (first lady)

Carlos Andrés Pérez

Date	Episode	Involved
Oct. 1989	Three hotels were privatized without public bidding: transferred to a private company partly controlled by Labor Federation (CTV).	Jesús Carmona (chief of staff)
Feb. 1990	VP of Aeropostal is fired for giving insurance contracts to companies other than winners of bidding.	Germán Pérez (VP of Aeropostal and Perez's nephew)
April 1990	Minister of information accused of harassment of journalists and manipulation of official advertising. AD's National Executive Committee calls for his removal.	Pastor Heydra (minister of the Central Information Office)
May 1990	Governor of Bolivar state accused Ministry of Transport of charging 10% kickback on projects.	Minister of transportation and communications
June 1990	Deputy accused three ministers of corruption.	Leopoldo Sucre Figarella (Guayana Development Corporation), Manuel Adrianza (minister of health), Eugenio de Armas (minister of agriculture)

Date	Episode	Involved
July 1990	Deputy accused minister of transportation of demanding kickbacks from French contractor.	Augusto Faria Viso (minister of transportation and communications)
Nov. 1990	Accusations that minister of justice transferred police funds to his personal account.	Luis Beltrán Guerra (minister of justice)
Dec. 1990	Accusations that president cancelled Isa Dobles's TV show (under pressure from Lusinchi).	C. A. Perez (CAP) and Cecilia Matos (his mistress), J. Lusinchi and Blanca Ibáñez (Lusinchi's mistress)
Jan. 1991	Crisis in Worker's Bank (BTV). Minister of finance had authorized financial bailout. President removed BTV's president.	José V. Sánchez Pina (president of BTV), Egleé Iturbe (ex–minister of finance)
Jan. 1991	Former minister of finance accused of negligence in dealing with a contraband scheme in the customs office.	Egleé Iturbe (ex–minister of finance), Eva Morales (ex–customs director)
March 1991	Copei deputy accused of extortion involves Cecilia Matos in corruption scandals.	Cecilia Matos (president's mistress)
May 1991	Minister of defense and C. Matos accused of receiving kickbacks from Italian shipbuilder.	Héctor Jurado Toro (minister of defense), C. Matos (CAP's mistress)
June 1991	CAP security chief was shareholder of military contractor that broke contracts with army. Copei demanded his resignation.	Orlando García (CAP's security chief), CAP indirectly
July 1991	Copei demanded resignation of minister of urban development for illegal contracts.	Penzini Fleury (minister of urban development)
July 1991	Accusations that CAP and Lusinchi spent millions on American PR advisors.	CAP, Lusinchi
Aug. 1991	Accusations that former minister of information tried to tap J.V. Rangel's phone.	P. Heydra (former OCI head, now deputy)
Nov. 1991	J.V. Rangel denounced "dirty war" against journalist A. Peña.	Ministry of Information
Feb. 1992	J.V. Rangel accused CAP's military aide of phony contracts for communication equipment.	Iván Carratú (chief military aide)

(continued)

Appendix Table to Chapter 5 *(continued)*

Date	Episode	Involved
May 1992	Accusations that CAP was hiring foreign bodyguards.	CAP, Cecilia Matos, Piñerúa Ordaz (minister of interior)
June 1992	Peña claimed that CAP ordered the military to investigate *El Nacional* after publication of an intelligence report.	CAP
Aug. 1992	Politicians called for congressional investigation of the "intimate entourage" of CAP.	Cecilia Matos (president's mistress)
Nov 1992	$17 million from secret account reported missing.	Minister of interior
Dec. 1992	Comptroller reported that $16.5 million was transferred to presidency.	CAP
Dec. 1992	Newspaper ads against CAP's opponents. Agency worked for the administration.	CAP
March 1993	Solicitor general resigns when he learns that administration had hidden documents.	CAP
	Ernesto Samper	
Aug. 1994	Tapes linking the Samper campaign and Cali cartel surfaced in late June.	
Jan. 1995	*Cambio 16* published list of Liberal leaders who received funds. Investigation is opened (in April) against nine members of Congress and Medina.	Santiago Medina (campaign treasurer)
April 1995	Comptroller accused of staying as a guest of the Cali cartel while campaigning for Samper.	David Turbay (comptroller general)
July 1995	Campaign treasurer arrested, accused Samper and Botero.	Santiago Medina (treasurer). Fernando Botero (minister of defense)
Aug. 1995	*Semana* published conversation of Samper with drug dealer Elizabeth Montoya.	Ernesto Samper
Jan. 1996	Former campaign manager (arrested in August) implicated Samper in TV interview.	Fernando Botero (ex–minister of defense)
April 1996	President of the lower house charged with illicit enrichment.	Alvaro Benedetti (speaker of house)
July 1996	United States cancelled Samper's visa.	Samper

Date	Episode	Involved
March 1997	Defense minister resigned after being involved in drug trafficking connections.	Guillermo González Mosquera (minister of defense)
May 1997	Transportation minister resigned, accused of lending helicopter to two *Samperista* congresswomen.	Carlos H. Lopez (minister of transportation)
Aug. 1997	*Semana* revealed that ministers of energy and communications granted FM radio frequencies to friends. Both resigned.	Rodrigo Villamizar (energy) and Saulo Arboleda (communications)
	Abdalá Bucaram	
Aug. 1996	Friendly courts dropped corruption case against sister of elected president; she returned from Panama.	Elsa Bucaram (Abdalá's sister)
Aug. 1996	President nominated partisan for comptroller and brother, brother-in-law for cabinet.	Fernando Rosero (comptroller), Adolfo Bucaram (welfare minister, brother); Pablo Concha (finance minister, brother-in-law)
Aug. 1996	President called former president R. Borja a "donkey." Congress members protested.	A. Bucaram
Sep. 1996	Minister of energy threatened union leader in Petroecuador.	Alfredo Adum (energy minister)
Oct. 1996	Minister of education accused of plagiarizing doctoral dissertation.	Sandra Correa (education minister)
Oct. 1996	President flew to Miami with his son (for undisclosed reason) without placing VP in charge.	A. Bucaram, Jacobo Bucaram (son)
Nov. 1996	Minister of energy accused of pointing gun at secretary.	Alfredo Adum (energy minister)
Nov. 1996	Two officials accused minister of health of appointing friends to key positions and potential mishandling of foreign loans.	Marcelo Cruz (minister of health)
Nov. 1996	President's son accused of order closing disco where show mocked first family.	Jacobo Bucaram (son)
Nov. 1996	Former president Osvaldo Hurtado denounced first rumors about the "party tax" charged to contractors.	First family

(continued)

Appendix Table to Chapter 5 *(continued)*

Date	Episode	Involved
Nov. 1996	Administration accused of charging 15% on all funds of FISE (Fondo Social de Emergencia).	
Nov. 1996	Deputy denounced episodes of political harassment and corruption.	Santiago Bucaram (brother), Leonidas Plaza (solicitor)
Dec. 1996	Minister of public works threatened EFE news agency after story about him losing his underwear in a hotel.	Vicente Estrada (minister of public works)
Dec. 1996	Administration accused of intervening in a lawsuit for the inheritance of Noboa family.	Alvaro Noboa (chair, Monetary Board)
Dec. 1996	Accusations that funds collected by the *Teletón* for social purposes were managed by the PRE.	A. Bucaram
Jan. 1997	Accusations about irregularities in customs. Complaints from U.S. ambassador.	(Undefined)

Raúl Cubas Grau

Date	Episode	Involved
Aug. 1998	Decree 117 freed Gen. Lino Oviedo. Congress protested law violation.	Gen. Oviedo, Raul Cubas
Dec. 1998	Supreme Court ruled that decree was unconstitutional and ordered arrest of Oviedo. President refused. *Oviedistas* staged protests.	Raul Cubas
Feb. 1999	New chief justice ordered enforcement within seventy-two hours. President ignored.	Raul Cubas
March 1999	Argaña killed; Oviedo suspected of conspiracy.	Lino Oviedo
March 1999	Snipers attacked pro-impeachment demonstration; Oviedo suspected of giving the order.	Lino Oviedo

Luis González Macchi

Date	Episode	Involved
Nov. 1999	Comptroller accused of embezzlement, money laundering, and corruption.	Daniel Fretes (comptroller general)
Dec. 1999	Investigation of irregular acquisition of medicines in October of 1999.	Social Security Institute (IPS)
Dec. 2000	Comptroller established that in 1999 Ministry of Public Works used funds collected at toll roads for purposes other than road maintenance.	José A. Planás (public works)

Date	Episode	Involved
Feb. 2001	Accusations that president ordered the Social Security Institute to use 46 percent of its funds to rescue a public bank.	L. Gonzalez Macchi
Feb. 2001	Japanese development bank complained that minister of public works manipulated contracting rules for road maintenance. He was also accused of the torture of detainees after the 2000 coup attempt (while minister of interior).	Walter Bower (public works)
March 2001	The press confirmed that an armored BMW used by the president had been stolen in Brazil.	L. Gonzalez Macchi
May 2001	The media suggested that the president's family benefited from the international laundering of $11 million stolen in the Asuncion airport in August of 2000.	Judith Gonzalez Macchi (sister)
May 2001	President was accused of transferring $16 million from two banks (Unión and Oriental) intervened by the Central Bank to a private account in New York. President of central bank resigned.	L. González Macchi, Julio González Ugarte (central bank)
Jan. 2002	Two leaders of the left, Juan Arrom and Anuncio Martí, were freed from a clandestine prison where they had been illegally arrested and tortured by police officers for thirteen days. Arrom and Martí were the prime suspects in the kidnapping of a woman who had been freed after sixty-four days.	Julio C. Fanego (interior minister), Oscar Latorre (prosecutor general)
April 2002	Government pays almost $600,000 to private notary to register the transfer of property from Antelco to Copaco. (Public transfer should be free.)	José Ignacio (brother) and Judith González Macchi (sister)

6

Building a Legislative Shield

THE INSTITUTIONAL
DETERMINANTS OF
IMPEACHMENT

Even when they are besieged by accusations and protests, presidents may avoid an impeachment if they can rely on loyal legislators. In this chapter, I explore how scandals and public outrage were translated into legislative action against the executive. Under ideal conditions, members of Congress would impeach the president only if there were sufficient proof of a "high crime," and would refrain from doing so if accusations were merely grounded in partisan or personal motivations. In reality, however, legislators are hardly able to detach themselves from the broader social and political context in which a presidential crisis takes place (Kada 2000; 2003b, 148–149). On the one hand, a partisan Congress may protect the chief executive even when – as in the case of Colombia – there are important reasons to pursue an in-depth investigation. On the other hand, legislators may press charges against the president even when there is no real proof or public sentiment in favor of impeachment – as in the cases of Panama in 1955 and the United States in 1998.

This issue is crucial for the credibility of Congress as a democratic institution. As a collective body, Congress should act in ways that strengthen its credibility and public standing. Individual legislators, however, may encounter personal incentives that run counter to this collective course of action (see Mayhew 1974).[1] Concerned about their own careers,

---

[1] Legislators are aware of this challenge. Colombian Representative Pablo Agámez Agámez noted that "[t]he trial against the President [Samper] has simultaneously become, for the national and the international public opinion, a trial against Congress" (*Gaceta del Congreso*, June 19, 1996, 466–467). During the critical session of May 21, 1993, in which the Venezuelan Senate authorized the Supreme Court to initiate the trial of President Pérez, Senator Rafael Caldera claimed that "Congress can save its prestige vis-à-vis a people that has recently questioned it, by giving [them] a provisional president, a new government that opens new horizons..." (*Diario de Debate del Senado*, May 21, 1993, 701).

members of the president's party may seek to shield the chief executive from any accusations, while opposition legislators may pursue an impeachment even if the evidence against the president is weak (Kada 2003a).

Given the presence of partisan incentives, what determines the congressional decision to protect or to impeach the president? I contend that this is the result of four factors: constitutional rules, the party system, the president's relation with Congress, and the overall political context (the nature of scandals and the electoral calendar, for instance). In the first section of this chapter, I compare different constitutional traditions and show that in every presidential system Congress has at least the power to *block* the impeachment process. It follows that the partisan composition of Congress interacts with key constitutional rules to facilitate the formation of a "legislative shield" to protect the president. In the second section, I present the stylized facts of this process. The model formalizes the role of legislative bodies as "veto players" with the capacity to block an impeachment. The third section takes a long historical detour in order to explore the ability of presidents to use these institutions to their advantage. The six case studies indicate that presidents who isolated themselves from Congress or who confronted Congress early in their terms became likely targets once media scandals enveloped their administrations. In the final section, I employ a statistical model to assess how different contextual factors encourage individual legislators to shield the president from impeachment. Although partisan affiliation is part of the story, the results indicate that presidential leadership truly matters: isolated presidents and, to a lesser extent, presidents who adopt a confrontational stance vis-à-vis Congress are more likely to be impeached, while presidents who build extensive legislative coalitions early in their terms are likely to be shielded (Coslovsky 2002). At the same time, electoral considerations also weigh in legislators' decisions: the more distant the next election is, and the higher the presidential approval rating, the more willing legislators are to protect the chief executive.

Constitutional Law and the Removal of the President

Impeachment

Presidential impeachment is the main constitutional procedure allowing Congress to remove the president from office. In the American constitutional tradition, the term "impeachment" refers to a trial of the president initiated by the lower house and conducted by the Senate. Although other presidential constitutions have altered this procedure, the impeachment trial is always authorized – though not always conducted – by the legislature.

I use "impeachment trial" to refer to the procedure conducted by the jury (say, the U.S. Senate) against the chief executive, and reserve the more general term "impeachment process" (or "impeachment crisis") to describe the political course of action that begins with a congressional investigation and crystallizes in a legislative vote (e.g., in the House of Representatives) to authorize the trial of the president. Thus, for instance, President Samper confronted an impeachment crisis even though he was never impeached because the lower house blocked the accusation. By contrast, Presidents Clinton (in 1999) and González Macchi (in 2003) were impeached but acquitted in the trial.

Understanding the unfolding of an impeachment *process* can be more relevant than understanding the specifics of the *trial*. In many constitutions, presidents are immediately suspended from office once legislators authorize the trial. Presumably, this decision is at least as controversial as the tribunal's final decision. Even if presidents are allowed to remain in power during the proceedings, sheer political embarrassment or the expectation of defeat may force them to resign in advance of the trial.

Depending on the constitution, the trial of the president may be conducted by the upper house of Congress or by the judiciary. Naoko Kada (2003a, 114–116) has referred to these models as *legislature-dominant* and *judiciary-dominant* impeachment processes. The congressional model was initially devised by the American Constitution of 1787 and later absorbed with minor modifications by most South American countries. After several debates on how to cast the British impeachment process in a republican mold, the members of the Constitutional Convention decided that the lower chamber would be in charge of the accusations for "bribery and other high crimes and misdemeanors" and that the Senate would operate as a jury in which at least two-thirds of the members would have to find the president guilty in order for him to be ousted (Gerhardt 1996, Chapter 1). Most bicameral systems in Latin America have followed this scheme, often expanding the requirement of a supermajority to the lower chamber. The Argentine constitution of 1853, for instance, required the vote of two-thirds of the deputies to indict the president and of two-thirds of the senators to remove the president from office (Serrafero 1997, 42). In the extreme case, the Dominican constitution required three-quarters of both chambers for an impeachment to succeed.

In the judicial model, Congress authorizes a trial of the president that is performed by the judiciary. Although from a strictly legal perspective this may not be considered an impeachment formula (since it does not involve a parliamentary trial of the chief executive), the political nature of the procedure becomes evident when we consider two factors. First, the judiciary cannot rule on the case against the president unless Congress authorizes the trial. Second, in most cases the trial must be conducted by the Supreme Court and not by an ordinary court. This design is typical of, but not restricted to, unicameral systems in which the absence of an upper house makes the American scheme hard to implement. The judicial system involves two stages: a "political" moment taking place in Congress – when the president can be shielded from prosecution – and the trial itself, which is supposedly dominated by strictly legal considerations.

A clear example of this scheme is provided by the 1949 Costa Rican constitution, in which the assembly authorizes the accusation against the president with the vote of two-thirds of its members and the trial is conducted by the Supreme Court (article 121). In El Salvador (articles 236, 237), the assembly approves the charges by a simple majority and suspends the president from office, but the trial of the chief executive is conducted by a court of appeals (Cámara de Segunda Instancia). The ruling of this court can be overturned by a chamber of the Supreme Court, and this decision can in turn be reviewed by the Supreme Court as a whole.[2]

Table 6.1 compares fifty-seven constitutions in force in Latin America and the Spanish Caribbean between 1950 and 2004 in terms of the structure of Congress and the role of the judiciary in the impeachment trial.[3] About 84 percent of the constitutions adopted in bicameral systems assigned no

---

[2] The constitutions of Guatemala, Honduras, and Nicaragua are vague about the impeachment procedure. They empower Congress to authorize crimimal charges against the executive, but there is no explicit provision for the suspension or ousting of the chief executive by impeachment.

[3] The constitutions included in the table were adopted in Argentina (1853, 1949, 1994); Bolivia (1945, 1961, 1967, 1995); Brasil (1946, 1967, 1969, 1988); Chile (1925, 1980); Colombia (1886, 1991); Costa Rica (1949); Cuba (1940); the Dominican Republic (1942, 1962, 1966, 1994, 2002); Ecuador (1946, 1967, 1978, 1998); El Salvador (1945, 1950, 1962, 1983); Guatemala (1945, 1956, 1965, 1985); Honduras (1936, 1957, 1965, 1982); Mexico (1917); Nicaragua (1948, 1950, 1974, 1987 with reforms in 1995); Panama (1946, 1972); Paraguay (1940, 1967, 1992); Peru (1933, 1979, 1993); Uruguay (1942, 1952, 1967); and Venezuela (1945, 1947, 1953, 1961, 1999). Three constitutions (Paraguay 1940, 1967; and Nicaragua 1987 before 1995) were excluded because they did not allow for *any* procedure against the president.

135

Table 6.1. *Bicameralism and models of impeachment (constitutions of Latin America, 1950–2004)*

| Congress | Impeachment Model | | | |
	Congressional	Hybrid	Judicial	Total
Unicameral	5	0	15	20
(Percentage)	(25.0)	(0.0)	(75.0)	(100.0)
Bicameral	20	11	6	37
(Percentage)	(54.1)	(29.7)	(16.2)	(100.0)
TOTAL	25	11	21	57
(Percentage)	(43.9)	(19.3)	(36.8)	(100.0)

Note: In the congressional model, legislators accuse and judge the president; in the judicial model, the judiciary always intervenes in the trial phase; in the hybrid model, the judiciary judges the president only for common crimes.

Source: Grijalva and Pérez-Liñán (2003).

role or only a marginal role to the judiciary, while in 75 percent of the unicameral constitutions the judiciary was in charge of conducting the trial.

Several countries have deviated from the principle relating bicameralism and the congressional model of impeachment. In spite of their bicameral systems, the Bolivian constitutions of 1967 and 1994 and the Venezuelan constitution of 1961 relied on the judicial model; Venezuela preserved this scheme when it moved to unicameralism in 1999. If the Venezuelan president is accused of a crime, the Supreme Court has to rule on the legal relevance of the charges – what Venezuelan constitutional law defines as a "pre-trial of merit" (*antejuicio de mérito*). After the charges are declared legitimate, it is up to the National Assembly (the Senate in the 1961 charter) to authorize the trial by a simple majority.[4] The Supreme Court is then in charge of the trial itself. In Bolivia, a joint session of Congress has to "authorize" the trial, which is similarly conducted by the Supreme Court.

The Ecuadorian constitutions of 1978 and 1998 and the Peruvian charter of 1993 display the opposite pattern. Despite unicameralism, they adhered to the congressional model. Ecuador's 1978 constitution established that the unicameral Congress was in charge of both the accusation and the trial. Section five of the Organic Law of the Legislative Function clarified the procedure: Congress had to authorize the accusation by a simple majority

---

[4] Under the 1961 constitution (which ruled the Pérez impeachment), the lower chamber played no role in the process. The 1999 charter is unclear about the voting threshold. I am indebted to Naoko Kada for her comments on this issue.

and remove the president by a vote of two-thirds of its members. In 1998, the two-thirds clause was clarified in a new constitutional text (article 130).

Some countries have adopted a hybrid scheme. The Brazilian constitution combines elements of the bicameral tradition and the judicial tradition by distinguishing between "accountability" crimes (*crimes de responsabilidade*) and "common" crimes.[5] In both cases, the Chamber of Deputies is in charge of the accusation, but accountability crimes are judged by the Senate, while all other crimes are tried by the federal Supreme Court. Similarly, the Colombian constitutions of 1886 and 1991 specified that the Chamber of Representatives issued the accusation and that the Senate authorized the trial by suspending the president from office.[6] For common crimes, the Supreme Court would perform the trial, but in cases of breach of public duties, the upper house would also play the role of jury. The Ecuadorian constitutions of 1946 and 1967 established a similar principle – although in this case common crimes were to be judged by an ordinary court. This dual procedure to conduct a trial against the president must be distinguished from the declaration, common in many constitutions, that the president is legally responsible for his or her crimes after being removed from office.

Although judicial involvement in the trial phase varies according to the constitutional design, legislative participation in the authorization phase is common to all constitutions. This fundamental involvement of Congress in the authorization of the trial of the chief executive makes impeachment, as Baumgartner has noted, essentially "a political, rather than a legal proceeding" (Baumgartner 2003a, 2).

Declaration of Incapacity

Under some constitutions, Congress may also remove the president from office after declaring his or her of physical or mental incapacity (e.g., the

---

[5] Article 85 defines *crimes de responsabilidade* as the actions of the president against the constitution – particularly those compromising the existence of the federal union, the independence of the other branches or local governments, political and civil rights, internal security, honesty in administration, the budget, and the law or judicial decisions.

[6] During the 1996 crisis, it was argued that the Colombian representatives were the "natural judges" of the president – implying that only a legislative solution was legitimate, and that they should act as "judges" and not as politicians. In my view, this thesis (supported by lawyers, most legislators, and the president himself) only created confusion regarding the proper function of the lower chamber. Not only was the House the natural *prosecutor* of the president (its constitutional role is not that of a jury), but political considerations are also, by definition, part of the legislative phase in every impeachment process.

clause used against President Bucaram in 1997) or his or her "permanent absence" from the position (enforced against President Pérez in 1993). In the United States, for instance, the vice president and a majority of the cabinet may declare that the president is "unable to discharge the powers and duties of his office"; but if the president challenges the decision, only Congress can declare the president impaired by a two-thirds vote in both houses (Twenty-fifth Amendment, 1967).

Originally, these rules were conceived as a way to replace a chief executive who was alive but unable to perform his or her duties. However, technical terms like "incapacity" and "permanent absence" may take on unexpected meanings in the midst of a presidential crisis. Incapacity clauses were artfully invoked to oust Presidents Manuel Estrada Cabrera of Guatemala in 1920 and Leonardo Argüello of Nicaragua in 1947. In 1955, the Brazilian Congress used the incapacity clause (article 79.1 of the 1946 constitution) to legalize the military ousting of President Carlos Luz (see Chapter 3). Legally speaking, Congress did not "declare" Luz incapacitated but "acknowledged" a situation: the president was hiding in a gunboat, under fire, in Guanabara Bay (Dulles 1970, 47; *Diario do Congresso Nacional, Seção I*, November 11, 1955, 8372–8382). Argentine legislators resorted to arguments about presidential incapacity in their attempts to depose President María Estela Martínez de Perón in 1976, but the president of the Senate refused to summon the joint session required to address the question (Serrafero 1997). Undoubtedly, the most interesting example of this sort is the ousting of Ecuadorian President Abdalá Bucaram on charges of insanity in February of 1997.

Political manipulation of the incapacity clause becomes more difficult when the procedure is highly restrictive. For example, the Chilean constitution of 1980 introduced a complex rule for declaring presidential incapacity: at least one-fourth of the Chamber of Deputies should ask the Supreme Court to consider the problem, and the Court must issue a report to the Senate before the latter could decide – by simple majority – on the question (articles 49 and 82). In practice, the Chilean arrangement called for an implicit agreement between the two chambers *and* the Supreme Court to declare the incompetence of the president.

The constitutions of El Salvador (article 131) and Guatemala (article 165) allow the legislature to declare the physical or mental incapacity of the president by a two-thirds majority after a committee of five physicians reports on the issue. The Colombian charter allows the Senate to declare the president's "permanent physical incapacity" by a simple majority. The term "physical" imposes some (vague) restrictions to this power, and the text of article 194, although not totally clear, implies that the president has already taken a leave of absence. In Ecuador, the constitutions of 1946 and 1967 demanded that the two chambers in *joint session* decide on incapacity – the 1967 charter also mentioned "indignity" – but this check disappeared with the return to unicameralism in 1979.

Table 6.2 summarizes the various provisions for impeachment and the declaration of incapacity in Latin America during the 1990s (the U.S. Constitution is included for comparative purposes). The table identifies the actors involved in the process (lower chamber, senate, courts) and the majorities required to oust the president. Nine of the eighteen Latin American countries rely on the congressional model of impeachment; four have a pure judicial model; and two others (Brazil and Colombia) have a hybrid model. Three other unicameral systems (Guatemala, Honduras, and Nicaragua) have constitutional clauses that resemble the judicial model but fail to outline clear impeachment procedures – no provisions for suspending or removing the president are established. Nine of the eighteen countries assign Congress a role in the declaration of presidential incapacity.

Rethinking the Role of Congress: Legislators as Veto Players

Tables 6.1 and 6.2 suggest a few conclusions about constitutional law. First, with the exception of rare authoritarian charters, virtually every presidential constitution includes some provision for impeachment and in many cases also for the declaration of presidential incapacity. Second, although Congress is not always the only player involved in the decision to remove the president from office, legislators *always* play a critical role in authorizing the trial. Third, it seems that constitutional arrangements do not affect the incidence of impeachments directly. In the 1990s, presidents were ousted under the congressional (Paraguay), the judicial (Venezuela), and the hybrid models (Brazil), and also following a declaration of incapacity (Ecuador).

In order to understand the role of institutions in the impeachment process, I propose that we consider legislators as "gatekeepers," members of a collective veto player with the capacity to activate or block the process. A veto player is "an individual or collective actor whose agreement is required

139

Table 6.2. *Constitutional rules on impeachment and declaration of incapacity in Latin America and the United States, 1990–2004*

Country	Date of Constitution	Rule	Majority Required			Articles (Sections)	Model
			LC	Senate	Court[b]		
Argentina	1853	i.	2/3	2/3		45, 51	Congressional
		d.i.				n/p	
	1994	i.	2/3	2/3		53, 59	Congressional
		d.i.				n/p	
Bolivia	1967	i.	1/2 [a, b]		1/2	68(12), 127(6)	Judicial
		d.i.				n/p	
	1994	i.	2/3 [a, c]		1/2	68(11), 118(5)	Judicial
		d.i.				n/p	
Brazil	1988	i.	2/3 [c]	2/3 [c]		52(I), 53(I), 86	Mixed
		c.c.	2/3 [c]		1/2	52(I), 86, 102(I)	
		d.i.				n/p	
Chile	1980	i.	1/2 [c]	2/3 [c]		48(2), 49(1)	Congressional
		d.i.	1/4 [c]	1/2	1/2	49(7), 82(9)	
Colombia	1886	i.	1/2 [b]	2/3		96, 97, 102	Mixed
		c.c.	1/2 [b]	2/3	1/2	96, 97, 103	
		d.i.		1/2 [b]		125	
	1991	i.	1/2 [b]	2/3		174, 175, 178	Mixed
		c.c.	1/2 [b]	2/3	1/2	174, 175, 235(2)	
		d.i.		1/2 [b]		194	
Costa Rica	1949 [d]	i.	2/3 [c]		1/2	121(9)	Judicial
		d.i.	1/2 [b]			121(8)	
Dominican Republic	1966	i.	3/4 [c]	3/4 [c]		23(4), 26	Congressional
		d.i.				n/p	
	1994	i.	3/4 [c]	3/4 [c]		23(4), 26	Congressional
		d.i.				n/p	
	2002	i.	3/4 [c]	3/4 [c]		23(4), 26	Congressional
		d.i.				n/p	
Ecuador	1978 [d]	i.	2/3 [e]			59(f)	Congressional
		d.i.	1/2 [b]			75(d), 75(e)	
	1998 [d]	i.	2/3 [c]			130(9)	Congressional
		d.i.	1/2 [b]			130(1)	
El Salvador	1983 [d]	i.	1/2 [b]	1/2	1/2 [f]	236, 237	Judicial
		d.i.	2/3 [c, g]			131(20)	
Guatemala	1985 [d]	i.	2/3 [c]			165(h)	Judicial? [b]
		d.i.	2/3 [c, g]			165(i)	
Honduras	1982 [d]	i.	1/2 [b]		1/2	205(15), 319(2)	Judicial? [b]
		d.i.				n/p	
México	1917	i.	1/2	2/3		74, 76, 110, 111	Congressional
		d.i.				n/p	

Country	Date of Constitution	Rule	Majority Required			Articles (Sections)	Model
			LC	Senate	Court[b]		
Nicaragua	1987[d]	i.				n/p	None
		d.i.				n/p	
	1995[d]	i.	1/2[c]		1/2	130	Judicial?[b]
		d.i.	2/3[c]			149	
	2000[d]	i.	2/3[c]		1/2	130	Judicial?[b]
		d.i.	2/3[c]			149	
Panama	1972[d]	i.	2/3[e]			154(1)	Congressional
		d.i.				n/p	
Paraguay	1967	i.				n/p	None
		d.i.				n/p	
	1992	i.	2/3	2/3[c]		225	Congressional
		d.i.				n/p	
Peru	1979	i.	1/2[b]	1/2[b]		183, 184, 210	Congressional
		d.i.	1/2[b]	1/2[b]		206(1)	
	1993[d]	i.	1/2[b,i]			99, 100	Congressional
		d.i.	1/2[b]			113(2)	
United States	1787	i.	1/2[b]	2/3		1(2.5, 3.6)	Congressional
		d.i.	2/3[k]	2/3[k]		Twenty-fifth Amendment (4)	
Uruguay	1967	i.	2/3[c,j]	2/3[c]		93, 102, 172	Congressional
		d.i.				n/p	
	1997	i.	1/2[b,j]	2/3[c]		93, 102, 172	Congressional
		d.i.				n/p	
Venezuela	1961	i.		1/2[c]	1/2	150(8), 215(1)	Judicial
		d.i.				n/p	
	1999[d]	i.	1/2[b]		1/2	233, 266(2)	Judicial
		d.i.	1/2[b]		1/2[l]	233	

Key: LC = lower chamber; i. = impeachment; d.i. = declaration of incapacity; c.c. = procedure for "common crimes"; n/p = no explicit provision.

[a] Joint session.

[b] No supermajority explicitly required (simple majority is assumed).

[c] Of total members (otherwise, of members present).

[d] Unicameral system.

[e] Supermajority established by law.

[f] A court of appeals rules on the issue; Supreme Court may review the case.

[g] Constitution requires a decision made by a commission of five physicians.

[h] Congress can lift presidential immunity only to authorize a court trial for common crimes; no provision for suspension or ousting.

[i] Permanent committee (25% of members) presents accusation; rest of Congress votes on trial.

[j] The House presumably authorizes trial with simple majority, but two-thirds are necessary to suspend president.

[k] Congress intervenes only if the president challenges declaration of incapacity issued by vice president and cabinet.

[l] The Supreme Court appoints a medical commission and the Assembly decides following its recommendation.

Sources: Grijalva and Pérez-Liñán (2003), Kada (2000), and specific constitutions.

for a policy decision" (Tsebelis 1995, 293).[7] Constitutional design determines not only the number of institutional players (chambers of congress, judicial bodies) that must agree in order to remove the president from office, but also the degree of internal cohesion (the decision threshold) that each of these collective bodies must achieve in order for an impeachment to move forward. If any of these players fails to achieve the required majority, the process is blocked and the president cannot be removed from office.

Although the number of institutions involved in the impeachment process potentially makes a difference for the resolution of a presidential crisis (the greater the number of veto players, the greater the possibility of a veto), I will not emphasize this explanation for three reasons. First, there is not much variance in the number of constitutional veto players across cases. Most presidential regimes have established a two-stage impeachment process – one chamber authorizes the process, and the other one (or the Supreme Court) conducts the trial. Second, even when the number of veto players increases, their preferences may remain highly congruent (Tsebelis 1995, 308–311). Veto players may not be fully independent of each other, not only for political reasons (e.g., the same party may control both chambers), but also for strategic ones. If there is mounting public outrage against the president, success at the first stage (the accusation) may increase the probability of success at the second stage (removal).[8] Last but not least, it is often the case that, as mentioned earlier, the most critical decision – the suspension of the president from office – takes place when the trial is authorized.

For these reasons, I will focus on a second set of constitutional rules: the legislative majorities required to proceed with an impeachment process. In contrast to judges, legislators represent the purely *political* component of the impeachment process, and as such they are required to intervene in every model of impeachment. No matter the constitutional framework, if

---

[7] The concept of "veto players" is part of a broader family of related terms that includes "veto points" (Birchfield and Crepaz 1998; Immergut 1992) and "veto gates" (Shugart and Haggard 2001; see Kada 2002 on the impeachment process). Because the term "veto player" has gained extensive currency (Ames 2001; Hallerberg and Basinger 1998; Kay 1999; Tsebelis 1999, 2002), I adopt it in this study.

[8] For instance, urging the vote against President Pérez, Venezuelan Senator Pedro P. Aguilar argued that "we must complete a foretold act. We had all agreed that if the Supreme Court found reasons to declare the trial germane, here, in the Senate, our hands would rise to authorize Court's prosecution of Carlos Andrés Pérez..." (*Diario de Debates del Senado*, Friday, May 21, 1993, 714).

the president is able to keep control over Congress, his or her constitutional removal is virtually impossible. The degree of legislative support necessary to prevent the initiation of an impeachment or the president's removal from office is therefore determined by the decision threshold required for each intervening chamber.

Interestingly enough, in the 1990s restrictive procedures involving two chambers and requiring supermajorities (like the ones employed in Brazil and Paraguay) were as lethal as the more flexible procedures required in Venezuela and Ecuador. Although we may be tempted to conclude that institutional design does not matter in the context of presidential crises, this is not necessarily the case. The role of constitutional rules can only be assessed vis-à-vis the capacity of specific presidents to mobilize support among members of Congress. Whether a "legislative shield" against impeachment is created depends upon both the number of loyal legislators in Congress and the constitutional voting thresholds required to prevent an impeachment.

A Model of Legislative Impeachment

Contemporary research on legislative behavior has emphasized the estimation of legislators' "ideal points." Given a certain number of observed roll call votes, political scientists have developed statistical models to locate the position of individual members of Congress in an underlying "policy space" in order to measure the ideological distance between legislators or between the legislators and the chief executive (e.g., Jackman 2001; Morgenstern 2004; Poole and Rosenthal 1997). Understanding the distribution of legislators in a given policy space is critical not only in characterizing the agents of legislative representation (parties, factions, and coalitions), but also in explaining the behavior of presidents, who must initiate viable bills, bargain, and build coalitions in order to get these bills passed (Morgenstern 2004).

It is interesting to note, however, that the problem confronted by presidents who anticipate an impeachment process is exactly the opposite. Imagine that the media unveil a major scandal, forcing Congress to consider the responsibility of the chief executive in an episode of corruption or abuse of power. Even if the president knows the exact position of each legislator in an underlying continuum of loyalty/opposition to the administration, there is little room to bargain along this continuum. Because the impeachment

143

proposal is by nature dichotomous, legislators are ultimately confronted with a discrete choice: to authorize an impeachment or not.[9] The combination of high stakes and the lack of a bargaining space gives the process a dramatic tone.

A Stylized Model of Impeachment　To illustrate this problem, assume for the state of simplicity that legislators locate themselves along a continuum with values ranging from zero, indicating no support for the executive (and extreme support for impeachment), to one, indicating extreme loyalty to the president. The dichotomous nature of the impeachment proposal will polarize the initial distribution of preferences, forcing legislators to adopt a public position from the set $\{0,1\}$, where 0 indicates support for impeachment and 1 indicates support for the executive. Other things being equal, legislators with positions below a certain threshold p^* on the underlying continuum will vote to authorize an impeachment, while their peers located above that threshold will vote to prevent the impeachment process. Because the voting rule induces a dichotomous choice, the location of the *median* legislator prior to the vote is of little theoretical relevance when compared to the expected position of the *mean* legislator *after* the vote – which simply indicates the proportion of legislators willing to move to the pro-president position (vote $= 1$) and act as veto players against impeachment.

Let P denote the proportion of the chamber loyal to the president (or the final position of the mean legislator), and let v denote the proportion of votes constitutionally required to prevent an impeachment. The difference between the two values denotes the size of the president's legislative shield, measured as the distance between the expected behavior of the mean legislator and the share of votes required to veto an impeachment. I will call this variable L, where $L = P - v$. Figure 6.1 illustrates the proportion of legislators backing the president in the vote authorizing the impeachment (or the declaration of incapacity, in the case of Bucaram) for the six cases discussed in Chapter 2. It is worth noting that in the cases of Bucaram, Collor, Cubas, and Pérez, this vote alone was sufficient to produce the separation of the president from office, either on a temporary basis (Collor, Pérez), or indefinitely because the president was ousted (Bucaram) or ultimately forced to resign (Cubas Grau, also Collor).

---

[9] Procedural rules allow for a third option – abstention. But an abstention counts as a nonvote if the rules demand a majority (or supermajority) of the members present, and as a vote against impeachment if the rules demand a majority of all the members.

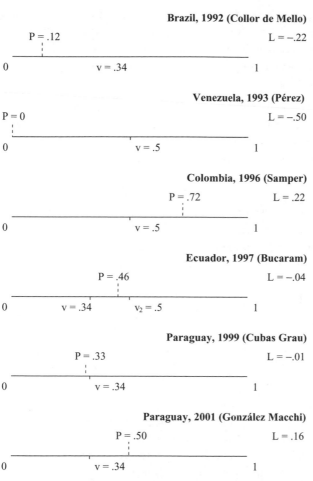

Figure 6.1 Support for the president in six impeachment crises. P = proportion of the chamber voting against impeachment; v = threshold required to prevent an impeachment; v_2 = threshold to prevent the declaration of incapacity; L = distance between the level of legislative support obtained and the level required by the constitution (L = P − v). *Sources*: Congressional records for the respective countries.

This model illustrates why constitutional rules do not operate in a vacuum. The analysis of constitutional voting thresholds is of little relevance unless we understand the capacity of the president to mobilize support in Congress. Presidents may lack a legislative shield (P < v) either because they have a small party *and* they are incapable of building a legislative coalition,

145

or because they are members of a large party controlled by an adversarial faction. This suggests that parameter P is in turn determined by three factors: the size of the president's party, its cohesion, and the capacity of the president to gain support among "opposition" legislators.

Sources of Support   At the core of the legislative shield is the president's party in Congress (Pérez-Liñán 2003a). Let us define P as a function of S, where S is the share of seats controlled by the president's party. It is hardly the case, however, that $P = S$, for two reasons. First, the administration may gather additional support from other parties or from independent legislators to oppose an impeachment (so that $P > S$). Let A be the share of votes supplied by allies in the president's coalition.[10] A second factor shaping P is party discipline. Weak party discipline may act both ways, by allowing the formation of an anti-impeachment coalition with undisciplined opposition legislators, and by depriving the president of support from members of his or her own party. It is the second problem ($P < S$) that I shall emphasize here. Members of the ruling party may abandon the president for many reasons, among them internal factionalism (as in Venezuela and Paraguay), the incentives created by the electoral system (as in Brazil), and their natural reluctance to sink with the president's boat. For the sake of simplicity, let parameter d capture the discipline displayed by members of the ruling party, where d ranges from 0 (if no legislator supports the president) to 1 (if all of them are loyal to the president).

To sum up, the degree of support for the president is determined by the proportion of members of the ruling party who remain loyal plus the contribution of outside members to the president's coalition. Formally, the legislative shield can be expressed as $L = dS + A - v$. The first term of the equation represents the contribution of "partisan powers" to the shield (Mainwaring and Shugart 1997b); the second term represents the role of coalition politics (Altman 2000; Amorim Neto 2002); and the last term represents the impact of constitutional rules (Kada 2003b).

In contrast to the size of the president's party, which in the absence of massive party switching is virtually fixed between elections, discipline and

---

[10] I use the term "coalition" to refer to the set of legislators who consistently vote with the administration on key issues – in this case, against impeachment – without assuming the existence of a previous electoral alliance, participation in the cabinet, or a formal legislative pact.

coalitions may fluctuate over time in response to the political environment and the president's strategy. I discuss the role of presidential leadership in the following section and the effects of the overall political environment in the last section of this chapter.

Rethinking the Role of the Executive: Nurturing Friendly Veto Players

What is the role of presidential leadership in the impeachment process? This section reconstructs the evolution of executive-legislative relations during the six administrations under study. The purpose of this histori-cal detour is to show how executive behavior may affect the prospects for impeachment. I treat presidential strategy as an independent variable shap-ing the executive's performance in office (in this case, presidential survival). This perspective follows a long-standing tradition in classical studies of the American presidency (e.g., Neustadt [1960] 1990; Skowronek 1997), but it is less common in the study of Latin American politics. The compara-tive literature has usually approached presidential behavior as a product of institutional factors (Carey and Shugart 1998) or as an equilibrium response to legislators' strategies (Cox and Morgenstern 2001), but it has been less willing to emphasize presidential agency.

As a notable exception to this pattern, Corrales (2002a) argued that dif-ferent presidential strategies in dealing with the ruling party promoted or hindered executive success in the implementation of economic reforms during the 1990s. "Party-neglecting" presidents (Carlos A. Pérez being the best example) failed to implement any reforms because their partisan sup-port evaporated, while "party-yielding" presidents (represented by Samper) failed to initiate any reforms because they acquiesced to the party's demands. In between, argued Corrales, lay "party-accommodating" pres-idents (like Carlos Menem in Argentina), who bargained with their par-ties and achieved major reforms even if they sacrificed their ideal policy positions.

I contend that the strategy adopted by the chief executive in order to deal with members of Congress early in the term is critical to shaping the legislators' response once an impeachment crisis explodes. Presidents who are more willing to accommodate congressional needs in terms of policy or pork may attract legislators to the upper end of the spectrum represented in Figure 6.1, building a critical mass of support early in their

147

terms. Even though later media scandals and popular discontent may drive many legislators "to the left" (i.e., closer to zero), the number of members of Congress above the support threshold may still be sufficient to prevent an impeachment process. By contrast, presidents who alienate members of Congress early in their terms (either by confronting them openly or by ignoring their needs) may be in an extremely weak position to confront an impeachment crisis. Frustrated legislators may leak critical information to the press in order to ignite media scandals; they may use their oversight powers to investigate and publicize the accusations; and they may ultimately refuse to act as veto players, triggering the fall of the administration.

This issue is particularly relevant when the president, out of preference or necessity, seeks to impose a policy agenda that most legislators oppose – for instance, neoliberal reforms in Venezuela or the liberation of Lino Oviedo in Paraguay. Faced with a potentially hostile Congress, the executive may adopt one of three possible strategies. The first one is to implement the policy, bypassing Congress and ignoring congressional leaders whenever possible. I refer to this strategy as *isolation*. For example, the president may refuse to bargain with a recalcitrant Congress, imposing policies by decree (Cox and Morgenstern 2001). Or, if his party controls a majority of the seats, the president may refuse to accommodate the party's needs, invoking rigid notions of party discipline (what Corrales dubbed party-neglecting behavior).

In other cases, presidents prefer to "go public" and openly defy Congress in the hope that this strategy will mobilize public opinion and induce legislative polarization to their benefit. The strategy of *confrontation* (close to what Corrales dubs "hostility") is less respectful of the institutional order, since presidents are often forced to denigrate legislators publicly. The third, and most expensive, strategy is to negotiate with legislative leaders on a regular basis, even if this leads to repeated concessions in terms of policy or patronage (or both). This strategy appropriate for presidents who are professional politicians with solid relationships in Congress (and who understand the existing room for party or opposition accommodation) or for presidents who lack strong policy preferences (and thus can afford to be party- or opposition-yielding). It is, however, a difficult strategy to implement when presidents claim to be anti-party politicians (Kenney 2004) or when they have rigid policy preferences. In the following sections, I show how these three strategies have worked for presidents with both small and large legislative contingents.

Small Parties and Weak Coalitions: Brazil and Ecuador

When presidents lack a strong partisan force in Congress, the formation of a broader coalition (A > 0) may be the only way to rule or to prevent an impeachment process. But stable coalitions cannot be forged overnight; a critical lesson of the cases under study is that presidents should nurture their legislative coalitions from their first day in office. Otherwise, the executive may be too isolated by the time media scandals reach the floor of Congress. Political isolation is hard to reverse once scandals have gained momentum, presidential popularity is low, and powerful elites are hurt. The experiences of Collor and Bucaram illustrate this problem.

Isolation: Brazil, 1990–1992

Fernando Collor won the 1989 Brazilian presidential election by campaigning aggressively against traditional parties and elites (Lins da Silva 1993a). According to Thomas Skidmore, Collor, the governor of a small state, was "used to making few concessions in dealing with other politicians. He seemed the modern incarnation of the infamous 'colonel' of northeastern politics, accustomed to giving orders rather than negotiating" (Skidmore 1999, 9).

Early in his term, Collor adopted several *medidas provisórias* (temporary decrees allowed by article sixty-two of the 1988 Brazilian constitution) to initiate his economic program and pushed them through Congress with the support of the right-wing parties – the Party of the Liberal Front (Partido da Frente Liberal, PFL), Brazil's Labor Party (Partido Trabalhista Brasileiro, PTB), the Democratic Social Party (Partido Democrático Social, PDS), the National Reconstruction Party (Partido da Reconstrução Nacional, PRN), and some dissident members of the Democratic Movement Party (Partido do Movimento Democrático Brasileiro, PMDB) (Figueiredo and Limongi 1999). The administration refused to grant any concessions or political appointments to these legislative allies until the *medidas provisórias* (MPs) were finally approved by Congress. The weekly *Veja* celebrated the uncompromising new legislative strategy:

In contrast to what we used to see in times of José Sarney,... Collor managed to gain parliamentary support without giving anything in exchange. He did not even compromise on important items of the plan as an instrument of negotiation. It was a victory without the "it is in giving that we receive," without the Persian market style of the Sarney administration. (*Veja*, April 18, 1990, 23)[11]

Willing to prove his independence from traditional parties, Collor vetoed congressional amendments to the plan – even those negotiated by the PRN leadership. Then the president delayed the appointment of some officials proposed by his congressional allies until Congress had swallowed the vetoes. By then, the largest party in Congress, the centrist PMDB, was clearly in the opposition, and members of the PFL (his largest ally on the right) began to complain about Collor's lack of flexibility. According to Ricardo Fiuza, the leader of the PFL in Congress, legislators accepted such "violent" economic measures only because of Collor's popularity at the time. "What is Congress anywhere in the world? Congress decides nothing; it is just a sounding board for the mood of the nation" (interview, October of 1999).

In the following months, legislative allies were repeatedly denied access to pork and patronage, or simply ignored by ministers and government officials. In May of 1990, with inflation coming back and presidential approval ratings falling to 46 percent, Congress began to rebel. The right-wing coalition passively allowed the defeat of a critical MP aimed at blocking the adjustment of salaries by labor courts. Within a month, indexation was widely expected throughout the economy and inflation bounced back to a monthly 12 percent.

A new test for the administration came with the congressional election of October of 1990, when the formation of a legislative majority was at stake. The president, however, remained aloof from the electoral process, and legislators of the right-wing parties felt that they owed nothing to the administration. The appointment of a new minister of justice, Jarbas Passarinho, suggested greater inclination to negotiate with the legislative branch after the election, but the press soon reported that Passarinho had complained to the president: "I am a general without troops, and Congress is like an army without a general" (*Veja*, November 21, 1990, 39). By the end of the year, as presidential approval ratings fell below 30 percent, Collor's strategy began to crumble: "After having 11 of 89 (12%) MPs rejected and 47 of 69 (68%) MPs amended by Congress he decided to give up the strategy of dictating policy by decree" (Negretto 2004, 550).

---

[11] The Brazilian press usually uses the phrase "franciscan politics" ("it is in giving that we receive") as a caustic allusion to pork barrel. The irony was coined by José Sarney's minister of industry and commerce, Roberto Cardoso Alves.

Octavio Amorim has argued that Collor sustained the strategy of ruling by decree for more than a year because the cost of making concessions to the largest parties would have been very high. Hoewever, political isolation bred increasing dissatisfaction both with the way he handled the relationship with Congress and with the overall performance of his government. In April of 1991, Congress debated and nearly approved the Jobim bill, intended to regulate the use of decrees by the executive (Amorim Neto 2002, 76).

Brazilian politicians, even those who followed President Collor to the end, confirm this diagnosis of isolation. According to Luiz Moreira (PTB-BA), one of the president's allies in Congress, Collor "adopted a rather authoritarian attitude. And besides that, creating antipathy among legislators, he made it very difficult to get access to him. He isolated himself and did not keep an open dialogue." Zé Gomes, a loyal congressman of the ruling PRN, also acknowledged the need for a "more professional relationship with Congress" during those years (personal interviews, October of 1999).

Ricardo Fiuza – a PFL leader appointed by Collor as his chief of staff to reorganize the congressional front in 1992 – reportedly told press secretary Cláudio Humberto Rosa e Silva: "forging a majority in the Chamber is the easiest thing in the word, *Claudinho*. It is just getting a list of the deputies and check, one by one, their political needs. I can do that in a week and the President will have a majority. But I need his authorization . . ." (Rosa e Silva 1993, 83–84).[12]

By the time Pedro Collor spoke to *Veja* and the impeachment process had begun in Congress, the legislative coalition was in shambles. Fiuza knew it was too late to form an anti-impeachment bloc: "With the accusations rolling against the president, with the left in the opposition, with an adversarial Congress because Collor had not taken care of the deputies, without [elite] support or any governability pact . . . Collor was not impeached,

---

[12] A few months earlier, while still a deputy, Fiuza had already complained to the press secretary that the administration was not giving enough attention to its allies:

Listen, son: I am the leader of the government [bloc in Congress], right? Well, I recommended Mrs. Rosane a candidate for the position of local head of the LBA – somebody who had been nominated by one of my mayors in the state of Pernambuco. She not only ignored my suggestion, but appointed another person who opposed the President during the campaign. The mayor can think only two things: either this deputy he has been supporting for 20 years is a moron (*bunda-mole*) with no prestige in the government whatsoever, or he made no effort to push his candidate. Whatever he thinks, I am on the losing side. Now, if that has happened to *me*, just imagine what is going on. . . . (quoted in Rosa e Silva 1993, 84)

he was not judged, he was *lynched*," explained his former chief of staff.[13] Another congressman who voted against impeachment recalls

...a fact that clearly exemplifies what happened.... Close to the time of the impeachment, President Collor began to telephone legislators requesting their support. One deputy from Paraná got the call and thought that it was a practical joke. He kept the conversation for a while and at the end he realized that, indeed, *it was* the president calling. Then he simply said: "Mr. President, how many times I attempted to talk to you and you never gave me an appointment. It is not now that I will take care of your request simply because you gave me a call." And he voted against [Collor]. This shows the kind of dissatisfaction that Collor had created among his legislative base. (Interview with Luiz Moreira, October 14, 1999)

Confrontation: Ecuador, 1996–1997

If the Collor strategy illustrates the risks of isolation, the Ecuadorian case presents a more dramatic example of failure driven by a confrontational style. Like Collor, Abdalá Bucaram won the 1996 election campaigning on an anti-elite platform. But in a highly fragmented legislative environment, where his Partido Roldosista Ecuatoriano (PRE) captured only 23 percent of the seats in the unicameral Congress and the average party controlled 9 percent of the seats, the formation of a comprehensive coalition appeared to be the only way to govern. However, the Bucaram administration opted for a confrontational strategy that ultimately sealed its fate.

Right after taking office in August of 1996, and lacking the votes to impose their own candidate, the *Roldosistas* backed Fabián Alarcón as the new president of Congress. Alarcón was the head of the FRA, a small electoral ally of the PRE with only two seats in the legislature. The Izquierda Democrática (ID), the Democracia Popular (DP), and several smaller parties agreed to support Alarcón in order to secure their presence on the permanent committees – which set the legislative agenda most of the year.[14] The largest congressional party, the coastal right-wing Partido Social Cristiano (PSC), and the left-wing parties (MPD, Pachakutik) remained in the opposition.

---

[13] Interview with Ricardo Fiuza, Brasília, October 19, 1999. In his memoirs, Samper (2000, 108) also uses the lynching metaphor.

[14] Votes to appoint Alarcón (on August 1, 1996) were distributed as follows: PRE, eighteen; DP, eleven; ID, four; FRA, two; LP, two; PCE, two; others, five (see Burbano de Lara and Rowland 1998, 82).

The agreement that tenuously linked the PRE with the ID and the DP did not survive the election of Alarcón. As explained in the previous chapter, the administration insisted on nominating Fernando Rosero, a staunch PRE politician, for the post of comptroller general. The leaders of the ID, the DP, and the PSC complained that the candidate was too close to the government to become an independent watchdog. The administration refused to replace the nominee, seeking instead to break party discipline among the opposition.[15] After two failed attempts (on August 20 and 21), the motion to appoint Rosero passed on August 22 by a vote of 38–5, while thirty-seven deputies abstained in a vain attempt to prevent the necessary quorum. In late October, the PRE reached a new agreement with the powerful Partido Social Cristiano (PSC) to appoint twelve Supreme Court justices. But the PSC leader, Heinz Moeller, made clear that the party would remain in the opposition and would demand the resignation of Education Minister Sandra Correa – by then already accused of plagiarizing her doctoral dissertation. President Bucaram publicly responded that PSC leaders were just "wasting their time" (*El Comercio*, October 25, 1996, A2).

By late November – when the first one hundred days of "truce" with the government were over – most legislators had overtly moved to the opposition camp. Bucaram had offended ID partisans by calling their leader, former president Rodrigo Borja, a "donkey." Bucaram had accused Alexandra Vela, a key DP representative, of obstructing justice in the investigation of the "assassination" of former president Jaime Roldós – to which Vela responded with a libel suit against the president.[16] The administration aroused the anger of the Pachakutik leaders by creating an "ethnic ministry" – breaking a previous deal with the indigenous movement, which saw

---

[15] Opposition deputies who voted in favor of Rosero explained to the press that the administration had promised investment for their districts (*El Comercio*, August 23, 1996). In later months, legislators denounced the presence of a "man with a briefcase" in charge of buying votes for the administration (Saltos 1997, 124). Politicians on both sides of the aisle depicted those actions as presidential attacks on the opposition parties' cohesion and not as logrolling. However, Paco Moncayo – at the time head of the military Joint Command and later an ID legislator – noted that the practice of buying votes was widely practiced by all parties (interview, November 1999).

[16] President Jaime Roldós (and first lady Marta Bucaram, Abdalá's sister) died in a plane crash in May of 1981. The Bucaram family claims that the crash was the result of sabotage (interview with Elsa Bucaram, November 17, 1999). Deputy Alexandra Vela believed that challenging the president in court would be a powerful signal to many people who feared the abuses of the Bucarams (interview with A. Vela, December 1999).

Because the constitutionality of the vote was dubious and the outcome of the crisis was uncertain, PRE legislators were reluctant to abandon the boat while Bucaram was still in office.[19] However, the *Roldosistas* controlled only 23 percent of the seats and were able to gather limited support from a few additional Conservative, CFP, and *Alfarista* deputies. This bloc would have sufficed to prevent the formation of a two-thirds majority, but it was unable to stop the simple majority needed for the declaration of incapacity. Bucaram's failure originated in the small size of his party and in his confrontational style (a hindrance for coalition building), rather than in the betrayal of his followers.

Large Parties and Strong Factions: Venezuela, Colombia, and Paraguay

Partisan powers are determined not only by the size of the president's party in Congress (parameter S in the model presented in the previous section), but also by the loyalty of those legislators to the chief executive (d). Therefore, impeachment is likely not only when the president's party is too small to act as a veto player, as in the cases of Collor and Bucaram, but also when a large party turns its back on the president. While Ernesto Samper and Luis González Macchi were willing to accommodate the demands of their own (and some opposition) legislators and ultimately survived in office, Carlos Andrés Pérez and Raúl Cubas Grau adopted an isolationist strategy and ultimately saw their partisan support crumble.

Isolation: Venezuela, 1989–1993

The removal of Carlos Andrés Pérez was in part the result of Pérez's inability to control the party machine, his reluctance to compromise with party leaders, and his decline in popularity after 1992. Pérez won the nomination for the 1988 presidential election against powerful sectors of his Democratic Action (AD) party. According to Michael Coppedge, the party became deeply divided "into a faction of 'Ortodoxos' commanded by general

---

[19] After the Alarcón administration had taken over, however, most of the nineteen PRE deputies disaffiliated and negotiated with the interim president. According to Burbano de Lara and Rowland (1998, 36): "The acute political crisis created by the demonstrations of February 5 and the ousting of President Bucaram had a demolishing effect on the ruling party, the PRE. One year after winning the presidential election, the PRE had lost 12 deputies."

secretary Luis Alfaro Ucero and aligned with former President Lusinchi, and a faction of 'Renovadores' led by Héctor Alonso López and aligned with incumbent President Pérez" (Coppedge 1994b, 103). Pérez won the presidential election with 53 percent of the vote, while his party obtained 48 percent of the seats both in the lower house and in the Senate, leaving him with the impression that he had won the popular election and that his opponents within the party had lost (interview with Carlos A. Pérez, July 10, 1998).

President Pérez had learned early in the presidential campaign of 1988 that the orthodox faction of AD opposed his economic reform program. After taking office, he appointed independent "technocrats" (well-trained professionals like Imelda Cisneros, Ricardo Hausmann, Moisés Naím, and Miguel Rodríguez) to key economic posts and followed a "party-neglecting strategy" in the implementation of public policy (Corrales 2000; 2002a). However, the orthodox faction won the 1991 internal elections and gained control of the powerful National Executive Committee (CEN) at the national convention.

According to Corrales (1997, 97), AD responded to Pérez's party-neglecting strategy in two ways. First, the party began to act as a "virtual opposition force." Second, its leaders relaxed the traditional party discipline in Congress, allowing a few dissidents to defy the government. After Hugo Chávez's coup attempt in February of 1992, the orthodox opposition within the party became stronger. Given the tradition of strong party loyalty within Acción Democrática, most criticism of the president had taken place behind closed doors rather than publicly; but party leaders now began to challenge the unpopular "technocrats" in an open way. Shortly after the coup attempt, for instance, AD's president, Humberto Celli, publicly called for a reshuffling of the cabinet, stating that the departure of the powerful head of the central bank (and former minister of planning) Miguel Rodríguez was a "point of honor" for the party.

As a result of the first coup attempt, presidential power began to vanish. Pérez appointed an eight-member advisory council that included opposition politicians and some "notables." In March, the president announced a series of measures in response to the committee's recommendations. A proposal for constitutional reform was introduced in Congress; price increases for oil and electricity were suspended; and price controls on some basic foodstuffs and medicines were reintroduced. As part of the negotiations, Pérez supported a reshuffling of the Supreme Court in which he lost several loyal justices.

The president's situation worsened with a second coup attempt in November, and approval ratings hit a floor (around 20 percent) after the second quarter of 1992. Senator Pedro Pablo Aguilar (Copei) proposed a referendum to shorten Pérez's term of office. On November 4, 1992, the Senate passed the proposal by a vote of 26–22. Jaime Lusinchi left the country to avoid being present for the vote, and senators from Copei and MAS supported the declaration. The Senate requested that President Pérez negotiate with the Superior Electoral Council the inclusion of a recall ballot concurrent with the local elections of December 6, 1992. Pérez refused. The press presented the situation as a "train collision" between Pérez and Lusinchi and depicted the position of AD leaders as a catch-22: they feared that a massive vote against Pérez at the recall would create negative coattails and harm AD in the local elections, but they were unwilling to defend the unpopular president.

Influenced by the Brazilian experience, the opposition began to explore accusations of corruption in late 1992. When the scandal of the $17 million erupted, Pérez, who still anticipated a positive Supreme Court vote in the pre-trial of merit, asked his party to "respect" the Court's decision (Kada 2003a, 126). On May 20, however, the Court declared that the case had legal merit and could proceed.

Although AD technically lacked a majority in the Senate, one additional vote could have been sufficient to prevent a Supreme Court trial. But with limited public support, a mounting scandal, and a party increasingly aligned with the opposition, Pérez found himself unable to control the subsequent Senate vote on May 21, 1993. No roll call vote was taken: the leaders of all parties unanimously authorized the suspension of Pérez from office in order to proceed with the trial. Three months later, when Congress met in joint session to declare the "permanent leave" (i.e., the effective removal) of the president from office, AD legislators symbolically voted against the decision (Kada 2003a, 127). Lacking a majority, it was clear that they would be defeated. Congress then appointed Ramón J. Velásquez, an independent *Adeco*, as the consensus interim president.

Negotiation: Colombia, 1994–1998

In contrast to the Pérez debacle, the case of Ernesto Samper illustrates how a partisan majority can shield a president who is willing to negotiate. In the 1994 election, Samper's Liberal Party obtained 54 percent of the seats in the Chamber of Representatives and 55 percent of the seats in the Senate. But aware of the internal opposition potentially represented by the *Gavirista* faction – the followers of former president César Gaviria, Samper's rival within the party – the president crafted a legislative coalition with the members of the Alliance for Colombia, a group of small parties that had supported his candidacy, and a few dissident Conservatives of the Dirección Oficial Conservadora led by Jaime Arias (Cepeda Ulloa 1996, 95).[20]

In a country where, prior to 2006, autonomous party factions presented separate lists for congressional elections, partisan majorities were never taken for granted, and the support of individual legislators was a matter of permanent bargaining – particularly in the midst of a crisis (Crisp and Ingall 2002; Pizarro 2002).[21] Samper's extensive coalition-building efforts proved successful: the Liberal Party remained cohesive despite internal tension between *Samperistas* and *Gaviristas*. Because the possibility of an impeachment looked remote, 89 percent of the Liberal representatives ultimately supported the president when the proposal to kill the impeachment charges reached the floor in June of 1996 (Hinojosa and Pérez-Liñán 2003, 75).

In personal interviews, Colombian politicians offered three explanations for this surprising pattern of party unity. The first one, present in Samper's own account, emphasized a carefully crafted relationship with Congress. "I met a lot with the legislators, especially to explain to them my own version of the [campaign finance] story. Many legislators requested individual meetings to hear my personal account of the campaign. Others came in groups. I think all that helped me to convey my perspective.... There was a dialog even with those who voted against [me]" (interview, May 22, 2000). One of those Liberal legislators who voted against Samper, the *Gaviirista*

---

[20] The Conservatives participated in the Samper cabinet until January of 1996, when they formally withdraw at the peak of the scandal (Samper 2000, 69). But a group of them (ironically called "*los lentejos*") remained in the cabinet and opposed an impeachment. The most prominent legislators in this group (which constituted almost half of the Conservative bloc) were Isabel Celis and Carlina Rodríguez (interview with Rep. Benjamín Higuita, C-Antioquia, May 24, 2000).

[21] According to Ungar Bleier (1995, 87): "The [1994] elections reinforced the atomization that was already present and the collapse of regional *cacicazgos* [bosses] which, with few exceptions, were replaced in Congress by 'small' bosses." On this process, see Pizarro (2002).

president of the Chamber of Representatives, Rodrigo Rivera, recalled that Samper's relationship with Congress was

... very positive; [he had] a very good personal relationship with Congress members. I would say that the last two presidents had an excellent relation with Congress – Gaviria and Samper, President Barco was too distant. Gaviria and Samper were presidents who met with Congress members, who explained their bills to them, who get them involved in their projects. They took care of Congress members, they returned their calls. They had a fluent relationship with Congress – with both Liberals and Conservatives. They had majorities in Congress, but besides such natural majorities, they crafted broader coalitions, political blocs beyond their own party. And that was useful for them because, since this is a Congress with no party discipline, there are issues on which even the members of the president's party may vote against [him]. (Interview, May 24, 2000)[22]

A second explanation, clearly related to the previous one, emphasizes the selective use of political appointments and pork in order to build an anti-impeachment coalition. Pork was presumably disbursed through the so-called co-financing funds, grants for local public works directed at the request of members of Congress. Samper has emphatically denied the use of the co-financing funds for political purposes (Samper 2000, 109; interview, May 2000). However, a nongovernmental organization that oversaw the impeachment process claimed that the 1995 budget tended to favor investment in regions that were political bailiwicks of members of the Investigation and Accusation Committee of the Chamber of Representatives (Comisión Ciudadana 1996, 34; but see Samper 2000, 109).

Although the evidence on the use of pork is somewhat inconclusive, scholarly observers have noted that the selective use of public investments is a normal way of building legislative coalitions in Colombia (interviews with Elisabeth Ungar and Germán Ruiz, May 2000; Behar and Villa 1991, 63–72). A statistical analysis of the distribution of co-financing funds during Samper's era showed that opposition deputies who received more pork in 1995 and 1996 were more likely to vote against impeachment – although this finding did not apply to the members of Samper's Liberal Party (Hinojosa and Pérez-Liñán 2003).

The third explanation for Liberal cohesion emphasizes the fact that campaign funds presumably donated by the Cali cartel had been widely distributed among Liberal legislators in order to "oil" the local machines before the runoff election (Comisión Ciudadana 1996, 33–34, 65–67).

---

[22] Rivera, a member of the *Gavirista* faction, voted in favor of impeachment on June 12, 1996.

Therefore, it was hard for some dissident Liberals to investigate the president. According to the head campaign treasurer, 69 of the 111 votes against impeachment were cast by legislators "who were treasurers themselves or received money from the regional treasurers for the Samper campaign in different districts" (Medina Serna 1997, 223).[23]

As a result of these factors, the Liberal Party (as well as some Conservatives) consistently shielded President Samper from impeachment.[24] The president invested his political capital to guarantee his survival in office rather than to push any controversial legislative agenda. In the end, the investigative committee rejected most of the evidence supplied by the prosecutor general and reported in favor of the president (Comisión Ciudadana 1996, 46–60). On June 12, 1996, the Chamber of Representatives finally voted 111–43 to close the investigation. The Liberal Party remained cohesive and the opposition divided: eighty out of ninety Liberals voted against impeachment, while only twenty-seven Conservatives (out of forty-eight) supported a trial.[25]

From Isolation to Confrontation: Paraguay, 1998–1999

As explained in previous chapters, Paraguayan President Raúl Cubas Grau was caught in the midst of a decade-long internal Colorado Party dispute. On one hand, Gen. Lino Oviedo, arrested on charges of sedition by the Wasmosy administration prior to the 1998 election, pressed Cubas for his immediate release from prison, and his followers demanded that Cubas honor his campaign promise. On the other hand, the president confronted the *Argañista* faction and the opposition parties in Congress – the

---

[23] Medina Serna (1997, 223) erroneously noted that the total number of votes in favor of Samper was 113 (instead of 111). Rodrigo Rivera, then president of the Chamber of Representatives, believes that this factor was marginal in deciding the Liberal vote. Because regional treasurers were not responsible for the fund-raising process, most legislators were not at risk in spite of the scandal (interview, May 2000).

[24] As a fourth explanation, Samper has claimed that American pressure (through decertification) heightened nationalism among members of Congress and strengthened his position (interview, May 22, 2000).

[25] Six legislators of smaller parties voted for impeachment and ten others against. I follow my own reconstruction of the roll call; because former Liberals and Conservatives tend to disguise themselves as "independents," figures vary slightly according to the source. See, for instance, Bermúdez (1999, 55), Hinojosa and Pérez-Liñán (2003, 75), and Ungar Bleier (1997, 77).

Authentic Radical Liberals (PLRA) and the Encuentro Nacional (PEN) – who opposed Oviedo's release as a threat to democracy.

In this context, Cubas adopted the course of releasing Oviedo swiftly and without consultation with either Vice President Argaña or the opposition. He appointed loyal *Oviedistas* to all key cabinet positions (justice, defense, treasury, interior, foreign affairs) and career officials to the rest of the ministries. Only his brother Carlos, appointed minister of industry, was somewhat closer to the *Argañista* faction. Within three days of taking office, Cubas released Gen. Oviedo from prison, opening the way for a presidential crisis.

A congressional coalition of *Argañistas*, Liberals, and *Encuentristas* under the name of the Democratic Front formally requested that the Supreme Court rule on the constitutionality of the decree that had freed the rebel military leader. In the meantime, the idea of an impeachment gained leverage as the ultimate weapon to pressure the Cubas administration. When the Court ruled against the decree and required the executive to return the general to prison, Cubas ordered the ruling to be archived and responded that enforcement was legally "impossible."[26] Acting in a way that could be construed as being in contempt of the Supreme Court, Cubas had now given Congress a constitutional excuse for impeachment.

By adopting an intransigent strategy, the president had taken the road of political isolation and created conditions for the coming confrontation led by Lino Oviedo himself. On December 10, speaking to seven thousand followers at a meeting, Oviedo promised that "we will take the appropriate measures to expel [the justices from the Court]" (quoted in Morínigo 1999, 54). Ten days later, violent demonstrators burned tires and threw stones at the Supreme Court building. The church offered to mediate in the conflict between the president and the opposition if Cubas agreed to enforce the decision of the Supreme Court.

It is ultimately a matter of historical speculation whether the confrontational outcome that followed could have been avoided. Firsthand accounts have indicated that the path of negotiation was not closed from the outset. "Cubas had everything to do a good administration," recalled Liberal Senator Gonzalo Quintana during an interview. "The vice president was not an obstacle for Cubas: Argaña could have been an ally because that's the

---

[26] As explained in previous chapters, while the Supreme Court deliberated the issue a new martial court had convened, revisited Oviedo's case, and declared the general not guilty. President Cubas thus claimed that there was no legal ground for him to recapture Oviedo.

logic of the Colorado Party – in the Colorado Party, the logic of building majorities always prevails.... It would have been possible for the president to work with the vice president, to pact."

Even the opposition was willing to compromise – with one condition:

On December the 27 [1998], I had the last conversation with [President Cubas]. We [the opposition] told him that we could guarantee governability and support for the policies he had outlined, only if he could distance himself from Oviedo. No way. We had to stop the meeting because he did not give a damn about his administration. (interview with Gonzalo Quintana, June of 2002)

The tensions escalated in January of 1999, after the chief justice gave Cubas seventy-two hours to capture Oviedo and reminded the president that he could be impeached if he remained in contempt. Vice President Argaña prepared for the takeover: by mid-March, the Committee of Constitutional Affairs of the Chamber of Deputies had drafted the accusation bill. Within days, the Chamber of Deputies modified its internal procedures to reduce the number of votes required to authorize an impeachment from 67 percent to 66.5 percent of the members present – a convenient interpretation of the two-thirds clause that could eventually save a vote or two. Inaugurating a new concept of filibustering, some Oviedista deputies cut the cords of the chamber's sound system in a vain attempt to block the approval of the new rule (*Ultima Hora*, March 11, 1999, 2).

At the same time, the national convention of the Colorado Party voted on March 14 to extend the terms of the *Argañista* authorities in control of the party. After a short battle in which Colorado politicians attacked each other with the convention chairs, the *Oviedistas* abandoned the meeting, formed a parallel convention, and occupied the party headquarters. The steering committee (Junta de Gobierno) of the ANR requested the intervention of the judiciary to evict the intruders and issued a communiqué stating that "President Cubas is not a representative of the Colorado Party."

Roberto Céspedes has explained the rise of the confrontational style of the *Oviedismo* in late 1998 and early 1999 as a response to its increasing political isolation: the Supreme Court turned against Oviedo; the Colorado convention outmaneuvered Unace; and Congress prepared for an impeachment. Oviedo responded with an escalation of conflict against the Court, the ANR, and Congress. "Without any citizen or partisan response, this escalation continued until the assassination of Vice President Luis María Argaña" (Céspedes 1999, 148).

163

On March 17, the *Oviedista* deputies attempted their last trick to derail the impeachment by bringing the accusations to the floor at a time when the opposition lacked the necessary votes, but floor consideration of the issue was rejected by a vote of 44–27. Instead, the chamber set a date for the debate, April 7. Although it was not at all clear that Argaña could produce a two-thirds majority by early April, it became evident that he was paving his way to the presidency. The brutal response came a few days later, when Argaña's car was intercepted by a death squad and he and his bodyguards were shot.

With the assassination, Cubas was left in a position of irreversible conflict with the Democratic Front. Public opinion immediately blamed Oviedo for the crime; the *Argañistas* feared for their lives; and the opposition parties feared a democratic breakdown. In the chaotic hours that followed, the president's attempts to reestablish links with the Democratic Front were doomed to failure. Cubas appointed his brother Carlos as the new minister of the interior, but the congressional leaders did not show up when the minister invited them to a meeting that night. Instead, they called for an extraordinary session of the Chamber of Deputies to take place in the early hours of March 24.

The deputies of the Democratic Front met in the chamber at dusk and carefully conducted a head count. As they initiated the session at 8:00 A.M., the crowds outside Congress cried for impeachment. The speaker ordered the security guards to ensure that nobody be allowed to enter the chamber after the session had started. In the meantime, the crowds prevented an *Oviedista* leader from reaching the building's entrance, until he drove his SUV over the building's metallic fence. The deputy run into the building holding a handgun and was intercepted by the guards, who disarmed him and locked him in a room. Fearing the arrival of more *Oviedista* deputies, the Democratic Front closed the debate and moved to a vote. The surprised *Oviedistas* saw the impeachment charges approved by a margin of a single vote (49–24). Within minutes, the Senate had been notified of the charges against the president (*Ultima Hora*, March 24, 1999, 2; interviews with Marcelo Duarte and Aristides González).

Negotiation: Paraguay, 1999–2003

With the resignation of President Raúl Cubas on March 28, 1999, and in the absence of the vice president, the speaker of the Senate, Luis "Lucho" González Macchi, was appointed as interim chief executive. The political pact that drove González Macchi to the López Palace involved, for the first time since 1946, the formation of a coalition cabinet. The *Argañistas* and some former officials of the Stroessner dictatorship ("Jurassic *Stronistas*" in local press parlance) gained control of six cabinet positions (interior, defense, treasury, education, health, and public works), the Liberals of two (foreign affairs and agriculture), and the Encuentro Nacional of the remaining two (justice and industry) plus the office of planning. Part of the agreement was that the coalition would present a common candidate for the coming vice presidential election, and that he would be a Liberal.

After eight months of confrontational politics under Cubas Grau, González Macchi presented himself as a natural negotiator. A pundit noted "the friendly, parliamentary face of *President Lucho*. We had not seen courtesy in the López Palace since [President] Rodríguez left office. The politics of friendship is nowadays a topic of praise and study among political scientists; it is not just gossip for the social pages or for the frivolous press" (Rodríguez 1999, 22).[27]

The ruling coalition of the Democratic Front began to disintegrate later in 1999, when internal disputes within the PLRA created tensions with the president regarding the Liberal leader to be appointed as minister of foreign affairs. González Macchi finally imposed his preferred Liberal candidate, but the losing factions within the PLRA began to distance themselves from the government (interview with José Moreno Rufinelli, June of 2002). In February of 2000, 759 of the 1,091 delegates at the PLRA national convention voted to abandon the government coalition and to nominate an opposition candidate for the coming vice presidential election to replace the late Argaña. The gamble paid off, and the Liberal candidate, Julio César "Yoyito" Franco, won the election in August (interview with Miguel A. Saguier, June of 2002).

Paradoxically, the Liberal triumph in the August election consolidated González Macchi's support among the *Argañistas*. They filled the two PLRA cabinet positions and realized that any attempt to oust González Macchi would drive Franco to the presidency, hurting their access to patronage and their capacity to win the presidential election in 2003. At the same time, González Macchi was able to preserve the support of Encuentro Nacional. But after the national convention of the party decided to remain in the coalition in April of 2000, internal voices of dissent grew louder. In September,

---

[27] For studies of the "politics of friendship" in the Paraguayan context, see Frutos and Vera (1993) and Caballero Carrizosa (1999).

a group of *Encuentristas* led by Carlos Filizzola broke with the party and formed a new organization called País Solidario (Solidary Country). In the end, the PEN preserved seven seats in the lower chamber and its splinter only two.

As the disgruntled *Oviedistas* regrouped their forces and later approached the Liberals to form an opposition front, inconclusive "social pacts" became part of the administration's style. In June of 1999, the coalition government and some social groups agreed on a government program that was rapidly forgotten. In July, a new attempt at "*concertación*" reached no solid conclusions. Four months later, the administration called for a new round of negotiations after a large peasant demonstration. At the time, the Liberals were already distancing themselves from González Macchi (*Ultima Hora*, June 15–16, 2002, 4).

By the end of 2000, the opposition camp was consolidated with the votes of the Liberals, the *Oviedistas*, and the País Solidario members of Congress. At the same time, corruption scandals began to erode the image of the administration. The president was soon accused of using a stolen BMW and of diverting $16 million from the central bank to private accounts in the United States. These scandals opened the way for a constitutional accusation led by the PLRA and the PEN dissidents (interviews with Rafael Filizzola and Miguel A. Saguier, June of 2002). Early in July of 2001, the government forces in the Chamber of Deputies attempted to reject the impeachment charges, but they were defeated in a 45–34 vote that postponed the treatment of the issue. With the government coalition unable to force a vote and the opposition incapable of reaching the two-thirds majority, González Macchi was now barely shielded from impeachment.

In late August of 2001, the church offered to coordinate a new round of social "dialogue" to promote governability. As part of the negotiations, the opposition in Congress finally agreed to subject the impeachment accusations to a vote even though that meant their defeat. On September 6, 2001, the impeachment charges were brought to the Chamber of Deputies and rejected in a 38–38 vote. The PLRA, the *Oviedistas*, País Solidario, and two Encuentro Nacional dissidents supported the accusation. The Argañistas and a majority of the PEN opposed the trial.

The dialog promoted by the church began in November of 2001 and lasted until March of 2002, with few tangible results. The opposition soon introduced new charges against the president for corruption and human rights violations. In early June, when peasant demonstrators marched to

Asunción to demand an end to the privatization of the public telephone company, the opposition sought to seize the moment and bring new accusations to a vote. The political climate was quite different from that of March of 1999, however, and the frustrated middle class never took to the streets to support an impeachment. To the horror of the IMF and the minister of finance, the president deactivated the protests by canceling the privatization process just few days before its completion. Facing a decline in popular mobilization and lacking enough votes to proceed, the opposition then closed the discussion of the impeachment charges in Congress for the second time (*Ultima Hora*, June 7, 2002, 3).

The final push of Liberals and *Oviedistas* came in late 2002. With presidential approval ratings below 10 percent, the *Oviedistas* returned the "surprise attack" that the opposition had mounted in March of 1999. On December 5, 2002, during a regular session of the lower house, a Liberal deputy unexpectedly requested the treatment on the floor of the impeachment charges. Realizing that they did not have enough deputies in their seats to block the accusation (which could be approved by two-thirds of the members present), the *Argañista* leaders ordered their legislators to abstain. The accusation then moved to the Senate, where the constitution required the vote of two-thirds of all members, and the *Argañistas* were fully prepared. On February 11, the Senate acquitted González Macchi after the opposition mustered only twenty-five votes (56 percent) in favor of his removal.

Summary

The extensive historical discussion presented here has shown how the pattern of executive-legislative relations established by a president early in his term may shape the willingness of legislators to shield the executive from impeachment at a later point. This view is consistent with Salo Coslovsky's interpretation of presidential crises in the 1990s. In his study of the Collor and Bucaram cases, Coslovsky argued that "presidents that did not respect the consultation and negotiation processes that characterize democracy provoked a deadlock that was solved through impeachment" (Coslovsky 2002, 8). Table 6.3 summarizes the situation of each president by the time the impeachment charges reached the floor of the legislature. The table presents the main presidential strategy adopted with regard to Congress and the structure of legislative support in terms of the analytical model described in the previous section.

Table 6.3. *Presidential strategies and support for the executive in six crises*

Administration	Strategy	Vote Held in (Date)	v	Support d	S	A	P	L = P − v
Collor de Mello	I	Deputies (9/29/92)	.34	.28	.06[a]	.10	.12	−.22
Pérez	I	Senate (5/21/93)	.50	.00	.48	.00	.00	−.50
Samper	N	House (6/12/96)	.50	.90	.54	.23	.72	.22
Bucaram	C	Congress (2/6/97)	.50	.95	.23	.24	.46	−.04
Cubas Grau	I/C	Deputies (3/24/99)	.34	.57	.57	.00	.33	−.01
González Macchi	N	Deputies (9/6/01)	.34	.77	.57	.07	.50	.16
		Deputies (12/5/02)	.34	.00	.57	.00	.00	−.34
		Senate (2/11/03)	.34	.48	.48	.20	.43	.09

Key: Strategies: I = isolation; N = negotiation; C = confrontation. Conditions: v = veto threshold; d = support within the president's party; S = size of the president's party (at the time of the vote if count is of members present); A = support provided by coalition members; P = overall support at the impeachment vote (P = dS + A); L = legislative shield.
[a] Figure for PRN alone. Including PFL forces, S = .23 (d = .27).
Sources: Congressional records from each country.

The historical evidence indicates that Fernando Collor and Carlos A. Pérez adopted a strategy of isolation in their relations with Congress. As a result, in September of 1992 Collor confronted a lethal combination of a small legislative party defecting from the executive and a coalition in shambles. Less than one-third of the PRN legislators supported the chief executive, and only 12 percent of all deputies opposed the impeachment. Carlos Andrés Pérez belonged to a strong party that had similarly ceased to support the president. Acción Democrática controlled 48 percent of the Senate, but in May of 1993 no senator opposed the trial.

Two other presidents, Abdalá Bucaram and Raúl Cubas Grau, adopted confrontational strategies before they found themselves enveloped in a presidential crisis. In the case of Cubas, the president was isolated rather than personally hostile to Congress, but the leader of his faction, Gen. Lino Oviedo, escalated the confrontation leading to the tragic events of March 1999. The result of the confrontational dynamic was in both cases political polarization and an unexpected takeover by opposition groups that, disregarding legal formalities, seized power in a volatile political context marked by chaos and mass protests. The uncompromising discourse of these administrations, the warlike political climate, and the uncertainty surrounding the outcome of the congressional vote fostered a relatively high degree of cohesion among the president's ranks (Bucaram's party and Oviedo's faction), but this cohesion was insufficient to shield the president in the midst of the crisis. Taken by surprise, the loyal legislators failed to prevent both Bucaram's declaration of incapacity and Cubas Grau's impeachment.

By contrast, the remaining two presidents adopted a policy of negotiation with Congress begining in their early days in office. Samper's negotiating style was not only the result of his affable personality and his experience as a seasoned politician, but also the product of informal institutions and coalition-building practices inherited from the days of the National Front. President "Lucho" González Macchi also had the right personality and professional experience for the role of negotiator, but his weak political skills, the atomization of the Paraguayan party system, and the tyranny of the electoral calendar – which first encouraged the defection of the Liberals from his coalition and later placed the *Argañistas* in an ambiguous position – increasingly left him isolated. Building on González Macchi's weaknesses, the opposition attempted to oust him from office time after time, each attempt coming closer to success than the previous one. Yet in the end both Samper and González Macchi bargained their way to the end of the term, even though this meant surviving without governing.

Political scientists are often inclined to see presidential behavior as an outcome that deserves explanation rather than as an independent factor operating in the political process, and therefore may wonder whether presidential styles are in fact a by-product of some other conditions that in turn drive presidential crises. For instance, presidents may be more willing to negotiate when they have a small party in Congress (or alternatively, they may be more likely to isolate themselves when they face a hostile legislature). I will address this problem in the following section, by analyzing the effect of presidential style on legislative behavior while controlling for other institutional and contextual factors. (I will also return to this issue in Chapter 7, by looking at a broad sample of presidential administrations in order to dispel risks of selection bias). Although the analysis of presidential strategies often involves processing large amounts of historical information and inevitably requires some degree of subjective assessment, a systematic treatment of this independent variable may yield valuable insights for the study of presidentialism in the future.

Presidents, Legislators, and the Political Environment

Presidential leadership and partisan motivations may not be the only factors shaping legislative behavior with regard to impeachment. The historical record suggests that the political environment also plays a critical role in determining the propensity of legislators to support an impeachment process. By "environment" I simply mean a set of factors that, although exogenous to executive-legislative relations, have the capacity to affect legislators' careers and therefore to alter their incentives to remain loyal to the president. The previous case studies indicate that three additional factors may be crucial to shaping the political environment in the midst of a presidential crisis: constituency pressures, the mass media, and the electoral calendar.

Constituency pressures, discussed in the previous chapter, are reflected in the collapse of presidential approval ratings and the emergence of mass protests calling for the resignation of the chief executive. Naoko Kada has distinguished between the "preconditioning" and the "resolution" effects of public opinion in the impeachment process. According to Kada, hostile public opinion may encourage legislators to investigate the president (preconditioning effect), but an incisive congressional investigation may also fuel public outrage, which in turn may increase public pressure for an impeachment (Kada 2003b, 148–49; see also Smulovitz and Peruzzotti 2000). Popular protest, a factor to be discussed in the concluding chapter in greater detail, represents a stronger form of pressure because legislators are confronted with a destabilizing escalation of public unrest.

The mass media, the focus of Chapter 4, also mold the environment for impeachment by investigating and publicizing the accusations against the president. The important question from the perspective of this chapter is whether media effects take place only indirectly, by shaping public opinion and constituency pressures, or also directly, by signaling to legislators the right course of action. Direct media influence over Congress could take place if legislators trusted the opinions or the investigations conducted by the mass media, or if they feared becoming the focus of media criticism for supporting the president. Meinke and Anderson, for instance, found that the members of the U.S. House were less likely to support the president on key bills during the Watergate, Iran–Contra, and Lewinsky scandals, even after controlling for presidential approval ratings (Meinke and Anderson 2001). On the other hand, it is also possible that politicians take media scandals seriously only when they ignite constituency pressures, but dismiss the accusations if their voters fail to react.

The third factor deserving consideration is the electoral calendar. Presumably, the proximity of elections increases strategic behavior on the part of politicians and potentially promotes party defection. According to

Barbara Geddes and Artur Ribeiro, Brazilian legislators became convinced that voters would punish Collor supporters at the polls not only because of the mass demonstrations, but also because municipal elections were scheduled for October 3, just a few days after the nationally televised roll call vote (Geddes and Ribeiro Neto 1999, 44). Naoko Kada has also argued that public opinion exercises greater leverage if legislators must vote on impeachment immediately prior to an election (Kada 2003b, 149).

Predicting the Strength of the Legislative Shield

How relevant are these contextual factors in explaining the vote on impeachment? In order to assess the impact of all the variables discussed in this chapter, I pooled in a single database all the roll call votes on impeachment or declaration of incapacity that took place while Presidents Collor, Samper, Bucaram, Cubas Grau, and González Macchi were in office. The indictment vote against President Collor held in the Brazilian Senate on December 29, 1992, was excluded from the sample because by then the president had already resigned; the votes against President Carlos Andrés Pérez could not be included in the dataset because the Venezuelan Congress failed to produce a roll call record. The remaining observations reflect the behavior of 956 legislators in four countries during seven different impeachment votes. These include decisions on the fate of Fernando Collor (9/29/1992), Ernesto Samper (6/12/1996), Abdalá Bucaram (2/6/1997), Raúl Cubas (3/24/1999), and Luis González Macchi (9/6/2001, 12/5/2002, and 2/11/2003).

The database documents whether each of those 956 legislators belonged to the president's party or the president's coalition. Members of the PRN in Brazil, the Liberal Party in Colombia, the PRE in Ecuador, and the Colorado Party (ANR) in Paraguay received a score of one for the dummy variable reflecting membership in the president's party; all other legislators were coded as zero. Coalition members were harder to identify, in part because the structure of legislative coalitions varied significantly from country to country, and in part because individual-level information was scarce. I relied on interview data and secondary sources to determine the parties or factions that were considered part of the presidential bloc in Congress at the time of the impeachment crisis. The inclusion in the cabinet of individual politicians does not always indicate that their congressional parties support the president, so I had to obtain subtler information.

171

In Brazil, I counted all members of the PDS, the PFL, the PL, the PRN, and the PTB as part of the president's coalition. In Paraguay, I took members of the *Oviedista* faction as the only legislative bloc supporting Raúl Cubas, and members of the *Argañista* faction plus the PEN as the coalition supporting Luis González Macchi. In the other two cases, the president's coalition coincided with his party. In Colombia, where information about factional identification was not available for the individual legislators, I simply assumed that the Liberals represented the president's coalition and that the Conservatives did not. In previous sections, I have shown that some Conservative factions supported Samper's policies while some Liberal factions opposed them, but it was impossible to identify the individual members of these factions. In Ecuador, I counted the PRE as the only member of the president's coalition because by early 1997 no other party was willing to support the Bucaram administration openly, even though the smaller parties may have been willing to secretly form "ghost coalitions" (Mejía Acosta 2003).

The dataset also includes two variables capturing the president's strategy vis-à-vis Congress. One dichotomous variable indicates the situation of legislators facing an isolationist president (Collor and Cubas, since votes for Pérez were not available), while a second dummy variable reflects the situation of legislators dealing with a confrontational administration (Bucaram and again Cubas Grau, given Oviedo's style). Legislators interacting with presidents prone to negotiation (Samper and González Macchi) were treated as the reference category.

Finally, three additional variables depict the political environment at the time of the vote. For the most part, these variables reflected conditions that varied across administrations rather than across individual legislators. The president's approval rating for the month in which the vote took place was used to capture constituency pressures (at the national level, since district-level approval data was of course not available). The scandal index (described in Chapter 5) corresponding to the same month was used to assess the role of the media. And the impact of the electoral calendar was measured by the number of days pending until the next legislative election. This indicator ranged from 1,495 days at the time the Paraguayan House charged Raúl Cubas Grau, to 75 days when the Senate acquitted Luis González Macchi. In the Brazilian case, because a municipal election took place few days after the impeachment vote, and because several observers have claimed that national legislators usually pursue careers at the subnational level (Mainwaring 1999b; Samuels 2003; Samuels and Mainwaring 2004), I identified the

Table 6.4. *Individual support for the president (logit models)*

	6.4.1	6.4.2	6.4.3
Member of president's party	0.843*	0.830*	0.826*
	(0.408)	(0.386)	(0.226)
Member of coalition	2.609*	2.616*	2.631*
	(0.437)	(0.441)	(0.306)
Days to next election	0.005*	0.005*	0.004*
	(0.001)	(0.001)	(0.000)
Scandal index	0.013*	0.015*	0.010*
	(0.004)	(0.004)	(0.002)
Approval rating	0.015*		0.017
	(0.004)		(0.002)
Popular protest		−0.418*	
		(0.029)	
Strategy of isolation	−4.174*	−4.402*	−3.965*
	(0.404)	(0.416)	(0.290)
Strategy of confrontation	−1.779*	−2.201*	−1.299*
	(0.437)	(0.458)	(0.309)
Constant	−4.322*	−4.339*	−3.899*
	(0.733)	(0.726)	(0.501)
Pseudo R^2	0.447	0.446	0.368
N	956	956	637

Note: Entries are logistic regression coefficients (standard errors clustered by country). Dependent variable is voting against impeachment (or against removal from office at the impeachment trial). Model 6.4.3 weights legislators so that all legislatures have an equal size (100 members).
* Significant at the .05 level (all coefficients passed the test).

eighty deputies running for mayor in the 1992 election and assigned them a very short time horizon (4 days to the municipal election), while all other deputies were assumed to have a longer horizon (734 days to the 1994 race).

Table 6.4 presents the results of three logistic regression models in which the dependent variable is the individual legislator's support for the president (i.e., a vote against impeachment). The results indicate that presidents who build extensive legislative coalitions are, not surprisingly, less likely to confront impeachment charges. They also suggest that strategies based on presidential isolation and, to a lesser extent, interbranch confrontation can be lethal once an impeachment crisis explodes.

The coefficients for the electoral calendar and the constituency pressure variables show the expected signs: the longer the time horizon and the higher the presidential approval rating, the more likely legislators are to support the executive. However, the sign of the scandal index coefficient defies the initial expectations – more scandals seem to encourage members of Congress to rally around the president, suggesting that the media exercise a powerful but indirect influence on the impeachment process. In the absence of constituency pressures, most legislators presumably interpret media scandals as political chicanery and close ranks with the executive. In model 6.4.2, I replaced presidential approval with an alternative measure of public outrage (a dummy variable indicating whether mass protests called for the resignation of the president) and obtained equivalent results. Model 6.4.3 corrected for the undue influence of large legislatures. For instance, the Brazilian Chamber of Deputies had 503 members, while the Paraguayan Chamber of Deputies had just 80 members. The model simulated a resizing of all chambers to the equivalent of one hundred seats. The results remained unchanged.

Table 6.5 compares the observed and the predicted values for the key parameter in the analytical model presented in this chapter: P, the proportion of legislators favoring the president. The predictions are highly accurate, with the exception of the ones referring to the final crisis of the González Macchi administration.

According to model 4.6.1, about 14 percent of the deputies should have voted against the impeachment of González Macchi in December of 2002

Table 6.5. *Observed and predicted support for the president*

Case (Date)[a]	Votes for Impeachment		Number of Legislators Voting	Support for the President (P)		Predicted L
	For	Against		Observed	Predicted	
Collor de Mello (9/29/92)	441	38	479	0.079	0.079	−0.26
Samper (6/12/96)	43	111	154	0.721	0.721	0.22
Bucaram (2/6/97)	44	34	78	0.436	0.436	−0.06
Cubas Grau (3/24/99)	49	24	73	0.329	0.329	−0.01
G. Macchi (9/6/01)	38	38	76	0.500	0.493	0.15
G. Macchi (House, 12/5/02)	52	0	52	0.000	0.136	−0.20
G. Macchi (Senate, 2/11/03)	25	19[b]	44	0.432	0.284	−0.06

Note: Observed P is the proportion of members voting against impeachment or removal from office. Expected P is the average probability of voting against impeachment or removal from office for all individuals voting (according to model 6.4.1). Predicted L is the anticipated size of the legislative shield based on v (Table 6.3) and the expected P.

[a] Roll call vote was not taken in Venezuela.

[b] Including one abstention, since the 1992 constitution requires a vote of two-thirds of the Senate to remove the president from office.

(while in reality no one backed the president), and only 28 percent of the senators should have supported the president in the trial vote a couple of months later (as opposed to 43 percent). The discrepancies in this case suggest that a complete model of legislative impeachment should probably incorporate additional measures of strategic behavior. In particular, further extensions of the model may need to capture the free-riding behavior of lower house legislators. In cases like Paraguay and the United States, where the president is not suspended from office before the impeachment trial, lower house members may allow the accusation to proceed, knowing that their partisan colleagues in the Senate will pay the political price for shielding the president.

Although the evidence presented in this chapter indicates that institutional factors play a major role in the impeachment process, it also suggests that there is a causal relationship between the style of presidential leadership and the strength of the legislative shield. Presidents who followed an isolationist strategy found themselves in a particularly weak position to prevent an impeachment process later in their terms. There was little uncertainty about the outcome of the votes against Fernando Collor and Carlos Andrés Pérez, because by the time of the crisis a large proportion of legislators were already detached from the executive. By contrast, presidents who adopted a confrontational style were in a stronger position even if they ultimately failed to survive in office. The outcome of the vote was highly uncertain in the cases of Abdalá Bucaram and Raúl Cubas Grau. Bucaram would have survived an impeachment, but he did not control enough support to prevent a declaration of incapacity. Cubas Grau's supporters in the Paraguayan Chamber of Deputies barely failed to prevent his impeachment by one vote. A sustained pattern of negotiation with Congress clearly appeared to be the best insurance against impeachment. The historical record shows that local observers easily anticipated the outcome in the cases of Ernesto Samper and (with the exception of the surprise in December of 2002) Luis González Macchi, because the political environment was more stable and a larger number of legislators were known to be loyal to the president.

7

Toward a New Pattern
of Political Instability

The episodes of impeachment described in previous chapters constitute part of a broader trend, a new pattern of political instability that emerged in Latin America in the 1990s. Between the fall of the Collor administration and the end of 2004, ten Latin American presidents were removed from office. In about half of the episodes, the outcome of the crisis was an impeachment or a declaration of incapacity. In the remaining cases, presidents were ousted by other means. In no case, however, was the demise of the president followed by the establishment of an authoritarian regime.

Why were some presidents ousted without an impeachment process? What do these cases tell us about the hypotheses developed in previous chapters? In the first section of this chapter, I discuss two paradigmatic episodes of presidential removal without impeachment proceedings: the fall of Presidents Fernando de la Rúa and Adolfo Rodríguez Saá of Argentina in 2001.[1] The Argentine crisis illustrates some of the general characteristics of the new pattern of instability. Similar cases of removal without impeachment took place in other countries, and they are summarized in the second section.

In the third section of the chapter, I identify the distinctive traits of the emerging pattern of instability and return to the hypotheses outlined in Chapter 2. The impact of declining military intervention, rising scandals, popular uprisings, and weak legislative support is tested in the next two sections, where I conduct a qualitative comparative analysis of twenty-four presidential crises and then perform a broader statistical test for seventy-five administrations. The conclusions explore three possible outcomes of

---

[1] The treatment of the Argentine crisis is based on Pérez-Liñán (2002b).

presidential crises in the new historical context: impeachments, failed military coups, and presidential downfalls.

Argentina, 2001

President Fernando de la Rúa won the 1999 election as the candidate of the Alianza, a coalition of the traditional Radical Party and the center-left Frepaso (Novaro 2002; Ollier 2001). The new administration inherited – and embraced – the so-called convertibility policy from its predecessor.[2] In 1991, in response to hyperinflation, the Menem administration had established a currency board, pegging the Argentine peso to the U.S. dollar at a 1:1 rate. This policy immediately stabilized the Argentine currency, brought inflation down, and allowed for the return of credit and some years of economic growth. Unable to rely on the inflationary tax, the Argentine government was forced to deal with its deficits by cutting expenditures and by borrowing, since a comprehensive tax reform proved politically infeasible and the revenues from privatization were soon exhausted (Corrales 2002b; Schamis 2002). After 1999 the limitations of this model became evident when Brazil, the largest partner in the Southern Cone Common Market, devalued its currency and Argentine leaders realized that the exchange rate policy was too rigid. As Argentine companies lost competitiveness in international markets, the unemployment rate skyrocketed to 17 percent by the end of the first Menem administration (in October of 1995), remaining at 14 percent by the end of his second term (in October of 1999).[3]

The de la Rúa administration inherited a budget deficit and soon realized that it had walked into a trap: any attempt to cut government spending or raise taxes would deepen the recession, while any attempt to boost the economy would worsen the fiscal imbalance. An orthodox strategy would facilitate access to the financial markets in the short run, but it would compound social tensions and compromise the federal tax base needed to serve

---

[2] Because many people had contracted debts in dollars and because of the harsh memories of hyperinflation, a large majority of the population opposed the devaluation of the Argentine currency. A Gallup poll conducted in the greater metropolitan areas of Buenos Aires, Rosario, Córdoba, Mendoza, and Tucumán on December 20, 2001 (already in the midst of the crisis) showed that 79 percent of the respondents opposed the devaluation of the Argentine peso; 78 percent rejected a full dollarization of the economy; and only 45 percent wanted to abolish the existing convertible peso (*La Nación*, December 23, 2001, 10).

[3] See "Tasa de Desocupación Abierta en los Principales Aglomerados Urbanos," Instituto Nacional de Estadística y Censos (INDEC), http://www.indec.mecon.ar/default.htm.

the debt in the long run. A gamble on economic growth, by contrast, would restrict immediate access to credit because financial operators were anticipating a slow recovery and therefore a likely default. Unable either to cut deficits or to curb unemployment, the administration increasingly projected an image of ineffective rule (Bonvecchi 2002).

Despite electoral promises of transparent administration and a more humane approach to the economy, the Alianza government was shaken in October of 2000 when trade union leaders denounced the minister of labor and the head of the intelligence service (a close friend of the president) for bribing twelve senators in order to get an unpopular labor law passed. As the scandal unfolded, presidential approval ratings dropped below 20 percent, and Vice President Carlos Alvarez, the leader of Frepaso, resigned to protest the corruption scheme (Weyland 2002, 201–204). According to Enrique Peruzzotti, the episode had deleterious effects because the administration had made the fight against corruption one of its prominent banners. Alvarez's resignation and the subsequent fracture of the government coalition around this issue indicated that the problem of corruption affected all political parties (Peruzzotti 2005, 243).

The president responded to this challenge by increasing his political isolation, "surrounding himself with 'friends and family' and shutting top Radicals out of his inner circle" (Schamis 2002, 87). By early 2001, it was clear that fiscal deficits had escalated, that access to the international capital markets had become too costly, and that a recovery in tax collection was unlikely. To make things worse, new authorities at the U.S. Treasury and the International Monetary Fund were increasingly reluctant to offer assistance, under the principle that unconditional support would encourage private lenders to behave imprudently (Corrales 2002b). A radical attempt to slash government expenditures by appointing a new minister of the economy in early March met political resistance and failed within days (Bonvecchi 2002, 139–147). Unable to pull the country out of a three-year recession, in March of 2001 the president appointed Domingo Cavallo – a former minister under Menem and the architect of the convertibility policy – as his economic czar, reinforcing his image as a weak leader who had virtually abdicated policy making in favor of Cavallo.

Paradoxically, this appointment created uncertainty about the future of the convertibility program. The new minister proposed to flexibilize the fixed exchange rate by pegging the Argentine peso to a basket of currencies that included the dollar and the euro. In July, facing skepticism in the financial markets, the administration turned to a more orthodox strategy and announced a "zero deficit" plan that slashed public salaries, pensions, and spending (Corrales 2002b).[4] A side effect of this policy may have been the reduction of local patronage resources and the disruption of the clientelistic networks that distributed food among the poor – with catastrophic consequences five months later (Auyero 2005). The Alianza lost the midterm elections in October of 2001, and the Peronist Party (Partido Justicialista, PJ) regained control of a plurality of the seats (45 percent) in the Chamber of Deputies and retained a majority (56 percent) in the Senate.[5]

The outcome of the midterm election led the government to reorient its strategy once again. In November, the Ministry of the Economy announced new social programs, minor tax cuts, and a plan to restructure the public debt. Investors reacted with skepticism, and capital flight accelerated. On the evening of December 1, 2001, Domingo Cavallo announced a set of desperate measures intended to prevent a run on banks and to save the convertibility policy: for a period of ninety days, citizens would be allowed to extract only 250 pesos (the equivalent of $250) in cash from their bank accounts every week; all other transactions would be restricted to checks, debit cards, and electronic transfers; and no person traveling outside of the country would be allowed to take more than a thousand dollars.

The announcements activated a ticking bomb in a country that had registered 18 percent unemployment during the previous month. As Christmas sales plummeted and the recession worsened, trade unions and shopkeepers mobilized to protest the economic policy. Early demonstrations appeared to be isolated episodes with little political weight, but in mid-December food riots erupted in several provincial cities. By December 19, 2001, food riots had reached the outskirts of Buenos Aires, unleashing a rapid chain of events that led to the collapse of the administration.

During the afternoon, as riots spread throughout the country, de la Rúa's chief of staff requested the resignation of all ministers to open the way for a coalition government. That night, in a vain attempt to show that he was still in control of the situation, the president made a televised speech announcing the declaration of a state of siege. Spontaneously, middle-class

---

[4] Feldstein (2002, 12) erroneously claimed that Argentine wages did not decline during the late 1990s. By contrast, the government cut public employees' salaries by 15 percent in May of 2000 and another 13 percent (including pensions for all retired people) in July of 2001 (Bonvecchi 2002, 125). The private sector followed the same course.

[5] The midterm election sent a clear signal of popular discontent to the Argentine elite, as 25 percent of the registered voters did not show up at the polls (even though voting is legally mandatory) and 21 percent of the voters annulled their ballots.

179

demonstrators defied the curfew, took to the streets, and began a pan-beating protest demanding the resignation of Domingo Cavallo. When police forces tried to repress acts of vandalism in downtown Buenos Aires later that night, seven people were killed. A few hours later, the president accepted the minister's resignation, but in the meantime, intense negotiations between Radical Party operatives and Peronist leaders to form a coalition government had reached a deadlock.

The next morning, the Peronist leaders politely excused themselves from meeting with the president. After two days of riots, demonstrations, and police repression, more than 30 people had died, more than 400 had been wounded, and more than 3,000 had been arrested all over the country. At 5 P.M., the leader of the Peronist bloc in the lower house announced that the party was ready to initiate impeachment proceedings against President de la Rúa. The president understood the message and submitted his resignation to Congress.[6]

The Rise and Fall of Rodríguez Saá

Without a vice president and with both chambers controlled by the opposition, it was clear that the new president would be a Peronist. But who was to be appointed? Several PJ governors had presidential ambitions and were unwilling to play the role of caretaker. After several rounds of negotiations, the provincial leaders reached an agreement: the governor of San Luis, Adolfo Rodríguez Saá – and old-fashioned local *caudillo* with a reputation as an efficient administrator – would be appointed as caretaker for ninety days, and presidential elections would be scheduled for March of 2002.

After twelve hours of legislative debate, a joint session of Congress approved the Peronist transition plan on the morning of December 23. The weakened Radical Party complained that the legislative majority was tampering with the electoral law to resolve its own internal disputes. Congressional leaders placed all the transition measures in a single bill to prevent any last-minute defections, and the plan was approved by a narrow 169–138 vote.

---

[6] Pablo Calvo and Rolando Barbano, "Represión en Plaza de Mayo: Una Batalla con Cinco Muertos," *Clarín*, December 21, 2001. Graciela Mochkofsky, Gabriela Litre, and Mariano Obarrio, "El Fallido Plan de De la Rúa para Sobrevivir," *La Nación*, December 23, 2001, 12.

As María Matilde Ollier (2003) has pointed out, the change in government had not resolved two major problems driving the crisis – the dependence on foreign credit and the fragmentation of political power. Within two days, it became clear that President Rodríguez Saá was planning to defy the transition pact and remain in office until the end of the de la Rúa term in 2003. In an attempt to gain the support of various factions within the Peronist Party, the new administration appointed some old-guard party leaders with an unpopular record of corruption. The betrayed PJ governors waited in silence.

On December 28, a federal judge ruled against restrictions on bank accounts, authorizing one citizen to withdraw his savings. Later that afternoon, however, the Supreme Court overruled the decision and upheld the restrictions by a vote of seven of its nine members – ordering the beneficiary of the initial ruling to *return* his money to the bank. That night, as they learned about the judicial decision on the news, upset middle-class demonstrators marched to the Supreme Court, calling for the resignation of the justices, and to the government palace, demanding the removal of public officials with well-known records of corruption. More than fifteen thousand people camped in the Plaza de Mayo, in front of the presidential palace. As young demonstrators began to burn tires and paint the doors of the government palace with graffiti, the police charged with tear gas and dissolved the demonstration. Some twelve officers were hurt; thirty-three demonstrators were arrested; and a new wave of looting of banks in the surrounding areas broke out. A few protesters entered the Congress building and sacked its offices until they were dispersed.

The protests of December 28 showed that public outrage was directed toward all politicians and institutions, not just against the defunct de la Rúa administration (Armony and Armony 2005; Peruzzotti 2005, 246). Even the Supreme Court, widely discredited after being taken over by *Menemista* justices in the early 1990s, became a major target of public outrage (see Helmke 2005; Larkins 1998). President Rodríguez Saá called for an emergency meeting with the Peronist governors on December 30, and all members of the cabinet submitted their resignations to allow for a new round of negotiations within the party. However, only six Peronist governors (of fourteen) showed up for the meeting, and new demonstrations erupted outside the president's summer house. Understanding that the leaders of the party had withdrawn their support in retaliation for his attempt to remain in office until 2003, Rodríguez Saá flew to his home province and announced his resignation on national television.[7]

After the failure of the Peronist takeover, it was imperative to create a new coalition. This time, Peronist leaders from the Buenos Aires province negotiated a new agreement with Radical and Frepaso politicians. The result of these negotiations was a broader congressional pact (Mustapic 2005). While supporters of Rodríguez Saá had barely gathered a 55 percent majority in Congress, the incorporation of the Alianza members allowed for the election of a new president with 93 percent of the legislative vote. On January 1, 2002, a joint session of Congress appointed Eduardo Duhalde (the PJ candidate who had lost the 1999 election) as new interim president by a vote of 262–21.

Three distinctive elements complicated the resolution of the Argentine political crisis: the restrictions on bank accounts (which created a self-fulfilling prophesy of financial catastrophe), the unresolved contest among the powerful governors, and the discrediting of the Supreme Court. But beyond such idiosyncratic elements, the Argentine crisis illustrates a broader pattern of political instability that emerged in Latin America after the third wave of democratization.

Other Episodes

Between 1990 and 2004, four other presidents were forced to leave office without the use of an impeachment or a declaration of incapacity. These episodes took place in Guatemala in 1993, in Ecuador and Peru in 2000, and in Bolivia in 2003.[8] Reasons of space prevent me from discussing these cases in great detail, but I offer a brief overview of them in order to concentrate on their comparative aspects in the next section.

Guatemala, 1993 Jorge Serrano won the Guatemalan presidential race of 1990–91, but his Movimiento de Acción Solidaria (MAS) captured just 16 percent of the seats in the unicameral Congress. Serrano failed to

---

[7] Mariano Obarrio, "La Fractura que Hizo Caer al Presidente," *La Nación,* December 31, 2001, 4

[8] Presidents were also ousted in Bolivia and Ecuador in 2005 – in ways that reinforced the conclusions of this chapter.

implement peace talks with the Guatemalan guerrillas and attempted a series of economic reforms. In 1993, the president was accused of corruption in the privatization of the electric industry, and mass demonstrations strongly protested austerity measures that included higher prices for electricity and public transportation. The congressional coalition that gave the administration a legislative majority collapsed, and the opposition began to collect signatures on a petition for Serrano's impeachment on charges of corruption. On May 25, 1993, Serrano launched a self-coup, dissolved Congress and the Supreme Court, imposed a media blackout, and ordered the arrest of the human rights ombudsman (Jonas 1993, 4). However, strong resistance from the press, civil society, and international institutions discouraged Serrano's allies. Although the army high command initially backed the president, middle-rank officers refused to support the coup, and the military ultimately asked Serrano to leave the country. The president was forced to resign, and the generals turned to the Supreme Court and to Congress looking for a constitutional solution. On June 5, 1993, Congress appointed Ramiro de León Carpio, the human rights ombudsman, as interim president (Villagrán de León 1993).

Ecuador, 2000   In 1998, Jamil Mahuad became the first elected president after the fall of Abdalá Bucaram. But Mahuad's situation deteriorated quickly in the midst of an economic crash that included a collapse of the exchange rate, the freezing of bank accounts, and a moratorium on Ecuador's foreign debt. The Mahuad administration proposed a "dollarization" plan that resembled Bucaram's convertibility program. As in 1997, the Indigenous Federation (Conaie) opposed the measures and led a popular uprising. This time, however, the social coalition against the executive was narrower, and the legislative conditions for impeachment were uncertain. Indigenous leaders overcame this obstacle through an alliance with middle-rank military officers (Pallares 2006). On January 21, 2000, a coalition of indigenous demonstrators and military officers led by Col. Lucio Gutiérrez occupied Congress and overthrew the president (Herrera Aráuz 2001). Although unable to remain in power, President Mahuad refused to submit his resignation, and the international community conveyed the message that a military junta would not be welcome. Inverting the Guatemalan situation, the top Ecuadorian generals outmaneuvered the middle ranks and turned to Congress in search of a constitutional outcome (Lascano Palacios 2001). Congress declared Mahuad out of office, and

183

Vice President Gustavo Noboa was sworn in to complete the rest of the term.

Peru, 2000   Peruvian President Alberto Fujimori took office in 1990 and immediately adopted a strategy of confrontation with Congress. The president was well known for his "arrogance towards political leaders, including his own advisers, [and his] vitriolic slander of civilian institutions" (McClintock 1993, 114). On December 6, 1991, six months before the Collor scandal erupted in Brazil, Fujimori almost became the first case of congressional removal in the decade. When he suggested that Congress was under the influence of drug-trafficking lobbyists, legislators met overnight and almost declared the president "morally unfit" to rule. The Senate approved the motion unanimously, but the Chamber of Deputies, fearing that they would incite a military coup, rejected the declaration of incapacity in a 51–60 vote (Kenney 2004, 177–191).

In April of 1992, taking advantage of the low popularity of Congress and his support among military officers, Fujimori closed the legislature, called for the election of a constituent assembly, and rewrote the constitution (Kenney 2004). (This episode was to inspire Guatemalan President Jorge Serrano a year later.) By 1995, a significant decline in inflation, the capture of the leader of the main terrorist organization, and spending targeted on social programs and public works allowed Fujimori to win reelection and to keep a majority in Congress (see Stokes 2001, Chapter 5; Weyland 2002, Chapter 7). But by the end of the second term, the administration's corruption and authoritarian leanings had eroded its popularity. Fujimori "won" the 2000 runoff election after the opposition candidate, Alejandro Toledo, refused to participate, anticipating electoral fraud. The administration confronted international criticism and increasing public unrest, and the situation only worsened when a TV station aired a video showing the head of the intelligence service and strongman of the regime bribing an opposition congressman.

In October of 2000, sensing the weakness of the administration, politicians began to realign. The vice president resigned, and at least ten members of Fujimori's legislative coalition switched parties. The president understood that his legislative shield was growing thin. In a context of media revelations, mounting demonstrations, and declining legislative support, Fujimori opted for a fast exit. On November 17, 2000, he flew to Japan and announced his resignation from Tokyo. Five days later, the stunned

Peruvian Congress voted to reject his resignation and to impeach the runaway president on the grounds of "moral incapacity."

Bolivia, 2003   Gonzalo Sánchez de Lozada left office following a popular revolt in October of 2003. After leading a successful administration from 1993 to 1997, Sánchez de Lozada was elected to a second term in 2002. This time, however, the president had to confront a dramatic financial situation, a more intransigent U.S. policy on coca eradication, and an increasingly mobilized popular sector organized by the Movimiento al Socialismo (MAS), the trade unions, and the indigenous party Pachakuti. When the administration attempted to raise taxes in February of 2003, rebel police officers staged a mutiny, and furious demonstrators sacked business and government buildings in the cities of La Paz and El Alto. Social conflicts escalated between February and October, when the administration proposed a plan to export natural gas using Chilean ports. Opponents to the plan mobilized in the city of El Alto and closed all access roads to La Paz (Verdesoto 2004). When the minister of defense ordered a military convoy to break the blockade, about sixty people were killed. In response, Vice President Carlos Mesa gave a televised speech in which he distanced himself from the administration and virtually offered himself as an alternative. Anticipating a collapse in political support, on October 17, 2003, President Sánchez de Lozada presented his resignation to Congress and went into exile; the vice president was then sworn into office. For the following months, Sánchez de Lozada's party, the Movimiento Nacionalista Revolucionario (MNR), consumed its political capital in Congress trying to fend off attempts to move forward with a post hoc impeachment of the former president.

The New Pattern of Instability

Like the Argentine debacle of 2001, political crises in Guatemala, Ecuador, Peru, and Bolivia did not result in an impeachment or a declaration of incapacity against the president. Just as in the Argentine case, it is not unthinkable that these episodes could have led to an impeachment, but the acceleration of political events led to the collapse of the government before such a course of action was even feasible. This fact underscores an important conclusion: the impeachment process was not the fundamental *cause* leading to the fall of the administrations discussed in previous chapters; it was just a particular *way* in which such collapses took place.[9]

A comparison of the cases of impeachment and the episodes of removal without impeachment offers important insights. Although these crises ultimately had different outcomes, the comparison underscores the relevance of the four historical conditions identified in Chapter 2: the reluctance (or inability) of military officers to take over, the impact of popular uprisings as the driving force behind the resignation of the president, the role of the mass media as a watchdog of public morality, and the intervention of Congress to guarantee a constitutional transition in the midst of the crisis. While the first two factors constitute common denominators for the ten cases of presidential removal, variations in the role of the media and the behavior of legislators have determined the different ways in which removals took place.

Demilitarization

Chapter 3 documented a sharp decline in military interventions since 1978. During the 1980s and 1990s, international and domestic factors greatly reduced the incentives for military intervention in Latin American politics, and military officers saw their influence in domestic affairs diminished (Hunter 1997). At the international level, the end of the Cold War encouraged changes in U.S. policy toward Central America and facilitated the attainment of peace accords in El Salvador (1992) and Guatemala (1996). The Organization of American States closed ranks to protect fledgling democracies and amended its charter in 1997 to suspend any member country when its "democratically constituted government is overthrown by force" (Chapter III, article 9). The United States (at least until the Venezuelan coup attempt of 2002) and the European Union consistently signaled low tolerance for military turmoil, threatening to cut economic and military aid to countries confronting the risk of a coup.

Internally, military intervention in politics was discredited by human rights violations and the poor economic performance of military governments in the 1970s. Political learning altered the perceptions of both civilian

---

[9] "The exact mechanism often comes down to a question of timing, such as whether Congress can put together a formal impeachment process, settles for a hasty vote to remove the president using other mechanisms, or the president simply resigns before formal proceedings are initiated" (Hochstetler 2006).

and military elites. J. Samuel Fitch reported a significant change in military belief systems in Argentina and, to a lesser extent, in Ecuador. Military officers increasingly abandoned ideas of direct control or tutelage of elected officials to embrace democratic values or, in most cases, a more tenuous conception of "conditional subordination" to civilian rulers (Fitch 1998).

In this context, military officers became reluctant to play a major role during presidential crises. In only two cases (Guatemala in 1993 and Ecuador in 2000) was military intervention critical for the ousting of the president. In all other cases, military leaders played at most an indirect role in the resolution of the crisis. In Brazil, the army was totally absent from the resolution of the Collor episode. In Venezuela, two frustrated coup attempts against President Pérez in 1992 convinced politicians that opposition to the government was widespread and ultimately encouraged a purely civilian solution. Ecuadorian generals acted as behind-the-scenes negotiators to facilitate a smooth transition between the Bucaram, Arteaga, and Alarcón governments in February of 1997 and blocked the rise of a military junta in 2000. In Paraguay, the *Oviedista* military leaders, who presumably backed the Cubas administration, were unable to intervene in defense of the government in 1999. The other Mercosur[10] countries strongly signaled the Paraguayan elite that any resolution of the presidential crisis would have to be cast in a constitutional mold. Indeed, it was following the invitation of Brazilian President Fernando Henrique Cardoso that Raúl Cubas Grau left the country in a Brazilian military airplane and sought refuge in Brazil.

Social Movements and Popular Protest

Kathryn Hochstetler has shown that between 1978 and 2003, 40 percent of the elected presidents in South America were challenged by civilian actors, and 23 percent of them were removed from office through impeachment or by other means. Hochstetler argues that street protests have played the most important role in determining which presidents are ousted, suggesting that social movements have become the new "moderating power" in civilian regimes (Hochstetler 2006).

Mass mobilization can weaken an elected president in three ways. First, extensive protests may signal political elites that the president has lost any trace of popular support and therefore is an easy target. Enemies may

[10] The Southern Cone Common Market is formed by Argentina, Brazil, Paraguay, and Uruguay, with Bolivia being an associate member.

187

organize, allies may defect, and an impeachment or a declaration of incapacity may easily move forward. Second, public unrest may acquire a violent character – in the form of lootings or riots – creating a situation of high uncertainty. In this situation, important political sectors that otherwise would back the president may withdraw their support in order to avoid an escalation of social conflict. Third, if popular protests are met with state repression, human tragedies may erode the government's legitimacy and accelerate the president's downfall.

Based on the findings presented in Chapter 5, I will emphasize the social scope of protests as the key factor shaping their political effectiveness. Public outrage can be the product of unpopular policies or watchdog politics, but mobilization, irrespective of its origins, is most lethal when it translates into broad social movements involving the participation of multiple political sectors. Unstructured "street coalitions" of the middle-class and popular sectors showed their power throughout Latin America in the 1990s and early 2000s. Maybe the most picturesque example of this trend was the colorful coalition of indigenous movements and Quito middle-class dwellers that toppled Abdalá Bucaram in February of 1997 (Luna Tamayo 1997). But broad protests were critical in most other episodes as well: in Brazil, the demonstrations against Fernando Collor were the largest since the movement to demand direct elections in 1984 (Avritzer 1999); in Venezuela, Carlos Andrés Pérez was received by the *Caracazo* and confronted middle-class demonstrations throughout his term (Kornblith 1998; López Maya 1999); in Paraguay, it was only after several days of tragic student and peasant protests that President Raúl Cubas Grau left the country (Abente Brun 1999); and in Argentina, the mobilizations of popular and middle-class sectors reinforced each other, even if they did not give rise to a true multiclass alliance (Armony and Armony 2005, 35).

Watchdog Politics

A new context of greater government respect for freedom of the press, combined with more powerful media outlets, has promoted the emergence of what Waisbord (2000) called "watchdog journalism." I documented in Chapter 4 how elected presidents, their families, and cabinet members became increasingly exposed to accusations and scandals. However, scandals were not present in all episodes of presidential removal, and the evidence suggests that exposés were not strictly necessary for the emergence of public outrage against the president. As shown in Chapter 5 (and as illustrated by the Argentine case), unpopular policies and negative social conditions were also important sources of popular discontent.

Even if scandals are not necessary to trigger the fall of an administration, two issues deserve serious consideration. First, scandals are probably necessary in order for *impeachments* to take place. If scandals are absent or play a secondary role in the crisis (as in Argentina in 2001, Bolivia in 2003, and Ecuador in 2000), it is hard for Congress to find a constitutional reason (or excuse) to question the president's right to rule. This argument is consistent with the historical evidence presented in Chapter 2. Second, although not necessary, scandals may be *sufficient* to ignite public outrage. Chapter 5 has shown that outrage is the likely outcome when accusations are recurrent and come to envelop the president.

Confronted with a scandal, presidents have defended themselves by claiming that the accusation is false, by placing responsibility on their subalterns, or by arguing that the charges do not represent an impeachable offense. In April of 1992, for example, President Rodrigo Borja insulted the Ecuadorian legislators by calling them "a gang of slackers." Congressional leaders threatened him with an impeachment, but his minister of the interior responded that "the constitution establishes only three causes for impeachment, and none of them includes calling the slackers, slackers."[11] (Four years later, President Bucaram returned the courtesy by asserting that Borja was a "donkey.") In a political context marked by public outrage, presidential attempts to cover up scandals have easily escalated into further investigations and a confrontation with Congress.

The New Role of Congress

Reflecting on revolutionary France, John Markoff noted that the activation of social movements can easily alter the relationship of power holders to one another (Markoff 1996, 23). In Latin America, popular uprisings against the executive have positioned legislators to play a critical role in almost every crisis since 1990. In a new international context that punished democratic instability and demanded institutional solutions to political conflicts, only Congress was able to cast the collapse of an administration in a constitutional mold. Legislators emerged as the last recourse to provide a "soft landing" for crises and preserve democratic stability. In some cases, they

---

[11] The three causes were the "betrayal of the motherland, graft, or crimes affecting national honor" (article 59 of the 1979 constitution).

played a proactive role, initiating the proceedings to remove the president from office. In others, they were merely reactive, indicting the president when he was already out of power or forming a legislative coalition to appoint a caretaker (Mustapic 2005; Schamis 2002).

The new role of Congress illustrates the deep transformation of Latin American politics documented in Chapter 3. The legislative removal of the president was virtually unthinkable in the polarized political environment of the 1960s and 1970s. For instance, in 1976 a group of Argentine legislators (including opposition Senator Fernando de la Rúa) attempted to initiate an impeachment against President María E. Martínez de Perón. Although dissident groups within the ruling Peronist Party adamantly opposed the president and hoped to prevent a much-anticipated military coup, the majority of the party refused to "betray" General Perón's widow. In the absence of a constitutional solution to the crisis, the military imposed a brutal authoritarian regime that lasted until 1983 (Serrafero 1997).[12]

The contrast between the fatal deadlock of the Argentine Congress in 1976 and the important role played by legislators in 2001 underscores a change in the elites' perceptions of social movements. Prior to the 1980s, popular mobilization was often interpreted as an indicator of underlying ideological polarization, and civilian elites responded by adopting radical postures – to the left or to the right – that facilitated the breakdown of democracy (Bermeo 2003). In the 1990s, elites construed the activation of multiclass street coalitions as an indicator of the president's own political isolation. Legislators were thus inclined to join the wave opposing the executive unless the protests had a narrow constituency (as in Samper's Colombia) or failed to produce a consistent mandate (as in González Macchi's Paraguay). The main exception to this pattern was Hugo Chávez's Venezuela: because popular protest was – much as in the past – read as a signal of underlying social polarization, Congress remained split, and some opposition leaders reacted with a radical strategy that led to a failed military coup and an "oil strike" in 2002.

Qualitative Comparative Analysis

The comparative discussion of presidential ousters without impeachment seems to corroborate the main hypotheses developed in this book. In a context of low military intervention, broad popular protests against the

---

[12] See also *Keesing's Contemporary Archives*, March 5, 1976, 27605–27608.

president typically determined the fall of an administration. But only the presence of media scandals and a proactive legislature allowed for the institutional;pattern of removal central to this study: presidential impeachment.

However, this comparison reintroduces the problem of selection bias presented at the end of Chapter 2. By dealing only with cases in which the president was removed from office, I have excluded from the previous discussion other episodes in which the hypothesized causal conditions (lack of military intervention, media scandals, popular protest, and weak legislative support for the president) may have been present, but in which the removal of the president was never an option (see Geddes 2003). In order to address this problem, I will extend the analysis in two ways. In this section, I will conduct a comparative analysis of the twenty-four presidential crises that took place between 1990 and 2004 (see Table 3.2). In the following section, I will conduct a statistical analysis of seventy-five presidential administrations (most of which never faced institutional turmoil) during the same period.

Table 7.1 summarizes the main characteristics of the presidential crises during the historical period covered in Chapter 2. In addition to the seven cases discussed in that chapter (the challenges to Luis González Macchi in 2001 and 2002 are listed in the table as separate events) and the six cases of removal without impeachment discussed in the previous sections, the table includes eleven other episodes in which neither an impeachment nor a presidential ouster took place.

The table provides information on four causal conditions. Military interventions (labeled M) were coded as present when there was a military operation intended to overthrow the president or to close Congress during the year in question, and coded as absent otherwise. Scandals (S) were coded as present when media exposés of corruption or abuse of power repeatedly compromised the situation of the chief executive and his or her close collaborators. In Ecuador in 1990, and later in Ecuador and Nicaragua in 2004, corruption scandals were present, but their incidence was probably lower than in the other cases.

Popular uprisings (U) were coded as present when mass protests demanded the resignation of the president *and* when they articulated a broad social coalition. In the case of Samper, for example, scattered protests took place, but they were narrow in scope (see Chapter 5). In the Dominican Republic, some protests against electoral fraud also occurred, but they were broader. In Paraguay in 2001, multiple public sectors mobilized, but the resignation of the president was not the only (or even the main)

Table 7.1. *Presidential crises in Latin America, 1990–2004*

Country	Year	Administration	M	S	U	L	I	R	C
Argentina	2001	Fernando de la Rúa	N	Y	Y	Y?	N	Y	N?
Argentina	2001	Adolfo Rodríguez Saá	N	N	Y	Y	N	Y	N?
Bolivia	1990	Jaime Paz Zamora	N	N	N	N	N	N	Y
Bolivia	2003	Gonzalo Sánchez de Lozada	N	N	Y	Y?	N	Y	N?
Brazil	1992	Fernando Collor de Mello	N	Y	Y	N	Y	Y	Y
Colombia	1991	César Gaviria	N	N	N	Y?	N	N	Y?
Colombia	1996	Ernesto Samper	N	Y	N	Y	N?	N	Y
Dominican Republic	1994	Joaquín Balaguer	N	N	Y?	Y	N	N?	N?
Ecuador	1990	Rodrigo Borja	N	N?	N	N	N	N	Y
Ecuador	1997	Abdalá Bucaram	N	Y	Y	N	Y	Y	Y
Ecuador	2000	Jamil Mahuad	Y	N	Y	Y?	N	Y	Y?
Ecuador	2004	Lucio Gutiérrez	N	Y?	Y?	Y?	N	N?	Y
Guatemala	1993	Jorge Serrano	Y	Y	Y	N	N	Y	Y
Guatemala	1994	Ramiro de León Carpio	N	N	N	N	N	N	Y?
Nicaragua	1992	Violeta Chamorro	Y	Y	N	Y?	N	N	Y
Nicaragua	2004	Enrique Bolaños	N	Y?	N	Y	N	N	Y
Paraguay	1999	Raúl Cubas Grau	N	Y	Y	N?	Y	Y	Y
Paraguay	2001	Luis González Macchi	N	Y	Y?	Y	N?	N	Y
Paraguay	2002	Luis González Macchi	N	Y	N	N?	Y	N	Y
Peru	1991	Alberto Fujimori	N	Y	N	N	N?	N	Y
Peru	1992	Alberto Fujimori	Y	Y	N	N	N	N	Y
Peru	2000	Alberto Fujimori	N	Y	Y	N?	N?	Y	Y
Venezuela	1993	Carlos A. Pérez	N	Y	Y	N	Y	Y	Y
Venezuela	1999	Hugo Chávez	N	N	N	N	N	N	Y

Key: M = military intervention; S = scandal involving the president; U = popular uprising against the president (broad protest coalition); L = legislative shield (party or coalition in Congress significantly larger than bloc necessary to block impeachment); I = impeachment or declaration of incapacity; R = president removed from office; C = presidential crisis (executive-legislative conflict); Y = causal condition was present; N = causal condition was absent; ? = process was completed only in part or present only in part.

Source: Presidential crises database (www.pitt.edu/~asp27).

goal of all sectors. Finally, the presence of a legislative shield (L) was acknowledged when the president controlled a legislative party or coalition with a proportion of seats significantly greater than the seats required to block an impeachment process. The dubious cases are those in which the party had only a marginal advantage, was divided, or relied on an uncertain coalition. Natural limitations of space prevent me from discussing the nuances of all coding decisions here, but more detailed case studies are presented in the qualitative database that accompanies this project (http://www.pitt.edu/~asp27/Presidential/Impeachment.html).

Table 7.1 also documents two possible outcomes. The column labeled "I" indicates whether an impeachment or a declaration of incapacity took place. I coded as qualified negatives the cases of Colombia in 1996, Peru in 1991, and Paraguay in 2001 because the process was initiated but terminated, and in the case of Peru in 2000 because the declaration of incapacity played only a symbolic role after the president had resigned. The next column (R) indicates whether the president was removed from office. Students of presidential crises have referred to such outcomes alternatively as presidential falls (Hochstetler 2006) or presidential interruptions (Marsteintredet and Berntzen 2006; Valenzuela 2004), but there is little doubt about the meaning. The only ambiguous cases in this column are the Dominican Republic in 1994, because President Balaguer negotiated his exit from power within a two-year period (for this reason I treated this case as an instance of stabilization with survival in Chapter 3), and Ecuador in 2004, because Gutiérrez survived the crisis in November but was ousted in April.[13]

The last column indicates the centrality of executive-legislative conflict in the process. As explained in Chapter 3, even though all the episodes discussed in this book involved an element of interbranch confrontation (and thus are treated as presidential crises), this element was critical to some historical events and peripheral to others. In the case of de la Rúa, for instance, the Peronist legislators anticipated the fall of the administration and placed one of their own in the line of succession (Mustapic 2005) but did not demand the resignation of the president until the last minute.

Qualitative comparative analysis offers a protocol for comparison that permits the systematic treatment of qualitative evidence (Ragin 1987; 2000). The algorithm employed in this study proceeds in two steps. In the first step, cases that display the outcome of interest (e.g., an impeachment) are compared in order to identify common necessary conditions. In the second step, all possible combinations of the causal conditions are analyzed in order to identify sufficient configurations for the outcome. With four dichotomous factors, eighty causal configurations are possible, although

---

[13] The Balaguer case resembles what Mustapic (2005) called the "presidential" way of terminating an administration – with the chief executive negotiating an anticipated election. Mustapic identified the cases of Raúl Alfonsín (1989) and Eduardo Duhalde (2003) as examples of this pattern in Argentina. In the case of Balaguer, Congress approved the required constitutional reforms; I have therefore counted this episode as a presidential crisis (see also Marsteintredet and Berntzen 2006).

Table 7.2. *Conditions for impeachment and removal from office (qualitative comparative analysis)*

Outcome	Crisp Sets	Fuzzy Sets	Presidential Crisis?
A. Impeachment	7.2.1	7.2.3	7.2.5
Necessary	¬M•S•¬L	¬M•S	¬M•S•C
Sufficient	None	None	None
Simplifying assumptions	None	None	None
B. Removal	7.2.2	7.2.4	7.2.6
Necessary	U	U	U
Sufficient	U•(M+¬L)	U•(M +¬L+¬S)	U•(M+¬S+¬L+¬C)
Simplifying assumptions	M•S•U•L	M•S•U•L	M•S•U•L•C
	M•¬S•U•¬L	M•¬S•U•L	M•S•U•L•¬C
	¬M•¬S•U•¬L	M•¬S•U•¬L	M•S•U•¬L•¬C
		¬M•¬S•U•¬L	M•¬S•U•L•C
			M•¬S•U•L•¬C
			M•¬S•U•¬L•C
			M•¬S•U•¬L•¬C
			¬M•S•U•L•¬C
			¬M•S•U•¬L•¬C
			¬M•¬S•U•L•C
			¬M•¬S•U•L•¬C
			¬M•¬S•U•¬L•C
			¬M•¬S•U•¬L•¬C

Note: Entries indicate Boolean configurations resulting from QCA analysis (veristic tests using inclusion algorithm; minimum frequency set at N = 1). Cases marked with question marks (?) in Table 7.1 were coded as having fuzzy membership scores of 0.5 in Models 7.2.3 through 7.2.6. Simplifying assumptions for configurations with no cases (i.e., empty subsets) reflect the patterns observed in the sample (listed configurations are assumed to yield the outcome of interest).

Key: M = military intervention; S = scandal involving the president; U = popular uprising (protest against the president involving broad social coalition); L = legislative shield (party or coalition in Congress significantly larger than seats necessary to block impeachment); C = presidential crisis (executive-legislative conflict); ¬ = negation (∼, !); • = conjunction (&); + = inclusive disjunction (∨).

configurations excluding necessary conditions can be eliminated from the analysis.[14]

The first column in Table 7.2 presents the results of the analysis of necessity and sufficiency for the occurrence of impeachment (7.2.1) and

[14] The analysis was conducted using fs/QCA 2.0. If every independent variable has j categories and there are k variables, the number of feasible sufficient configurations (considering the possibility that each variable may or may not have a significant impact) equals $(j + 1)^k - 1$.

for the removal of the president (7.2.2). Models 7.2.1 and 7.2.2 treat all variables as dichotomous factors (without any adjustment for the question marks in Table 7.1; that is, they rely on conventional crisp sets). Given the small number of cases, all tests in Table 7.2 are "veristic": the presence of a deviant case is enough to eliminate a particular solution (Ragin 2000).

The results of the analysis reinforce the previous conclusions: the absence of military intervention, the presence of scandals, and a weak legislative shield are necessary for an impeachment to take place. However, those conditions do not pass a test of sufficiency because in two cases, Peru in 1991 and 2000, the three elements were present to some extent, but no impeachment took place (however, note that Congress attempted a declaration of incapacity in 1991 and declared Fujimori unfit for the post after he had resigned in 2000).

Model 7.2.2 indicates that, during this historical period, popular uprisings were the only condition necessary to remove an elected president from office. Uprisings often interacted with other factors (military action, as in Ecuador in 2000, or partisan opposition, when the president lacked a legislative shield) to trigger the collapse of an administration. The table also reports the simplifying assumptions made to reach those conclusions: although no case in Table 7.1 displays military intervention combined with protests and legislative support, or protests without scandals and no legislative shield, it is assumed that such configurations would also trigger the fall of an administration.

Models 7.2.3 and 7.2.4 accommodate some of the historical nuances discussed earlier by treating the analytical categories as fuzzy sets (Zadeh 1965). Conventional comparison assumes "crisp" categories: cases belong to a particular category (set) or not (e.g., Sartori 1970). The analysis of fuzzy sets relaxes this restriction, allowing for a continuous membership function ranging between zero (full exclusion from the set) and one (full inclusion in the category). The assignment of partial membership scores may rely on various procedures (Verkuilen 2005); for the sake of simplicity, I will just assume that cases with partial membership in any of the categories presented in Table 7.1 always lie at the crossover point (0.5). The goal of this procedure is not just to "split the difference" in cases that involve difficult coding decisions. By acknowledging the ambiguity of the historical record explicitly, this strategy forces us to reconsider the results of the previous comparative analysis and to verify the results under an alternative coding scheme. Because categories are not strictly dichotomous, the equivalent of negation ("not a member of") for fuzzy sets corresponds to

$1 - m$, where m is the membership score for the case in any given set. Membership in an intersection (e.g., M *and* S) is determined by the minimum membership score in any of the components, while membership in a union (M *or* S) is determined by the maximum membership score in any of the sets.

The second column in Table 7.2 presents the results of the analysis based on this approach. Two of the factors previously identified (no military intervention and scandals) were confirmed as necessary conditions for an impeachment, but a weak legislative shield was dropped from the list. This change was driven by four cases in which an impeachment took place despite partial legislative support (Paraguay in 1999 and 2002) or in which an impeachment was attempted even though the president had articulated a shield (Colombia in 1996 and Paraguay in 2001). The presence of the four "deviant" cases also prevented the detection of any sufficient configurations.

Similarly, model 7.2.4 confirmed the role of popular uprisings as necessary conditions for the fall of elected presidents. The sufficient configurations detected in the sample suggest that popular protests may lead to this outcome in at least three different ways: by prompting a military intervention against the president (Ecuador in 2000) or preventing an *autogolpe* (Guatemala in 1993);[15] by empowering an adversarial majority in Congress (which may initiate an impeachment); and by destabilizing an unpopular government, even if no scandals have taken place and therefore, according to model 7.2.3, an impeachment is not feasible.

The last two models incorporate questions about the relevance of executive-legislative conflict into the fuzzy set analysis. The assumption in those models is that the twenty-four cases that constitute the sample may belong to the underlying population to varying degrees. The results of this analysis suggest, not surprisingly, that a significant level of executive-legislative conflict is necessary for an impeachment to take place, and that mass protests may be sufficient to force the exit of the president even in the absence of interbranch confrontation. However, given that all cases in Table 7.1 have at least some degree of membership in the set of presidential crises, the number of simplifying assumptions in this analysis is quite large.

---

[15] Note the ambiguity of the M term in Model 7.2.4, which may indicate that the protests support the military or that they oppose their action.

Quantitative Evidence

The last column in Table 7.2 underscores the need to analyze a broader sample of cases including administrations that never faced a presidential crisis. Consider, for instance, the findings about the legislative shield presented in Chapter 6. The evidence suggests that presidents who are willing to negotiate with the opposition from the outset are less likely to confront an impeachment crisis later in the term. At the same time, willingness to logroll may be correlated with being a minority president. For reasons of personality or for other reasons, some minority presidents (such as Fernando Collor, Alberto Fujimori, and Abdalá Bucaram) may not be willing to negotiate, but most minority presidents probably will. If this is the case, weak partisan powers could be a blessing because they would force presidents to bargain with the legislature from the first day in office. But this strategic behavior would create a paradox: presidents with smaller parties (a small parameter S according to the terminology of Chapter 6) would also work harder (and earlier) to secure broader coalitions (a larger A) and also to keep their followers happy (achieving greater cohesion, d). By looking only at presidential crises, we would not be able to perceive this effect because only "unreasonable" minority presidents would self-select into the sample.

The obvious solution to this problem is to select a representative sample of administrations irrespective of whether they confronted a presidential crisis. Unfortunately, the small number of impeachments and declarations of incapacity complicates any quantitative analysis. Moreover, presidential crises are better analyzed as a process than as a discrete outcome. There are at least three stages in the process leading to a successful impeachment: the emergence of the presidential crisis, the decision by Congress to authorize (or block) an impeachment or declaration of incapacity, and the removal of the president from office. As the previous sections of this chapter have shown, different variables may play different roles at these stages.

To develop a large-N comparative test, a research team at the University of Pittsburgh collected information on seventy-five presidential administrations in eighteen Latin American countries between 1990 and 2004.[16] The dataset includes all administrations considered democratic or

[16] Data collection was supported by the Center for Latin American Studies and by the Faculty of Arts and Sciences at the University of Pittsburgh. I am indebted to Andrea Castagnola, Agustín Grijalva, Germán Lodola, and Juan Carlos Rodríguez Raga for their assistance with this project.

semidemocratic during this period (see Mainwaring, Brinks, and Pérez Liñán 2001). The units of analysis are administration-years (for instance, the de la Rúa administration during 2000).

In this database, scandals were coded following the criteria outlined in Chapter 5, using the *Latin American Weekly Report* (LAWR) as the general source.[17] An index of government exposure to scandals was constructed by counting the cumulative number of media scandals involving the president, the cabinet, or the first family reported by LAWR by the end of each year and dividing this tally by the number of years the administration had been in office. This index is thus equivalent to the one presented in Chapter 5, except that the denominator (time elapsed) is measured in years and not in months. A dichotomous indicator also documented whether LAWR reported that the president was personally involved in the scandal.

Popular protest was also coded using the LAWR as the main source. The team identified where and when six social groups (trade unions, state workers, peasant or indigenous federations, the urban poor, middle-class demonstrators, and upper-class groups) took to the streets to demand the resignation of the president. In order to capture the breadth of the protest coalition, we computed a simple score ranging from zero (in years when no group participated in protests) to one (in years when all six groups joined a popular uprising). A score of 0.5 indicates that three of these groups demonstrated against the government, irrespective of which ones formed the "street coalition."

To establish the impact of institutional factors, we collected four pieces of information: (a) the chamber of Congress in charge of authorizing the impeachment process;[18] (b) the percentage of votes constitutionally necessary to block the authorization (i.e., parameter v as discussed in Chapter 6); (c) the percentage of votes controlled by the president's party in the chamber (i.e., a proxy for parameter P);[19] and (d) any reference in LAWR to

[17] *Latin American Weekly Report* (London: Latin American Newsletters Ltd., 1990–2001).

[18] As shown in Chapter 6, in most countries the lower (or only) house authorized the impeachment process. Exceptions to this pattern were Bolivia (where a joint session authorizes the impeachment, which is conducted by the Supreme Court) and Venezuela before 1999, where the Senate authorized a trial conducted by the Supreme Court.

[19] For four administrations, I used the percentage of seats controlled by the president's coalition rather than the share of his or her party. Three of them corresponded to the Concertación's governments in Chile (Aylwin, Frei, and Lagos). I treated the size of the Concertación as a better indicator of the level of support for the president in Congress because Carey (2002) has shown that the coalition behaves cohesively as a unified actor. The other case was the Endara administration in Panama, where I treated the anti-PRD

situations in which the president's party was controlled by an adversarial faction. With this information, we computed a proxy for P − v, measured as the share controlled by the president's party in the authorizing chamber minus the proportion of votes required to block the process. When the president's party was controlled by an adversarial faction, it was assumed that the bloc was prone to act against the executive.[20] Unfortunately, no reliable indicators of the president's leadership style were available for all administrations.

Three dichotomous dependent variables captured the outcome of presidential crises. The first dummy identified situations in which Congress openly debated the possibility of a presidential impeachment or a declaration of incapacity (Brazil in 1992, Colombia in 1996, Ecuador in 1997 and 2004, Nicaragua in 2004, Paraguay in 1998–99 and 2001–02, Peru in 1991 and 2000, and Venezuela in 1993). A second indicator coded all cases in which the authorizing chamber refused to exercise its veto power and accused the president in office. These cases included Brazil in 1992, Ecuador in 1997, Paraguay in 1999, Peru in 1991, and Venezuela in 1993. The third variable captured the episodes of removal from office, irrespective of the circumstances (impeachment, declaration of incapacity, failed coup, or strategic resignation) in Argentina (twice in 2001), Bolivia (2003), Brazil (1992), Ecuador (1997 and 2000), Guatemala (1993), Paraguay (1999), Peru (2000), and Venezuela (1993).

Because the dependent variables are dichotomous and because the density of events is very low, I analyzed the data using rare-event logistic regression (King and Zeng 2001). The rare-event estimator corrects for the low density of events (the low number of crises *relative* to noncrises), but it does not solve the inherent problems created by the small number of cases. Therefore, the results reported in Table 7.3 must be interpreted with caution. The evidence suggests that presidents who become enveloped by scandals are more likely to confront a challenge from Congress (model 7.3.1). At the same time, the greater the size of the legislative shield, the greater the probability that friendly legislators will block the process (model 7.3.2).

Model 7.3.3 pinpoints the factors driving the collapse of presidential administrations in the 1990s and early 2000s. This model also includes

coalition as a unit, and adjusted its size to account for its decline after a couple of years. (A similar case was the Chamorro administration in Nicaragua, but the Nicaraguan constitution did not contemplate an impeachment process until 1995.)

[20] If LAWR reported factional disputes in the ruling party, I computed the legislative shield as $L = P/3 - v$.

Table 7.3. *Predictors of presidential crises, impeachments, removals, and mass protests, 1990–2004*

Type of Model	7.3.1 Crisis RELogit	7.3.2 Accusation RELogit	7.3.3 Removal RELogit	7.3.4 Protest Fixed Effects
Scandal index	0.005	**0.012****	0.002	**0.001****
	(0.004)	(0.005)	(0.007)	(0.000)
President involved	**1.255****	−0.246	0.802	**0.089****
	(0.603)	(1.164)	(1.119)	(0.027)
Protest coalition	**3.603****	**4.552****	**5.985****	
	(0.993)	(1.378)	(1.311)	
Legislative shield, P − v	−4.063*	−4.335**	−2.834	0.013
	(2.401)	(1.909)	(2.324)	(0.114)
Military rebellions			0.861	
			(1.701)	
Inflation				0.010
				(0.010)
Unemployment				0.005
				(0.005)
Constant	−4.413**	−5.554**	−4.725**	−0.061
	(0.601)	(1.049)	(0.668)	(0.058)
R^2 (within)				.080
Pseudo R^2	.263	.368	.486	
Events	12	5	10	
N	311	311	311	311

Note: Entries are regression coefficients. Rare-events logistic for models 1–3 (standard errors corrected for clustering on administration); OLS with fixed effects for model 4.
* Significant at .1 level; ** significant at .05 level.

a dummy variable for military rebellions directed against the executive (Argentina 1990, Ecuador 2000, Honduras 1999, Paraguay 1996 and 2000, and Venezuela 1992).[21] Consistent with the findings of the previous section, military rebellions have not been the main force behind the collapse of elected governments. By contrast, the size of the coalition mobilized against the president emerged as the key factor explaining the demise of these governments.

But what drives popular protests? Model 7.3.4 is a fixed-effects regression of the size of the protest coalition against other predictors, which include

---

[21] Military interventions in Peru (1992) and Guatemala (1993) were not coded because they were initially directed against Congress and not against the president. Additional tests showed that including the Guatemalan crisis would not alter the results.

macroeconomic conditions. The results confirm the findings presented in Chapter 5, indicating that scandals – more than any economic forces – tend to ignite public outrage. The quantitative evidence presented in Table 7.3 tends to corroborate the qualitative analysis of the previous section: the military is not the main force behind the new pattern of instability, and presidents are likely to fall when vast coalitions demand their resignation. In this context, congressional action (via impeachment or declaration of incapacity) has emerged as a common way to depose weak executives when media scandals provide good reasons for a congressional investigation. Media scandals also ignite popular outrage, creating the downward spiral described in Chapter 5.

On the other hand, if the fall of the administration takes legislators by surprise, Congress will be left in a purely reactive position – able to orchestrate a constitutional transfer of government only after the president has abandoned power. The concentration of several resignations in the late 1990s and early 2000s (Fujimori, de la Rúa, Rodríguez Saá, Sánchez de Lozada) may indicate a learning curve among presidents. Aware of the preceding episodes of impeachment, executives without hope may increasingly opt for a planned exit before their removal takes place.

The Political Consequences of Crises without Breakdown

Latin America is marked by the paradox of recurrent government collapse in the midst of democratic stability. It is not hard to see why this historical context has bred presidential impeachments: when broadly mobilized sectors demanded the ousting of the president and military officers refused to do the job, Congress emerged as the only institution able to replace the chief executive in a constitutional way. This pattern was disrupted only when the military attempted to fill the role, or when the president anticipated the reaction of Congress.

In most of the cases discussed in this book, Congress adopted a proactive stance by promoting the impeachment of an unpopular president, by questioning his mental health, by removing him from office, or by forcing him to resign. Legislators were willing to adopt this position if partisan and electoral incentives discouraged them from shielding the president. Chapter 6 showed that legislators were willing to pursue an impeachment when the president had failed to build a lasting coalition, when factionalism had divided the ruling party, or when elections approached and pressure from public opinion was mounting. On the other hand, legislators were *able* to play this proactive role because repeated media scandals had eroded the president's credibility and mass protests had made the survival of the administration untenable.

Alternative outcomes occurred when military officers ignored the historical conditions that restricted their role in politics, or when the president resigned, anticipating his downfall. The first example of deviation from impeachment happened when the armed forces disregarded the trend toward demilitarization and sought to disrupt the democratic process. Although these coups ultimately failed, they accelerated the fall of presidents in Guatemala (in 1993) and Ecuador (in 2000). The second kind of deviation happened when the president acted strategically before Congress could consider his removal. This pattern was characteristic of situations marked by spiraling social conflict, when presidents feared facing criminal charges (or furious mobs) unless they could manage their exit from power. Popular protests outpaced the articulation of a legislative front, and the president resigned before an impeachment process could be set in motion.

In those cases, Latin American legislators worked reactively, providing a constitutional framework for the government transition once the fall of the administration was already in sight. In Guatemala in 1993, in Ecuador and Peru in 2000, in Argentina in 2001, and in Bolivia in 2003, legislators contained the disruptive effects of the crisis by legitimizing the president's removal – and sometimes by offering a parliamentary mechanism to replace the ousted leader (Marsteintredet and Berntzen 2006; Mustapic 2005).

8

Rethinking Latin American Presidentialism

A new pattern of political instability has emerged in Latin America. It took shape in the 1990s and consolidated in the early 2000s. In contrast to the experience of past decades, this trend is unlikely to compromise the stability of democratic *regimes*, but it is lethal for democratic *governments*. Within a few years, political crises without regime breakdown have become a common occurrence in Latin American politics – and presidential impeachment has become the main institutional expression of this trend.

I argued in Chapter 7 that those crises have shared several distinctive traits. First, military officers – bounded by international constraints and by the disastrous experience of military rule in the 1970s – have refused to intervene in politics (or failed on the few occasions when they have tried). Second, the mass media have played a new role as guardians of public morality. Third, popular uprisings against corruption or bad economic performance have driven – in the absence of military coups – the resignation of the president. And, last but not least, given the previous conditions Congress has shouldered the enormous responsibility of guaranteeing the constitutional transfer of power in the midst of the political debacle. This historical context has created conditions for the multiplication of presidential impeachments, although several political crises have led to alternative outcomes for reasons discussed in the previous chapter.

Until recently, this trend was virtually ignored in the specialized literature. Studies of democratization concerned with the possibility of authoritarian reversals usually focused on the survival of democratic regimes. To the extent that old-fashioned military takeovers have virtually disappeared from Latin America, most democracies in the region seemed on their way to "consolidation." In this context, neo-institutional studies focused on the specifics of institutional design and its implications for voters, for politicians' careers, and for the formation of public policy.[1] From time to time, country specialists were puzzled by crises without breakdown, but they tended to analyze those episodes in isolation (see Chapter 2).

What are the theoretical and normative implications of the new pattern of political instability? Are crises without breakdown mere functional equivalents of traditional military coups, or do they demonstrate the presence of checks and balances in Latin America? Are they signals of democratic erosion, or of democratic vitality? Students of comparative politics have only begun to address those questions, and I suspect that we will see heated debates in the years to come. Although analysts are naturally inclined to interpret presidential crises according to their own intellectual frameworks and ideological propensities, debates will not be settled easily because crises without breakdown leave multiple and sometimes contradictory legacies. Among them are the ability of civilian elites to resolve conflicts without military intervention, the emergence of unexpected checks and balances, and the capacity of social movements to exercise vertical accountability through insurrectional politics. Those legacies – and the paradoxes they embody – constitute the focus of this concluding chapter. Exploring those paradoxes may not yield conclusive answers, but it will force us to rethink much of our current understanding of Latin American presidentialism.

Stable Presidentialism with Unstable Presidents

Arguments about the destabilizing effects of executive-legislative conflict became conventional wisdom as part of the debate on the "perils of presidentialism" in the late 1980s. The issue was at the core of Juan Linz's (1990, 1994) claim that presidential democracies are more likely to break down than parliamentary ones. In this view, because the president and members of the Congress are independently elected for fixed terms in office, any significant disagreement between the two branches of government can lead to an institutional deadlock. In contrast to parliamentary regimes, presidential systems do not have flexible mechanisms for the replacement of the head of government or the legislators, and there is no "natural" solution to the problem of gridlock. Tensions can escalate and ultimately destabilize the

---

[1] For instance, as Latin American governments displayed a "surprising resilience" (Mainwaring 1999a), the literature on presidential institutions abandoned its concern for regime breakdown and emphasized problems of deadlock in the policy-making process (Ames 2001; Cox and McCubbins 2001; Eaton 2000; Mainwaring 1999b).

democratic regime (Lamounier 1994; Linz 1990; Riggs 1988; Shugart and Mainwaring 1997; Stepan and Skach 1993; Valenzuela 1994).

In the 1990s, new voices questioned this view by pointing out that not every form of presidentialism is equally dangerous. The argument was reframed in terms of destabilizing veto players (Tsebelis 1995, 321–322). According to Cox and McCubbins, the separation of powers characteristic of presidential constitutions breeds deadlock when the two branches also display a separation of purpose (Cox and McCubbins 2001). Thus, the presence of different partisan players in control of the two branches of government was seen as a potential source of turmoil. Scott Mainwaring showed that the interaction between presidentialism and multipartyism constitutes a difficult combination for democracy (1993, 212–213), and Mark Jones claimed that stable presidentialism usually requires an executive able to command a legislative majority (Jones 1995, 160).

As the debate on the perils of presidentialism cast shadows on the fate of the new Latin American democracies, the multiplication of crises without breakdown in the 1990s challenged the terms of the debate (Mainwaring 1999a, 109–110; Pérez-Liñán 2003b). How should these cases be interpreted? Were they another manifestation of presidential instability, a challenge to the theory, or just a few irrelevant anomalies?

For Arturo Valenzuela, the collapse of fourteen presidential administrations[2] between 1985 and 2004 simply underscored the well-known problems of presidentialism: in presidential systems, disputes about specific grievances may easily escalate into debates about whether the chief executive should resign, and the related polarization may in turn transform the governmental crisis into a full-blown crisis of the constitutional order (Valenzuela 2004, 12).

There is little doubt – and the historical evidence presented in Chapter 3 proved this point – that the underlying propensity of presidential systems toward interbranch confrontation has not subsided after the third wave of democratization. But Valenzuela's interpretation poses an obvious question: if current presidential crises do not trigger democratic breakdowns, where exactly do the *perils of presidentialism* lie? Instability is now installed at the level of the government, not at the level of the regime. Based on this fact, most studies of recent presidential crises have drawn an almost diametrically

---

[2] In addition to the ten cases discussed in Chapter 7, Valenzuela discussed the fall of presidents Hernán Siles Zuazo of Bolivia (1985), Raúl Alfonsín of Argentina (1989), and Jean Bertrand Aristide of Haiti (in 1991 and again in 2004).

opposite conclusion: executive-legislative conflict is not, per se, enough to destabilize presidential democracies (Carey 2005; Marsteintredet and Berntzen 2006; Mustapic 2005; Pérez-Liñán 2003b).

These scholars often embraced the thesis of the "parliamentarization" of presidential regimes, suggesting that the repeated use of impeachments or declarations of incapacity resembles the vote of no confidence characteristic of parliamentary systems (Carey 2005; Mustapic 2005; Pérez-Liñán 2005; Schamis 2002). In other terms, irrespective of whether the Linzean view was an accurate depiction of presidentialism in the past, the current situation may increasingly resemble a parliamentary world. John Carey noted that "even while Latin American constitutions remain presidential...the replacement of presidents in practice increasingly displays a more parliamentarized flavor, with a priority on legislative discretion" (Carey 2005, 115). In an optimistic tone, Marsteintredet and Berntzen claimed that "Latin American presidentialism...is adapting more and more flexible and parliamentary features" (2006, 20).

Valenzuela's concerns should probably temper our optimism. Because these are, after all, presidential regimes, the congressional removal of the president is typically indicative of a political catastrophe, not a mere partisan realignment. Consider, as a mental experiment, the career expectations of a prime minister who has lost a vote of no confidence as against those of a president who has been impeached: the former often returns to the party headquarters to prepare for the next election; the latter often leaves the country to find safe heaven and write bitter memoirs. The evidence presented in the last chapter showed that popular uprisings, rather than legislative action, are the main force behind the collapse of elected administrations. Congressional action provides the framework – the best available framework – for a government collapse, but it often plays a merely reactive role.

Horizontal Accountability with Recurring Abuse of Power

Maybe the most enduring image of Latin American presidentialism is one of executive dominance unconstrained by institutional checks. The "Caesaristic" executive has a long intellectual tradition among Latin Americanists. Early in the twentieth century, the Venezuelan historian Laureano Vallenilla Lanz argued that "democratic Caesarism" was a sociological necessity – the deterministic outcome of cultural, racial, and historical conditions in the Latin American lowlands. According to Vallenilla, a strong president was needed to perform the role of guardian, "representative and protector of national unity" for the unruly peoples of Latin America (Vallenilla Lanz [1919] 1991, 106).

Although Vallenilla's classic work depicted the Venezuela of José Antonio Páez and Juan Vicente Gómez more than the one of Rómulo Betancourt and Carlos Andrés Pérez, executive dominance was also emphasized by later representations of presidential democracies. In a seminal essay published in the 1940s, William Stokes compared a few Latin American examples of congressional government to the modal pattern:

"Democratic Caesarism," whether by military *caudillo* or *doctor en filosofía*, has discouraged administrative efficiency and contributed to political disorganization in Latin America. Concentration of executive authority without responsibility has given free rein to the worst administrative practices of poor presidents without demanding the best from competent chief executives; and, with minority groups in Congress dominated by a rubber-stamp majority – the entire legislature gasping in the shade of strong executive government – active groups have turned to revolution as an outlet for political and administrative expression. (Stokes 1945, 522)

The concern with unconstrained presidents has survived into the present, sometimes inspiring stereotypical representations. Maybe the most dramatic depiction of Third World presidentialism was put forward by Carles Boix, who suggested that because elected presidents are not fully accountable to the other branches of government, they may seize most of the nation's fixed assets and impose a dictatorship (Boix 2003, 152).

A much more nuanced image of presidential dominance pervaded the debate about delegative democracy in the 1990s. Guillermo O'Donnell argued that many new democracies "rest on the premise that whoever wins election to the presidency is thereby entitled to govern as he or she sees fit, constrained only by the hard facts of existing power relations and by a constitutionally limited term of office" (O'Donnell 1994, 59).

O'Donnell's ideal type emphasized three different but related problems: the absence of horizontal accountability (i.e., control over the executive exercised by Congress or other institutions); a pattern of politically isolated and highly technocratic economic decision making; and a cycle leading from presidential "omnipotence" early in the president's term to political "impotence" by the end of the administration. Subsequent work on this topic emphasized the problems of horizontal accountability (e.g., Larkins 1998; O'Donnell 1998) and unilateral policy making (e.g., Ghio 2000; Panizza 2000), but for the most part ignored the cyclical nature of presidential power that became so evident in most presidential crises (as partial exceptions, see Helmke 2002; Schmidt 2000; Weyland 1993).

The multiplication of impeachments in the early 1990s posed an important question for this traditional view. In the absence of horizontal accountability, how could Congress have challenged presidential dominance, held the president accountable, and removed him from office time after time?

The first possible solution to this puzzle is that impeachments took place in countries that were not delegative democracies. But this answer is clearly unsatisfactory. Brazil, the nation that initiated the wave in 1992, was one of the cases that O'Donnell identified with the ideal type, and among the examples of weak horizontal accountability were established polyarchies such as Colombia and Venezuela (O'Donnell 1998, 112).

A second way to account for this paradox is by discarding the concept of delegative democracy altogether, claiming that it fails to reflect the true attributes of Latin American presidentialism in the 1990s. Neo-institutional studies have revisited the role of legislatures vis-à-vis the executive branch, noting that delegation is one among several possible strategic interactions between the executive and Congress (Carey and Shugart 1998; Cox and Morgenstern 2001; Palanza 2006). Thus, when legislators failed to exercise their oversight they may have done so for strategic reasons rather than as a result of institutional impotence. Congressional leaders may have realized that challenging a popular president would not help their political careers, or they may have wanted the executive branch to take sole responsibility for unpopular policies. Yet, when confronted with popular demands to do so, they were fully capable of conducting an investigation and removing the president from office.

The problem with this answer is that, paradoxically, it ignores the strategic effects of horizontal accountability. It is true that the multiplication of impeachments proved that congressional oversight could *ultimately* be exercised, but these outbursts of congressional action represented an intermittent form of accountability, very different from the institutionalized form that is (at least in theory) characteristic of well-established democracies. Like any other form of law enforcement, impeachment is successful only when its shadow discourages the perpetration of misdeeds. This strategic effect is imperfect anywhere, but the surprise and skepticism with which many Latin Americans observed the unfolding of impeachment processes indicates that horizontal accountability was not an institutionalized trait of these regimes.

I suspect that there is a third and more complex answer to this puzzle, an answer that fits O'Donnell's thesis of presidential power cycles as well as Smulovitz and Peruzzotti's thesis about the emergence of societal accountability in Latin America (Peruzzotti 2005; Smulovitz and Peruzzotti 2000). In the 1990s, the multiplication of impeachments signaled the emergence of a model of checks and balances consistent with, and embedded in, the new pattern of political instability. The search for presidential accountability took place in a context marked by a traditional Latin American dynamic – executive dominance punctuated by presidential failure – but also by new conditions, namely, the inability of military leaders to take over and the related emergence of new decisive actors like the mass media and the protest movements (Smulovitz and Peruzzotti 2000).

The model of horizontal accountability that emerged in this context can best be characterized as politicized and spasmodic. By "politicized," I mean that short-term electoral, partisan, and personal considerations drive legislators' decisions about impeachment as much as their concerns about presidential dominance or institutional maintenance (Mayhew 1974). By "spasmodic," I mean that the impeachment mechanism is activated intermittently as a way to handle extreme situations, without a more continuous exercise of congressional oversight during "normal" times (see Siavelis 2000). The elites used impeachments as a way to control presidents who had become too unpopular, too unpredictable, or too unwilling to compromise. But institutional checks were activated intermittently in order to dethrone undesirable presidents rather than to prevent presidential dominance and misdemeanors at an early stage.

This position lies somewhere between a pessimistic image of Latin America as a vast institutional wasteland and an optimistic image of societies governed by well-established "rules of the game." In a presidential regime deprived of any effective mechanism of horizontal accountability, we would expect presidential excesses to be common and impeachment to be unknown. In a context of strong horizontal accountability, we would expect high crimes and misdemeanors to be rare – and impeachment to be equally unusual. By contrast, presidential misbehavior was frequent in Latin America during the 1990s, but impeachment emerged as an unexpected phenomenon. Impeachments proved that legislators were strong enough to hold the president accountable when media scandals and popular protest gave them enough leverage, but not strong enough to discourage the occurrence of presidential abuse on a regular basis.

Popular Empowerment with Limited Democratization

By now it is clear that social movements have played a decisive role in recent presidential crises. In the absence of military intervention, the mobilization of popular sectors and middle-class demonstrators has emerged as the main force capable of overthrowing corrupt or unpopular governments.

In a region plagued by some of the highest levels of inequality in the world, the decisive agency of the popular sectors is not a minor achievement, and several authors have celebrated this fact. Marsteintredet and Berntzen (2006) characterized presidential removals resulting from popular protests as the functional equivalent of popular recalls. Kathryn Hochstetler noted that popular mobilization has worked as a democratic instrument to fight exclusion and construct rights through political contestation (Hochstetler 2006).

One of the most interesting analyses of the role of popular movements in the removal of presidents was elaborated by León Zamosc (2006). Zamosc coined the term "popular impeachments" to refer to episodes in which "presidents have resigned or have been removed from office as a result of political interactions in which popular protest mobilizations expressly demanding the president's ouster played a central role" (2006, 1). For Zamosc, popular protests exercised a particular form of vertical accountability in a context in which ordinary mechanisms of control had failed; they constituted a distinctive manifestation of the new societal accountability in Latin America (Zamosc 2006, 6–8; see also Smulovitz and Peruzzotti 2000).

In this view, popular protests were the natural consequence of democratization, because freedom of expression and organization facilitated the action of social movements and the articulation of their grievances. Moreover, popular impeachments may have promoted the consolidation of democracy in the long run by creating more responsible and legitimate governments (Zamosc 2006, 12).

This interpretation is powerful and sensible; but just as in the case of the parliamentarization thesis, optimism about popular impeachments may need to be qualified. In order to explore this issue, consider two ideal-typical situations: a military revolt and a popular uprising against an elected president. Most readers would probably accept without hesitation the idea that military uprisings against an elected president constitute a threat to democracy. Two underlying assumptions make this argument self-evident. First, military officers have not been popularly elected and therefore cannot represent the popular will. The military revolt, of course, may be popular, but the officers have no right to speak for the people. Second, a military revolt by definition violates a democratic taboo – the use of violence to achieve power. By contrast, an ideal-typical uprising seems to reverse those assumptions: it is the people who make their voices heard in the streets, and any form of violence – to the extent that it takes place – is just indicative of a desperate situation, proof that the elected rulers have not represented the people's interests.

Time after time, these two assumptions have informed the understanding of popular uprisings. Unfortunately, the difference between a "popular impeachment" and a "popular coup" is often blurred, as the example of January 2000 in Ecuador illustrates (Pallares 2006; see also Munck 2006, 11). For this reason, the two underlying assumptions deserve some careful consideration.

First, there is the issue of representation. In principle, there is no clear democratic principle to support the argument that protests should trump votes. In other words, why should the will of the people currently trying to oust the president prevail over the will of the people who cast votes in favor of the same president in the last election? Working in the midst of crises, politicians have eschewed abstract philosophical debates in favor of practical solutions to this dilemma. The evidence presented in previous chapters has shown that the scope of social protests is critical to determining their political leverage. The presence of a broad street coalition conveys the message that something resembling a supermajority wants the president out of office.

Unfortunately, after a broad coalition succeeds in deposing a president, the task of representation only begins. Who has the right to set the new agenda? Interpretations of popular protest often assume that uprisings have unified goals, convey clear mandates, and have foundational consequences for the political system; but the evidence in this regard is mixed. Just like the horizontal accountability exercised by legislators, the vertical accountability exercised by social movements is often politicized and spasmodic. Two dynamics account for this outcome: popular movements may divide over the new agenda and ultimately play into the hands of traditional actors, or they may displace those actors from power only to create new unaccountable governments.

Popular uprisings do not occur in isolation, and they are often shaped by complex interactions between emerging social forces and conventional political structures (Pallares 2006). The experience of Argentina after the 2001 crisis is illustrative. The middle-class assemblies that proliferated under the shadow of a monetary drought vanished without leaving much of a trace, but the Peronist machine that activated the food riots in December of 2001 remained alive and well. And the protest movements (the "*piqueteros*") whose leaders failed to join this structure for the most part languished (see Auyero 2005).

This is not to say that traditional party structures always capitalize on popular outrage – in cases like Bolivia and Venezuela, where the traditional parties had abandoned their popular constituencies, new leaders mobilized those sectors. The evidence seems to confirm Ollier's (2003) thesis that presidential crises tend to occur in contexts of high political fragmentation. Popular uprisings may bring new leaders to power, but, as the Venezuelan example suggests, the reconstitution of political power that follows does not always create a more accountable executive branch.

Second, there is the issue of violence. Although most protests have been peaceful in nature, others – like the Venezuelan *Caracazo* and the Argentine food riots – have involved widespread looting. Moreover, the experience of popular struggles has taught social movements to put a strain on other segments of the population (often through the use of barricades and road blocks) in order to attract the attention of the mass media and public officials. In a context of democratization, protests of this sort present a catch-22 for elected governments. Riots and blockades make the president look weak and ineffective; they encourage the defection of former allies and promote the conspiracies of emboldened enemies. At the same time, the use of repression against demonstrators infuriates the public, triggers international criticism, and usually accelerates the collapse of the administration. In Argentina and Bolivia, the deaths caused by the confrontation between security forces and protestors ultimately triggered the fall of Fernando de la Rúa and Gonzalo Sánchez de Lozada before any impeachment process could even be considered. Maybe the most dramatic example of this situation was the use of snipers to disperse the peaceful demonstrations for impeachment during the "Paraguayan March." As explained in Chapter 2, the attacks created a chaotic situation that quickly forced the resignation of President Raúl Cubas Grau.

Because popular protests represent a reaction against government corruption, abuse of power, or abysmal economic conditions, they have established an asymmetry in the legitimate use of violence. Domestic and international observers make an effort to understand (and even condone) spontaneous riots, while they overtly condemn state repression. This reaction has foreclosed the authoritarian options of cornered administrations, but at the same time has legitimized the potential use of popular protest as a "democratic" form of praetorian politics. As a positive by-product, this asymmetric situation has encouraged the emergence of a restrained style of presidential rule. In the early 2000s, presidents as dissimilar as Eduardo Duhalde and Néstor Kirchner in Argentina or Hugo Banzer and Carlos Mesa in Bolivia bowed to the proliferation of popular protests, trying to funnel them through a dense web of negotiations, social programs, and patronage rather than confronting them with security forces (Gamarra 2004).

A debate about the democratic legitimacy of insurrectional politics is still pending. Defenders of popular uprisings will be tempted to dress them in epic narratives, but they will have a hard time convincing other democrats that social movements have an intrinsic right to forceful political action while other nonstate actors should commit to human rights and abide by the rule of law. Critics of popular uprisings will be tempted to cast this problem as a Hungtingtonian tension between social incorporation and democratic institutions, but they will have a hard time convincing other democrats that this approach is not a latent justification for social exclusion and institutional rigidity.[3]

Maybe the most important lesson taught by recent presidential crises is that presidents who exercise virtually unconstrained power in a context of high popularity often become easy targets when their approval ratings plummet and mass protests consume their political capital. The impeachment process has emerged as the most effective way to manage the downfall of an elected administration while protecting a democratic constitution, but it has generally failed to prevent a new cycle of presidential dominance and government collapse. Military coups may be the drama of the past, but there are reasons to believe that crises without breakdown will be Latin America's drama for years to come.

---

[3] Interestingly, the recent popular uprisings proved that conflict-ridden incorporation is not simply a by-product of the modernization process. Street coalitions were often formed by the poor, but they did not represent new social groups created by the process of economic development. (For the classic work on this topic, see Huntington 1968.)

References

Abente Brun, Diego. 1999. "People Power in Paraguay." *Journal of Democracy* 10(3): 93–100.

Acosta, Alberto. 1997. "El Bucarmismo en el Poder." In *¿Y Ahora Qué? Una Contribución al Análisis Político-Histórico Actual*. Quito: Eskeletra Editorial, 47–90.

Acosta Cerón, Ramiro. 1997. "El Levantamiento del 5 de Febrero: Una Visión Jurídica." In *5 de Febrero: La Revolución de las Conciencias*. Quito: CECS–FETRAPEC–Fundación José Peralta, 85–111.

Acuña, Carlos, and William C. Smith. 1994. "The Political Economy of Structural Adjustment: The Logic of Support and Opposition to Neoliberal Reform." In *Latin American Political Economy in the Age of Neoliberal Reform*, ed. William C. Smith, Carlos H. Acuña, and Eduardo A. Gamarra. Miami: North-South Center Press, 17–66.

Agresti, Alan. 1996. *An Introduction to Categorical Data Analysis*. New York: John Wiley and Sons.

Allen, Philip M. 2003. "Madagascar: Impeachment as Parliamentary Coup d'Etat." In *Checking Executive Power*, ed. J. C. Baumgartner and N. Kada. Westport, CT: Praeger, 81–94.

Altman, David. 2000. "The Politics of Coalition Formation and Survival in Multi-Party Presidential Democracies: The Case of Uruguay, 1989–1999." *Party Politics* 6(3): 259–283.

Alves, Rosental Calmon. 1997. "Democracy's Vanguard Newspapers in Latin America." Paper presented at the forty-seventh annual conference of the International Communication Association, Montreal, Quebec, Canada, May 22–26.

Ames, Barry. 2001. *The Deadlock of Democracy in Brazil*. Ann Arbor: University of Michigan Press.

Amorim Neto, Octavio. 2002. "Presidential Cabinets, Electoral Cycles, and Coalition Discipline in Brazil." In *Legislative Politics in Latin America*, ed. S. Morgenstern and B. Nacif. Cambridge: Cambridge University Press, 48–78.

Armony, Ariel C., and Victor Armony. 2005. "Indictments, Myths, and Citizen Mobilization in Argentina: A Discourse Analysis." *Latin American Politics and Society* 47(4): 27–54.

215

Auyero, Javier. 2005. "Protests and Politics in Contemporary Argentina." In *Argentine Democracy: The Politics of Institutional Weakness*, ed. S. Levitsky and M. V. Murillo. University Park: Pennsylvania State University Press, 250–268.

Avritzer, Leonardo. 1999. "The Conflict between Civil and Political Society in Postauthoritarian Brazil: An Analysis of the Impeachment of Fernando Collor de Mello." In *Corruption and Political Reform in Brazil: The Impact of Collor's Impeachment*, ed. Richard Downes and Keith S. Rosenn. Miami: North-South Center Press, 119–140.

Ayala Bogarín, Oscar, and José María Costa. 1996. *Operación Gedeón: Los Secretos de un Golpe Frustrado*. Asunción: Editorial Don Bosco.

Banco de la República (Colombia). 1997. "Indice de Precios al Consumidor: Inflación Total y 'Básica'." *Revista del Banco de la República* 70(842): 255.

Baumgartner, Jody C. 2003a. "Comparative Presidential Impeachment: Introduction." In *Checking Executive Power: Presidential Impeachment in Comparative Perspective*, ed. J. C. Baumgartner and N. Kada. Westport, CT: Praeger, 1–19.

Baumgartner, Jody C. 2003b. "Impeachment, Russian Style (1998–99)." In *Checking Executive Power: Presidential Impeachment in Comparative Perspective*, ed. J. C. Baumgartner and N. Kada. Westport, CT: Praeger, 95–112.

Baumgartner, Jody C., and Naoko Kada, eds. 2003. *Checking Executive Power: Presidential Impeachment in Comparative Perspective*. Westport, CT: Praeger.

Beck, Nathaniel. 1991. "Comparing Dynamic Specifications: The Case of Presidential Approval." *Political Analysis* 3(1): 51–87.

Behar, Olga, and Ricardo Villa S. 1991. *Penumbra en el Capitolio*. Santafé de Bogotá: Planeta.

Belejack, Barbara. 1997. "Sound Bites and Soap Operas: How Mexican Television Reported the 1994 Presidential Elections." In *A Culture of Collusion: An Inside Look at the Mexican Press*, ed. William A. Orme, Jr. Miami: North-South Center Press, 49–58.

Bermeo, Nancy. 2003. *Ordinary People in Extraordinary Times: The Citizenry and the Breakdown of Democracy*. Princeton, NJ: Princeton University Press.

Bermúdez, Jaime. 1999. *Battles for Public Opinion: Mass Media, Political Scandal, and Presidential Popularity in Colombia (1994–1996) and Venezuela (1989–1993)*. Ph.D. dissertation, University of Oxford.

Berry, William D. 1984. *Nonrecursive Causal Models*. Thousand Oaks, CA: Sage.

Betancourt Pulecio, Ingrid. 1996. *Sí Sabía: Viaje a Través del Expediente de Ernesto Samper*. Santafé de Bogotá: Ediciones Temas de Hoy.

Birchfield, Vicki, and Markus Crepaz. 1998. "The Impact of Constitutional Structures and Collective Veto Points on Income Inequality in Industrialized Democracies." *European Journal of Political Research* 34(2): 175–200.

Bloom, Howard S., and H. Douglas Price. 1975. "Voter Response to Short-Run Economic Conditions: The Asymmetric Effects of Prosperity and Recession." *American Political Science Review* 69(4): 1240–1254.

Boix, Carles. 2003. *Democracy and Redistribution*. Cambridge: Cambridge University Press.

References

Bonvecchi, Alejandro. 2002. "Estrategia de Supervivencia y Tácticas de Disuasión." In *El Derrumbe Político en el Ocaso de la Convertibilidad*, ed. M. Novaro. Buenos Aires: Norma, 107–193.

Boorstin, Daniel J. 1987. *The Image: A Guide to Pseudo-Events in America*. New York: Vintage Books.

Botana, Natalio. 1979. *El Orden Conservador: La Política Argentina entre 1880 y 1916*. Buenos Aires: Editorial Sudamericana.

Bray, Donald. 1961. *Chilean Politics during the Second Ibañez Government*. Ph.D. dissertaton, Stanford University.

Bresser Pereira, Luiz Carlos. 1991. *Os Tempos Heróicos de Collor e Zélia: Aventuras da Modernidade e Desventuras da Ortodoxia*. São Paulo: Nobel.

Buckman, Robert. 1996. "Birth, Death, and Resurrection of Press Freedom in Chile." In *Communication in Latin America: Journalism, Mass Media, and Society*, ed. Richard R. Cole. Wilmington, DE: Scholarly Resources, 155–181.

Buendía, Jorge. 1996. "Economic Reform, Public Opinion and Presidential Approval in Mexico, 1988–1993." *Comparative Political Studies* 29(5): 566–591.

Burbano de Lara, Felipe, and Michel Rowland García. 1998. *Pugna de Poderes: Presidencialismo y Partidos en el Ecuador, 1979–1997*. Quito: Corporación de Estudios para el Desarrollo.

Bushnell, David, and Neill Macaulay. 1994. *The Emergence of Latin America in the Nineteenth Century*. New York: Oxford University Press.

Caballero Carrizosa, Esteban. 1999. "Los Poderes del Estado Después de los Sucesos de Marzo." In *Marzo de 1999: Huellas, Olvido y Urgencias*, ed. J. N. Morínigo. Asunción: Universidad Católica, 121–144.

Cameron, Maxwell. 1994. *Democracy and Authoritarianism in Peru: Political Coalitions and Social Change*. New York: St. Martin's Press.

Cameron, Maxwell. 1997. "The *Eighteenth Brumaire* of Alberto Fujimori." In *The Peruvian Labyrinth: Polity, Society, Economy*, ed. Maxwell Cameron and Philip Mauceri. University Park: Pennsylvania State University Press, 37–69.

Caplow, Theodore. 1968. *Two Against One: Coalitions in Triads*. Englewood Cliffs, NJ: Prentice-Hall.

Carey, John M. 2002. "Parties, Coalitions, and the Chilean Congress in the 1990s." In *Legislative Politics in Latin America*, ed. S. Morgenstern and B. Nacif. Cambridge: Cambridge University Press, 222–253.

Carey, John M. 2005. "Presidential versus Parliamentary Government." In *Handbook of New Institutional Economics*, ed. C. Menard and M. M. Shirley. Dordrecht: Springer, 91–122.

Carey, John M., and Matthew S. Shugart. 1998. "Calling Out the Tanks or Filling Out the Forms?" In *Executive Decree Authority*, ed. J. M. Carey and M. S. Shugart. Cambridge: Cambridge University Press, 1–29.

Carrión, Andrés. 1997. "Y Llegó el Comandante y Mandó a Parar." In *¿Y Ahora Qué? Una Contribución al Análisis Político-Histórico Actual*. Quito: Eskeletra Editorial, 117–144.

Casar, Ma. Amparo. 2002. "Executive-Legislative Relations: The Case of Mexico (1946–1997)." In *Legislative Politics in Latin America*, ed. S. Morgenstern and B. Nacif. Cambridge: Cambridge University Press, 114–144.

Castañeda, Jorge G. 1997. "Limits to Apertura: Prospects for Press Freedom in the New Free-Market Mexico." In *A Culture of Collusion: An Inside Look at the Mexican Press*, ed. William A. Orme, Jr. Miami: North-South Center Press, 131–140.

Cepeda Ulloa, Fernando. 1996. "El Congreso Colombiano ante la Crisis." In *Tras las Huellas de la Crisis Política*, ed. Francisco Leal Buitrago. Santafé de Bogotá: TM Editores–FESCOL–IEPRI, 75–97.

Céspedes, Roberto L. 1999. "Los Actores Sociales en el Marzo Paraguayo de 1999." In *Marzo de 1999: Huellas, Olvido y Urgencias*, ed. J. N. Morínigo. Asunción: Universidad Católica, 145–178.

Chappell, Henry W., and William R. Keech. 1985. "A New View of Political Accountability for Economic Performance." *American Political Science Review* 79(1): 10–27.

Chehabi, H. E., and Juan J. Linz. 1998. *Sultanistic Regimes*. Baltimore: Johns Hopkins University Press.

Cheibub, José Antonio. 2002. "Minority Governments, Deadlock Situations, and the Survival of Presidential Democracies." *Comparative Political Studies* 35(3): 284–312.

Chernick, Marc. 1997. "The Human Rights Crisis in Colombia: It's Time to Internationalize the Peace Process." *LASA Forum* 28(3): 20–23.

Chitty La Roche, Nelson. 1993. *Doscientos Cincuenta Millones: La Historia Secreta*. Caracas: Pomaire.

Cima. 1998. *Informe Anual de Opinión Iberoamericana, 1997–1998*. Bogotá: Consorcio Iberoamericano de Empresas de Investigación de Mercados y Asesoramiento.

Collier, David, ed. 1979. *The New Authoritarianism in Latin America*. Princeton, NJ: Princeton University Press.

Collier, David, and James Mahoney. 1996. "Insights and Pitfalls: Selection Bias in Qualitative Research." *World Politics* 49(1): 56–91.

Collier, David, James Mahoney, and Jason Seawright. 2004. "Claiming Too Much: Warnings about Selection Bias." In *Rethinking Social Inquiry: Diverse Tools, Shared Standards*, ed. H. E. Brady and D. Collier. Lanham, MD: Rowman and Littlefield, 85–101.

Collor de Mello, Pedro. 1993. *Passando a Limpo: A Trajetória de Um Farsante*. Rio de Janeiro: Record.

Comisión Ciudadana de Seguimiento (Colombia). 1996. *Poder, Justicia e Indignidad: El Juicio al Presidente de la República Ernesto Samper Pizano*. Santafé de Bogotá: Utópica Ediciones.

Conaghan, Catherine M. 1996. "Public Life in the Time of Alberto Fujimori." Working Paper No. 219. Washington, DC: Woodrow Wilson International Center for Scholars.

Conaghan, Catherine M. 1998. "The Permanent Coup: Peru's Road to Presidential Reelection." *LASA Forum* 29(1): 5–9.

Conaghan, Catherine M. 2005. *Fujimori's Peru: Deception in the Public Sphere*. Pittsburgh: University of Pittsburgh Press.

Coppedge, Michael. 1994a. "Prospects for Democratic Governability in Venezuela." *Journal of Interamerican Studies and World Affairs* 36(2): 39–64.

References

Coppedge, Michael. 1994b. *Strong Parties and Lame Ducks: Presidential Partyarchy and Factionalism in Venezuela*. Stanford, CA: Stanford University Press.

Corrales, Javier. 1997. "El Presidente y Su Gente: Cooperación y Conflicto entre los Ámbitos Técnicos y Políticos en Venezuela, 1989–1993." *Nueva Sociedad* (152): 93–107.

Corrales, Javier. 2000. "Presidents, Ruling Parties, and Party Rules: A Theory on the Politics of Economic Reform in Latin America." *Comparative Politics* 32(2): 127–49.

Corrales, Javier. 2002a. *Presidents without Parties: The Politics of Economic Reform in Argentina and Venezuela in the 1990s*. University Park: Pennsylvania State University Press.

Corrales, Javier. 2002b. "The Politics of Argentina's Meltdown." *World Policy Journal* 19(3): 29–42.

Coslovsky, Salo Vinocur. 2002. *Neoliberalism, Populism, and Presidential Impeachments in Latin America*. M.A. thesis, Tufts University.

Cox, Gary W., and Mathew D. McCubbins. 2001. "The Institutional Determinants of Economic Policy Outcomes." In *Presidents, Parliaments, and Policy*, ed. S. Haggard and M. D. McCubbins. Cambridge: Cambridge University Press, 21–63.

Cox, Gary W., and Scott Morgenstern. 2001. "Latin America's Reactive Assemblies and Proactive Presidents." *Comparative Politics* 33(2): 171–189.

Crisp, Brian F. 2000. *Democratic Institutional Design: The Powers and Incentives of Venezuelan Politicians and Interest Groups*. Stanford, CA: Stanford University Press.

Crisp, Brian, and Rachael E. Ingall. 2002. "Institutional Engineering and the Nature of Representation: Mapping the Effects of Electoral Reform in Colombia." *American Journal of Political Science* 46(4): 733–748.

Crisp, Brian, and Michael J. Kelly. 1999. "The Socioeconomic Impacts of Structural Adjustment." *International Studies Quarterly* 43(3): 533–552.

Crisp, Brian, Daniel Levine, and Juan Carlos Rey. 1995. "The Legitimacy Problem." In *Venezuelan Democracy under Stress*, ed. Jennifer McCoy, Andrés Serbin, William C. Smith, and Andrés Stambouli. New Brunswick, NJ: Transaction Books, 139–170.

D'Amico, Margarita. 1992. "TV Años 50: La Epoca de Oro." *Feriado, no.* 506 (November 22).

Dassin, Joan. 1984. "The Brazilin Press and the Politics of *Abertura*." *Journal of Interamerican Studies and World Affairs* 26(3): 385–414.

de la Torre, Carlos. 1996. *Un Solo Toque: Populismo y Cultura Política en Ecuador*. Quito: Centro Andino de Acción Popular.

de la Torre, Carlos. 1997. "Populism and Democracy: Political Discourses and Cultures in Contemporary Ecuador." *Latin American Perspectives* 24(3): 12–24.

de Lima, Venicio A. 1993. "Brazilian Television in the 1989 Presidential Campaign: Constructing a President." In *Television, Politics, and the Transition to Democracy in Latin America*, ed. Thomas Skidmore. Washington, DC: Woodrow Wilson Center Press, 97–117.

de Lima, Venicio A. 1998. "Política de Comunicações no Brasil: Novos e Velhos Atores." Paper presented to the twenty-first International Congress of the Latin American Studies Association, Chicago, September 24–26.

Di Palma, Giuseppe. 1977. *Surviving without Governing: The Italian Parties in Parliament.* Berkeley: University of California Press.

Díaz Rangel, Eleazar. 1994. *La Prensa Venezolana en el Siglo XX.* Caracas: Fundación Neumann.

Dion, Douglas. 1998. "Evidence and Inference in the Comparative Case Study." *Comparative Politics* 30(2): 127–145.

Dugas, John C. 2001. "Drugs, Lies, and Audiotape: The Samper Crisis in Colombia." *Latin American Research Review* 32(2): 157–174.

Dulles, John W. F. 1970. *Unrest in Brazil: Political-Military Crises, 1955–1964.* Austin: University of Texas Press.

Eaton, Kent. 2000. "Parliamentarism versus Presidentialism in the Policy Arena." *Comparative Politics* 32(3): 355–376.

Eckstein, Susan. 2001. "Where Have All the Movements Gone? Latin American Social Movements at the New Millenium." In *Power and Popular Protest: Latin American Social Movements*, ed. S. Eckstein. Berkeley:. University of California Press, 351–406.

Economic Commission for Latin America and the Caribbean (ECLAC). 1997. *Statistical Yearbook.* Santiago: United Nations.

Escallón, María del Pilar, and Juan Pablo Ferreira. 1996. "Cronología, Junio de 1994–Junio de 1996." In *Tras las Huellas de la Crisis Política*, ed. Francisco Leal Buitrago. Santafé de Bogotá: TM. Editores–FESCOL–IEPRI, 273–298.

Fausto Neto, Antônio. 1995. *O Impeachment da Televição: Como se Cassa um Presidente.* Rio de Janeiro: Diadorim.

Feldstein, Martin. 2002. "Argentina's Fall." *Foreign Affairs* 81(2): 8–14.

Figueiredo, Argelina, and Fernando Limongi. 1999. *Executivo e Legislativo na Nova Ordem Constitucional.* Rio de Janeiro: Editora FGV.

Fischle, Mark. 2000. "Mass Response to the Lewinsky Scandal: Motivated Reasoning or Bayesian Updating?" *Political Psychology* 21(1): 135–159.

Fitch, John Samuel. 1977. *The Military Coup d'Etat as a Political Process: Ecuador, 1948–1966.* Baltimore: Johns Hopkins University Press.

Fitch, John Samuel. 1998. *The Armed Forces and Democracy in Latin America.* Baltimore: Johns Hopkins University Press.

Fitzgibbon, Russell. 1952. "Adoption of a Collegiate Executive in Uruguay." *Journal of Politics* 14(4): 616–642.

Flynn, Peter. 1993. "Collor, Corruption and Crisis: Time for Reflection." *Journal of Latin American Studies* 25(2): 351–371.

Fossum, Egil. 1967. "Factors Influencing the Occurrence of Military Coups d'Etat in Latin America." *Journal of Peace Research* 4(3): 228–251.

Fox, Elizabeth. 1998. "Latin American Broadcasting and the State: Friend and Foe." In *Communicating Democracy: The Media and Political Transitions*, ed. Patrick H. O'Neil. Boulder, CO: Lynne Rienner, 21–40.

Francia, Néstor. 2002. "¿Un Paso Adelante?" In *Venezuela: La Crisis de Abril*, ed. A. Francés and C. Machado Allison. Caracas: Ediciones IESA, 139–143.

References

Freidemberg, Flavia. 2003. *Jama, Caleta y Camello: Las Estrategias de Abdalá Bucaram y el PRE para Ganar las Elecciones.* Quito: Corporación Editora Nacional.

Frutos, Julio César, and Helio Vera. 1993. *Pactos Políticos.* Asunción: Editorial Medusa.

Galperín, Hernán. 2002. "Transforming Television in Argentina: Market Development and Policy Reform in the 1990s." In *Latin Politics, Global Media*, ed. E. Fox and S. Waisbord. Austin: University of Texas Press, 22–37.

Gamarra, Eduardo. 2004. "Carlos Mesa's Challenges in Bolivia: Will He Succeed against Overwhelming Odds?" *LASA Forum* 35(1): 4–5.

Geddes, Barbara. 2003. *Paradigms and Sand Castles: Theory Building and Research Design in Comparative Politics.* Ann Arbor: University of Michigan Press.

Geddes, Barbara, and Artur Ribeiro Neto. 1999. "Institutional Sources of Corruption in Brazil." In *Corruption and Political Reform in Brazil: The Impact of Collor's Impeachment*, ed. K. S. Rosen and R. Downes. Miami: North-South Center Press, 21–48.

George, Alexander L., and Andrew Bennett. 2005. *Case Studies and Theory Development in the Social Sciences.* Cambridge, MA: MIT Press.

Gerhardt, Michael J. 1996. *The Federal Impeachment Process. A Constitutional and Historical Analysis.* Princeton, NJ: Princeton University Press.

Gervasoni, Carlos. 1998. "El Impacto de las Reformas Económicas en la Coalición Electoral Justicialista (1989–1995)." *Boletín SAAP* 4(6): 67–101.

Ghio, José María. 2000. "América Latina Después de la Reforma: Incertidumbre Institucional y Crecimiento Económico." *Reforma y Democracia* (16):65–82.

Ginsberg, Benjamin, and Martin Shefter. 1990. *Politics by Other Means: The Declining Importance of Elections in America.* New York: Basic Books.

González, Luis Eduardo, and Charles Guy Gillespie. 1994. "Presidentialism and Democratic Stability in Uruguay." In *The Failure of Presidential Democracy: The Case of Latin America*, ed. Juan J. Linz and Arturo Valenzuela. Vol. 2. Baltimore: Johns Hopkins University Press, 151–178.

Grijalva, Agustín, and Aníbal Pérez-Liñán. 2003. *Presidential Powers Database* [computer file]. Department of Political Science, University of Pittsburgh.

Gronke, Paul, and John Brehm. 2002. "History, Heterogeneity, and Presidential Approval: A Modified ARCH Approach." *Electoral Studies* 21(3): 425–452.

Hagopian, Frances, and Scott Mainwaring, eds. 2005. *The Third Wave of Democratization in Latin America: Advances and Setbacks.* Cambridge: Cambridge University Press.

Hallerberg, Mark, and Scott Basinger. 1998. "Internationalization and Changes in Tax Policy in OECD Countries: The Importance of Domestic Veto Players." *Comparative Political Studies* 31(3): 321–52.

Hartlyn, Jonathan. 1988. *The Politics of Coalition Rule in Colombia.* New York: Cambridge University Press.

Hartlyn, Jonathan. 1994. "Presidentialism and Colombian Politics." In *The Failure of Presidential Democracy: The Case of Latin America*, ed. Juan J. Linz and Arturo Valenzuela. Vol. 2. Baltimore: Johns Hopkins University Press, 220–253.

Hartlyn, Jonathan. 1998. *The Struggle for Democratic Politics in the Dominican Republic.* Chapel Hill: University of North Carolina Press.

Helmke, Gretchen. 2002. "The Logic of Strategic Defection: Court-Executive Relations in Argentina under Dictatorship and Democracy." *American Political Science Review* 96(2): 291–304.

Helmke, Gretchen. 2005. "Enduring Uncertainty: Court-Executive Relations in Argentina during the 1990s and Beyond." In *Argentine Democracy: The Politics of Institutional Weakness*, ed. S. Levitsky and M. V. Murillo. University Park: Pennsylvania State University Press, 139–162.

Helmke, Gretchen, and Steven Levitsky. 2004. "Informal Institutions and Comparative Politics: A Research Agenda." *Perspectives on Politics* 2(4): 725–740.

Herrera Aráuz, Francisco. 2001. *Los Golpes del Poder al Aire: El 21 de Enero a Través de la Radio*. Quito: Abya Yala.

Hesli, Vicki L., and Elena Bashkirova. 2001. "The Impact of Time and Economic Circumstances on Popular Evaluations of Russia's President." *International Political Science Review* 22(4): 379–398.

Hinojosa, Victor, and Aníbal Pérez-Liñán. 2003. "Presidential Impeachment and the Politics of Survival: The Case of Colombia." In *Checking Executive Power: Presidential Impeachment in Comparative Perspective*, ed. Jody C. Baumgartner and Naoko Kada. Westport, CT: Praeger, 65–79.

Hinojosa, Victor J., and Aníbal Pérez-Liñán. 2007. "Presidential Survival and the Impeachment Process: The United States and Colombia in Comparative Perspective." *Political Science Quarterly* 121(4): 653–675.

Hirmas, María Eugenia. 1993. "The Chilean Case: Television in the 1988 Plebiscite." In *Television, Politics, and the Transition to Democracy in Latin America*, ed. Thomas Skidmore. Washington, DC: Woodrow Wilson Center Press, 82–96.

Hochstetler, Kathryn. 2006. "Rethinking Presidentialism: Challengers and Presidential Falls in South America." *Comparative Politics* 38(4): 401–418.

Hommes, Rudolf. 1992. "Challenges to the Private Sector in the Nineties: Colombian Economic Policies and Perspectives." In *The Colombian Economy: Issues of Trade and Development*, ed. Alvin Cohen and Frank R. Gunter. Boulder, CO: Westview Press, 87–92.

Hughes, Sallie. 2006. *Newsrooms in Conflict: Journalism and the Democratization of Mexico*. Pittsburgh: University of Pittsburgh Press.

Hunter, Wendy. 1997. *Eroding Military Influence in Brazil: Politicians against Soldiers*. Chapel Hill: University of North Carolina Press.

Huntington, Samuel. 1968. *Political Order in Changing Societies*. New Haven, CT: Yale University Press.

Huntington, Samuel. 1991. *The Third Wave: Democratization in the Late Twentieth Century*. Norman: University of Oklahoma Press.

Immergut, Ellen. 1992. *Health Policies: Interests and Institutions in Western Europe*. Cambridge: Cambridge University Press.

International Labor Organization (ILO). 1998. "Empleo: Un desafío para Colombia (Documento preliminar para discusión)." Bogotá: Oficina de Area y Equipo Técnico para los Países Andinos, OIT.

J. Walter Thompson de Venezuela, C.A. 1970. "El Mercado Venezolano." Caracas: unpublished report.

References

Jackman, Simon. 2001. "Multidimensional Analysis of Roll-Call Data via Bayesian Simulation: Identification, Estimation, Inference, and Model Checking." *Political Analysis* 9(3): 227–241.

Jiménez Sánchez, Fernando. 1994. *Una Teoría Sobre el Escándalo Político*. Madrid: Instituto Juan March de Estudios e Investigaciones, Centro de Estudios Avanzados en Ciencias Sociales.

Jonas, Sussane. 1993. "Text and Subtext of the Guatemalan Political Drama.". *LASA Forum* 24(4): 3–9.

Jones, Mark P. 1995. *Electoral Laws and the Survival of Presidential Democracies*. Notre Dame: University of Notre Dame Press.

Kada, Naoko. 2000. "For Whom Is the Whistle Blown? Politics of Impeachment." Paper presented at the twenty-second International Congress of the Latin American Studies Association, Miami, March 16–18.

Kada, Naoko. 2002. *The Politics of Impeachment*. Ph.D. dissertation, University of California, San Diego.

Kada, Naoko. 2003a. "Impeachment as a Punishment for Corruption? The Cases of Brazil and Venezuela." In *Checking Executive Power: Presidential Impeachment in Comparative Perspective*, ed. J. C. Baumgartner and N. Kada. Wesport, CT: Praeger, 113–135.

Kada, Naoko. 2003b. "Comparative Presidential Impeachment: Conclusions." In *Checking Executive Power: Presidential Impeachment in Comparative Perspective*, ed. J. C. Baumgartner and N. Kada. Westport, CT: Praeger, 137–156.

Karl, Terry L. 1987. "Petroleum and Political Pacts: The Transition to Democracy in Venezuela." *Latin American Research Review* 22(1): 63–94.

Karl, Terry L. 1997. *The Paradox of Plenty: Oil Booms and Petro-States*. Berkeley: University of California Press.

Kasuya, Yuko. 2003. "Weak Institutions and Strong Movements: The Case of President Estrada's Impeachment and Removal in the Philippines." In *Checking Executive Power: Presidential Impeachment in Comparative Perspective*, ed. J. C. Baumgartner and N. Kada. Westport, CT: Praeger, 45–63.

Kaufman, Edy. 1979. *Uruguay in Transition: From Civilian to Military Rule*. New Brunswick, NJ: Transaction Books.

Kaufman, Edy. 1988. *Crisis in Allende's Chile: New Perspectives*. New York: Praeger.

Kay, Stephen J. 1999. "Unexpected Privatizations: Politics and Social Security Reform in the Southern Cone." *Comparative Politics* 31(4): 403–422.

Keck, Margaret. 1992. "Brazil: Impeachment!" *NACLA Report on the Americas* 26(3): 4–7.

Keenan, Joe. 1997. "*La Gacetilla*: How Advertising Masquerades as News." In *A Culture of Collusion: An Inside Look at the Mexican Press*, ed. William A. Orme, Jr. Miami: North-South Center Press, 41–48.

Kenney, Charles. 1996. "¿Por Qué el Autogolpe? Fujimori y el Congreso, 1990–1992." In *Los Enigmas del Poder: Fujimori 1990–1996*, ed. Fernando Tuesta Soldevilla. Lima: Fundación Friedrich Ebert, 75–104.

Kenney, Charles D. 2004. *Fujimori's Coup and the Breakdown of Democracy in Latin America*. Notre Dame, IN: University of Notre Dame Press.

Kiewe, Amos, ed. 1994. *The Modern Presidency and Crisis Rhetoric*. Westport, CT: Praeger.

Kinder, Donald, and Roderick Kiewiet. 1981. "Sociotropic Politics: The American Case." *British Journal of Political Science* 11(2): 129–162.

King, Gary, and Langche Zeng. 2001. "Logistic Regression in Rare Events Data." *Political Analysis* 9(2): 137–163.

Kornblith, Miriam. 1998. *Venezuela en los '90: Las Crisis de la Democracia*. Caracas: Ediciones IESA.

Kuypers, Jim A. 1997. *Presidential Crisis Rhetoric and the Press in the Post-Cold War World*. Westport, CT, and London: Praeger.

Kvaternik, Eugenio. 1987. *Crisis sin Salvataje: La Crisis Político-Militar de 1962–63*. Buenos Aires: Ediciones del IDES.

Lamounier, Bolivar. 1994. "Brazil: Toward Parliamentarism?" In *The Failure of Presidential Democracy*. Volume 2, *The Case of Latin America*, ed. Juan J. Linz and Arturo Valenzuela. Baltimore: Johns Hopkins University Press, 179–219.

Larkins, Christopher. 1998. "The Judiciary and Delegative Democracy in Argentina." *Comparative Politics* 30(4): 423–442.

Lascano Palacios, Mario. 2001. *La Noche de los Coroneles: La Rebelión de los Mandos Medios*. Quito: Editorial KESS.

Lavieri, Omar. 1996. "The Media in Argentina: Struggling with the Absence of a Democratic Tradition." In *Communication in Latin America: Journalism, Mass Media, and Society*, ed. Richard R. Cole. Wilmington, DE: Scholarly Resources, 183–198.

Lerin, François, and Cristina Torres. 1987. *Historia Política de la Dictadura Uruguaya (1973–1980)*. Montevideo: Ediciones Nuevo Mundo.

Lewis, Paul H. 2005. *Authoritarian Regimes in Latin America: Dictators, Despots, and Tyrants*. Lanham, MD: Rowman and Littlefield.

Lewis-Beck, Michael S., and Martin Paldam. 2000. "Economic Voting: An Introduction." *Electoral Studies* 19(2): 113–121.

Lewis-Beck, Michael S., and Mary Stegmaier. 2000. "Economic Determinants of Electoral Outcomes." *Annual Review of Political Science* 3: 183–219.

Lins da Silva, Carlos Eduardo. 1993a. "The Brazilian Case: Manipulation by the Media?" In *Television, Politics, and the Transition to Democracy in Latin America*, ed. Thomas Skidmore. Washington, DC: Woodrow Wilson Center Press, 137–144.

Lins da Silva, Carlos Eduardo. 1993b. "Brazil's Struggle with Democracy." *Current History* 92(572): 126–129.

Linz, Juan. 1978. *Crisis, Breakdown, and Reequilibration*. Vol. 1 of *The Breakdown of Democratic Regimes*, ed. Juan J. Linz and Alfred Stepan. Baltimore: Johns Hopkins University Press.

Linz, Juan. 1990. "The Perils of Presidentialism." *Journal of Democracy* 1(1): 51–69.

Linz, Juan. 1994. "Presidential or Parliamentary Democracy: Does It Make a Difference?" In *The Failure of Presidential Democracy: The Case of Latin America*, ed. Juan J. Linz and Arturo Valenzuela. Baltimore: Johns Hopkins University Press, 3–90.

References

López, Bruno. 1997. "Balancing Act: Surviving as a Television Reporter in Mexico." In *A Culture of Collusion: An Inside Look at the Mexican Press*, ed. William A. Orme, Jr. Miami: North-South Center Press, 89–96.

López Caballero, Juan Manuel. 1997. *La Conspiración: El Libro Blanco del Juicio al Presidente Samper*. Bogotá: Planeta.

López Maya, Margarita. 1999. "La Protesta Popular Venezolana entre 1989 y 1993 (En el Umbral del Neoliberalismo)." In *Lucha Popular, Democracia, Neoliberalismo: Protesta Popular en América Latina en los Años de Ajuste*, ed. Margarita López Maya. Caracas: Nueva Sociedad, 211–238.

López Maya, Margarita. 2005. *Del Viernes Negro al Referendo Revocatorio*. Caracas: Alfadil.

López Maya, Margarita, David Smilde, and Keta Stephany. 2002. *Protesta y Cultura en Venezuela: Los Marcos de Acción Colectiva en 1999*. Buenos Aires: CLACSO.

Luna Tamayo, Milton. 1997. "Bucaram, ¡¡Fuera!! La Voz de los Movimientos Profundos." In *¿Y Ahora Qué? Una Contribución al Análisis Político-Histórico Actual*. Quito: Eskeletra Editorial, 197–228.

Lustick, Ian S. 1996. "History, Historiography, and Political Science: Multiple Historical Records and the Problem of Selection Bias." *American Political Science Review* 90(3): 605–618.

MacKuen, Michael, Robert Erikson, and James Stimson. 1992. "Peasants or Bankers? The American Electorate and the US Economy." *American Political Science Review* 86(3): 597–611.

Mainwaring, Scott. 1993. "Presidentialism, Multipartyism and Democracy: The Difficult Combination." *Comparative Political Studies* 26(2): 198–228.

Mainwaring, Scott. 1999a. "The Surprising Resilience of Elected Governments." *Journal of Democracy* 10(3): 102–114.

Mainwaring, Scott. 1999b. *Rethinking Party Systems in the Third Wave of Democratization: The Case of Brazil*. Stanford, CA: Stanford University Press.

Mainwaring, Scott, Daniel Brinks, and Aníbal Pérez-Liñán. 2001. "Classifying Political Regimes in Latin America, 1945–1999." *Studies in Comparative International Development* 36(1): 37–65.

Mainwaring, Scott, Daniel Brinks, and Aníbal Pérez-Liñán. 2007. "Classifying Political Regimes in Latin America, 1945–2004." In *Regimes and Democracy in Latin America: Theories and Methods*, ed. G. L. Munck. Oxford: Oxford University Press.

Mainwaring, Scott, and Aníbal Pérez-Liñán. 2005. "Latin American Democratization since 1978: Regime Transitions, Breakdowns, and Erosions." In *The Third Wave of Democratization in Latin America: Advances and Setbacks*, ed. F. Hagopian and S. Main.waring. Cambridge: Cambridge University Press, 14–59.

Mainwaring, Scott, and Matthew S. Shugart. 1997a. "Juan Linz, Presidentialism, and Democracy: A Critical Appraisal." *Comparative Politics* 29(4): 449–471.

Mainwaring, Scott, and Matthew S. Shugart. 1997b. "Conclusion: Presidentialism and the Party System." In *Presidentialism and Democracy in Latin America*, ed. S. Mainwaring and M. S. Shugart. Cambridge: Cambridge University Press, 394–439.

Markoff, John. 1996. *Waves of Democracy: Social Movements and Political Change.* Thousand Oaks, CA: Pine Forge Press.

Marsteintredet, Leiv, and Einar Berntzen. 2006. "Latin American Presidentialism: Reducing the Perils of Presidentialism through Presidential Interruptions." Paper read at the Workshop on Parliamentary Practices in Presidential Systems, ECPR Joint Sessions of Workshops, Nicosia, Cyprus, April 25–30.

Mata, Aquilino José. 1992. "TV Años 70. La Década que Sacudió a la Televisión." *Feriado, no.* 506 (November 22).

Mayhew, David R. 1974. *Congress: The Electoral Connection.* New Haven, CT: Yale University Press.

Mayobre, José Antonio. 2002. "Venezuela and the Media: The New Paradigm." In *Latin Politics, Global Media*, ed. E. Fox and S. Waisbord. Austin: University of Texas Press, 176–186.

McClintock, Cynthia. 1993. "Peru's Fujimori: A Caudillo Derails Democracy." *Current History* 92(572): 112–119.

McConnell, Shelley. 1993. "Rules of the Game: Nicaragua's Contentious Constitutional Debate." *NACLA Report on the Americas* 27(2): 20–25.

McConnell, Shelley. 1997. "Institutional Development." In *Nicaragua without Illusions: Regime Transition and Structural Adjustment in the 1990s*, ed. Thomas W. Walker. Wilmington, DE: Scholarly Resources, 45–63.

Medina Serna, Santiago. 1997. *La Verdad Sobre las Mentiras.* Santafé de Bogotá: Planeta.

Meinke, Scott R., and William D. Anderson. 2001. "Influencing from Impaired Administrations: Presidents, White House Scandals, and Legislative Leadership." *Legislative Studies Quarterly* 26(4): 639–659.

Mejía Acosta, Andrés. 1999. "Indisciplina y Deslealtad en el Congreso Ecuatoriano." *Iconos* (6):13–21.

Mejía Acosta, Andrés. 2002. *Gobernabilidad Democrática: Sistema Electoral, Partidos Políticos y Pugna de Poderes en Ecuador, 1978–1998.* Quito: Fundación Konrad Adenauer.

Mejía Acosta, Andrés. 2003. "Through the Eye of a Needle: Veto Players, Informal Institutions and Economic Reform in Ecuador." Paper presented at the annual meeting of the Latin American Studies Association, Dallas, Texas, March 27–29.

Menendez, Cristina, and Mercedes Kerz. 1993. *Autocracia y Democracia: Brasil, Un Camino al Mercosur.* Buenos Aires: Editorial de Belgrano.

Miller, Marjorie, and Juanita Darling. 1997. "The Eye of the Tiger: Emilio Azcárraga and the Televisa Empire." In *A Culture of Collusion: An Inside Look at the Mexican Press*, ed. William A. Orme, Jr. Miami: North-South Center Press, 59–70.

Morgenstern, Scott. 2004. *Patterns of Legislative Politics: Roll-Call Voting in Latin America and the United States.* Cambridge: Cambridge University Press.

Morínigo, José N. 1999. "La Disolución del Poder Dual y el Orígen de una Nueva Legitimidad Política." In *Marzo de 1999: Huellas, Olvido y Urgencias*, ed. J. N. Morínigo. Asunción: Universidad Católica, 29–97.

References

Moura, Alkimar R. 1991. "Introdução à Política Monetária 'Collorida': Um Excercício de Monetarismo Tropical." In *A Economia Pós Plano Collor II*, ed. Clovis de Faro. São Paulo: Livros Técnicos e Científicos Editora.

Moura, Alkimar R. 1993. "Stabilization Policy as a Game of Mutual Distrust: The Brazilian Experience in Post-1985 Civilian Governments." In *Brazil: The Challenges of the 1990s*, ed. Maria D'Alva G. Kinzo. London: Institute of Latin American Studies, University of London, and British Academic Press, 5–23.

Munck, Gerardo. 2006. "Latin America: Old Problems, New Agenda." *Democracy at Large* 2(3): 10–13.

Murillo, María Victoria. 2001. *Labor Unions, Partisan Coalitions, and Market Reforms in Latin America*. Cambridge: Cambridge University Press.

Mustapic, Ana María. 2005. "Inestabilidad sin Colapso. La Renuncia de los Presidentes: Argentina en el Año 2001." *Desarrollo Económico* 45(178): 263–280.

Nadeau, Richard, and Michael S. Lewis-Beck. 2001. "National Economic Voting in U.S. Presidential Elections." *Journal of Politics* 63(1): 158–181.

Naím, Moisés. 1993. *Paper Tigers and Minotaurs: The Politics of Venezuela's Economic Reforms*. Washington, DC: Carnegie Endowment for International Peace.

Narváez, Iván. 1997. "Resistencia al Gobierno Neopopulista de Abdalá Bucaram." In *5 de Febrero, la Revolución de las Conciencias*. Quito: CECS–Fetrapec–Fundación José Peralta, 31–82.

Needler, Martin C. 1966. "Political Development and Military Intervention in Latin America." *American Political Science Review* 60(3): 616–626.

Negretto, Gabriel L. 2004. "Government Capacities and Policy Making by Decree in Latin America: The Cases of Brazil and Argentina." *Comparative Political Studies* 37(5): 531–562.

Neustadt, Richard E. [1960] 1990. *Presidential Power and the Modern Presidents: The Politics of Leadership from Roosevelt to Reagan*. New York: The Free Press.

Nickson, Andrew. 1997. "Corruption and the Transition." In *The Transition to Democracy in Paraguay*, ed. P. Lambert and A. Nickson. New York: St. Martin's Press, 24–44.

Norpoth, Helmut. 1996. "Presidents and the Prospective Voter." *Journal of Politics* 58(3): 776–792.

Novaro, Marcos. 2002. "La Alianza, de la Gloria del Llano a la Debacle del Gobierno." In *El Derrumbe Político en el Ocaso de la Convertibilidad*, ed. M. Novaro. Buenos Aires: Norma, 31–105.

O'Donnell, Guillermo. 1988. *Bureaucratic Authoritarianism: Argentina, 1966–1973, in Comparative Perspective*. Berkeley: University of California Press.

O'Donnell, Guillermo. 1994. "Delegative Democracy." *Journal of Democracy* 5(1): 55–69.

O'Donnell, Guillermo. 1998. "Horizontal Accountability in New Democracies." *Journal of Democracy* 9(3): 112–126.

O'Donnell, Guillermo, and Philippe C. Schmitter. 1986. *Transitions from Authoritarian Rule: Tentative Conclusions about Uncertain Democracies*. Baltimore: Johns Hopkins University Press.

Ohnesorge, John. 2006. "Impeachments Compared: Presidents Roh and Clinton in Law and Politics." Paper presented at the second International Forum on Korean Studies, International Center for Korean Studies, Korea University, Seoul, July 6–7.

Ollier, María Matilde. 2001. *Las Coaliciones Políticas en Argentina: El Caso de la Alianza*. Buenos Aires: Fondo de Cultura Económica.

Ollier, María Matilde. 2003. "Argentina: Up a Blind Alley Once Again." *Bulletin of Latin American Research* 22(2): 170–186.

Orme, William A., Jr. 1997. "Overview: From Collusion to Confrontation." In *A Culture of Collusion: An Inside Look at the Mexican Press*, ed. William A. Orme, Jr. Miami: North-South Center Press, 1–17.

Oviedo, Gerardo. 1997. "Fuentes de Información y Sistemas Políticos en el Diarismo." In *Comunicación: Múltiples Escenarios, Diversas Confrontaciones*, ed. Asalia Venegas. Caracas: Universidad Central de Venezuela, 53–82.

Pachano, Simón. 1997 "Bucaram, ¡Fuera! Bucaram, ¿Fuera?" In *¿Y Ahora Qué? Una Contribución al Análisis Político-Histórico Actual*. Quito: Eskeletra Editorial, 229–264.

Palanza, Valeria. 2006. "Legislative Delegation to Executives in Separation of Powers Systems." Paper presented at the annual meeting of the Midwest Political Science Association, Chicago, April 20–23.

Palermo, Vicente. 2002. "El Enemigo del Pueblo." In *El Derrumbe Político en el Ocaso de la Convertibilidad*, ed. M. Novaro. Buenos Aires: Norma, 289–335.

Pallares, Amalia. 2006. "Mass Mobilization and Presidential Removal in Ecuador: Entre la Ira y la Esperanza." *Lasa Forum* 37(1): 22–25.

Pangrazio, Miguel Angel. 2000. *Historia Política del Paraguay*. Vol. II. Asunción: Intercontinental Editora.

Panizza, Francisco. 2000. "Beyond 'Delegative Democracy': 'Old Politics' and 'New Economics' in Latin America." *Journal of Latin American Studies* 32(3): 737–763.

Paredes, Roberto. 2001a. *Los Colorados y la Transición*. Asunción: Etigraf.

Paredes, Roberto. 2001b. *Los Opositores y la Transición*. Asunción: Grafía Press.

Paredes, Willington. 1997. "Guayaquil, Ciudad-Puerto y Bahía." In *¿Y Ahora Qué? Una Contribución al Análisis Político-Histórico Actual*. Quito: Eskeletra Editorial, 145–172.

Patterson, Thomas E. 1994. *Out of Order*. New York: Vintage Books.

Paz Ballivián, Ricardo, and Galo Cevallos Rueda. 2001. *Los Rostros del Neopopulismo*. La Paz: Fundemos-Hanns Seidel Stiftung.

Pérez-Liñán, Aníbal. 2000. "¿Juicio Político o Golpe Legislativo? Sobre las Crisis Constitucionales en los Años Noventa." *América Latina Hoy* (26):67–74.

Pérez-Liñán, Aníbal. 2001. *Crisis without Breakdown: Presidential Impeachment in Latin America*. Ph.D. dissertation, University of Notre Dame.

Pérez-Liñán, Aníbal. 2002a. "Television News and Political Partisanship in Latin America." *Political Research Quarterly* 55(3): 571–588.

Pérez-Liñán, Aníbal. 2002b. "Argentina y el Nuevo Patrón de Inestabilidad Política en América Latina." *Revista SAAP* 1(1): 167–185.

Pérez-Liñán, Aníbal. 2003a. "Presidential Crises and Democratic Accountability in Latin America, 1990–1999." In *What Justice? Whose Justice? Fighting for*

References

Fairness in Latin America, ed. S. E. Eckstein and T. P. Wickham-Crowley. Berkeley: University of California Press, 98–129.

Pérez-Liñán, Aníbal. 2003b. "Pugna de Poderes y Crisis de Gobernabilidad: ¿Hacia un Nuevo Presidencialismo?" *Latin American Research Review* 38(3): 149–164

Pérez-Liñán, Aníbal. 2005. "Democratization and Constitutional Crises in Presidential Regimes: Towards Congressional Supremacy?" *Comparative Political Studies* 38(1): 51–74.

Perkins, William B. 2003. "The Political Nature of Presidential Impeachment in the United States." In *Checking Executive Power*, ed. J. C. Baumgartner and N. Kada. Westport, CT: Praeger, 21–44.

Peruzzotti, Enrique. 2005. "Demanding Accountable Government: Citizens, Politicians, and the Perils of Representative Democracy in Argentina." In *Argentine Democracy: The Politics of Institutional Weakness*, ed. S. Levitsky and M. V. Murillo. University Park: Pennsylvania State University Press, 229–249.

Petkoff, Teodoro. 2002. "Chávez y los Medios." In *Venezuela: La Crisis de Abril*, ed. A. Francés and C. Machado Allison. Caracas: Ediciones IESA, 89–100.

Pierson, William W., and Federico G. Gil. 1957. *Governments of Latin America*. New York: McGraw-Hill.

Pinheiro do Nascimento, Elimar. 1992. *Renúncia e Impeachment no Presidencialismo Brasileiro: "L'affaire" Collor de Mello*. Cahiers du Centre d'Etudes Politiques Brésiliennes, No. 15–16. Paris: C.E.P.B.

Pippin, Larry L. 1964. *The Remón Era: A Decade of Events in Panama, 1947–1957*. Stanford, CA: Institute of Hispanic American and Luso-Brazilian Studies.

Pizarro Leongómez, Eduardo. 2002. "La Atomización Partidista en Colombia: El Fenómeno de las Micro-Empresas Electorales." In *Degradación o Cambio: Evolución del Sistema Político Colombiano*, ed. F. Gutiérrez Sanín. Bogotá: Norma, 357–401.

Pizzurno Gelós, Patricia, and Celestino A. Aráuz. 1996. *Estudios sobre el Panamá Republicano (1903–1989)*. Panamá: Manfer.

Poole, Keith T., and Howard Rosenthal. 1997. *Congress: A Political-Economy History of Roll-Call Voting*. New York: Oxford.

Pricto, Helios. 1973. *Chile: Los Gorilas Estaban entre Nosotros*. Buenos Aires: Tiempo Contemporaneo.

Ragin, Charles C. 1987. *The Comparative Method: Moving beyond Qualitative and Quantitative Strategies*. Berkeley: University of California Press.

Ragin, Charles C. 2000. *Fuzzy Set Social Science*. Chicago: University of Chicago Press.

Restrepo M., Luis Alberto. 1996. "El Ejecutivo en la Crisis: Dimensiones, Antecedentes y Perspectivas." In *Tras las Huellas de la Crisis Política*, ed. Francisco Leal Buitrago. Santafé de Bogotá: TM. Editores–FESCOL–IEPRI, 46–73.

Rey, Juan Carlos. 1993. "La Crisis de Legitimidad en Venezuela y el Enjuiciamiento y Remoción de Carlos Andrés Pérez de la Presidencia de la República." *Boletín Electoral Latinoamericano* (9):67–112.

Ribadeneira, Alejandro. 1997. "El Paro Cívico del 5 de Febrero: ¡Que se vaya!" In *¡Que se vaya! Crónica del Bucaramato*. Quito: Diario Hoy, 13–19.

Ribadeneira, Jorge, José Hernández, and Marco Aráuz. 1997. *Ecuador Frente al Vértigo Fatal*. Quito: El Comercio.

Riggs, Fred W. 1988. "The Survival of Presidentialism in America: Para-Constitutional Practices." *International Political Science Review* 9(4): 247–278.

Riva Palacio, Raymundo. 1997. "A Culture of Collusion: The Ties That Bind the Press and the PRI." In *A Culture of Collusion: An Inside Look at the Mexican Press*, ed. William A. Orme, Jr. Miami: North-South Center Press, 21–32.

Rodríguez, Juan Carlos. 1999. "Unidad Nacional: Un Desafío del Gobierno y de la Ciudadanía." *Última Hora – Correo Semanal* (April 3–4): 22.

Rodríguez-Valdés, Angel. 1993. *La Otra Muerte de CAP*. Caracas: Alfadil Ediciones.

Romeu, José Vicente. 2000. *Del Caso Remón-Guizado*. Panamá: Editorial Mariano Arosemena.

Rosa e Silva, Cláudio Humberto. 1993. *Mil Dias de Solidão: Collor Bateu e Levou*. São Paulo: Geração Editorial.

Saad Herrería, Pedro. 1997. *La Caída de Abdalá: Un Análisis Actual*. Quito: Editorial El Conejo.

Sabato, Larry. 1993. *Feeding Frenzy: How Attack Journalism Has Transformed American Politics*. New York: The Free Press.

Saltos, Napoleón. 1997. "Testigo de Cargo." In *5 de Febrero, la Revolución de las Conciencias*. Quito: CECS–Fetrapec–Fundación José Peralta, 117–136.

Samper Pizano, Ernesto. 2000. *Aquí Estoy y Aquí me Quedo: Testimonio de un Gobierno*. Santafé de Bogotá: El Áncora Editores.

Samuels, David. 2003. *Ambition, Federalism, and Legislative Politics in Brazil*. Cambridge: Cambridge University Press.

Samuels, David, and Scott Mainwaring. 2004. "Strong Federalism, Constraints on the Central Government, and Economic Reform in Brazil." In *Federalism and Democracy in Latin America*, ed. E. L. Gibson. Baltimore: Johns Hopkins University Press, 85–130.

Sarmiento, Sergio. 1997. "Trial by Fire: The Chiapas Revolt, the Colosio Assassination and the Mexican Press in 1994." In *A Culture of Collusion: An Inside Look at the Mexican Press*, ed. William A. Orme, Jr. Miami: North-South Center Press, 33–39.

Sartori, Giovanni. 1970. "Concept Misinformation in Comparative Politics." *American Political Science Review* 64(4): 1033–1053.

Saunders, J. V. D. 1964. "A Revolution of Agreement among Friends: The End of the Vargas Era." *Hispanic American Historical Review* 44(2): 197–213.

Schamis, Hector. 2002. "Argentina: Crisis and Democratic Consolidation." *Journal of Democracy* 13(2): 81–94.

Schmidt, Gregory D. 2000. "Delegative Democracy in Perú? Fujimori's 1995 Landslide and the Prospects for 2000." *Journal of Interamerican Studies and World Affairs* 42(1): 99–132.

Seiferheld, Alfredo M., ed. 1987. *La Caída de Federico Cháves: Una Visión Documental Norteamericana*. Asunción: Editorial Histórica.

Serrafero, Mario Daniel. 1997. "Juicio Político y Derrumbe Institucional en la Argentina (1976)." *Estudios Interdisciplinarios de América Latina y el Caribe* 8(2): 41–66.

References

Shah, Dhavan V., Mark D. Watts, David Domke, and David P. Fan. 2002. "News Framing and Cueing of Issue Regimes: Explaining Clinton's Public Approval in Spite of Scandal." *Public Opinion Quarterly* 66(3): 339–370.

Shugart, Matthew S., and John Carey. 1992. *Presidents and Assemblies: Constitutional Design and Electoral Dynamics*. Cambridge: Cambridge University Press.

Shugart, Matthew S., and Stephan Haggard. 2001. "Institutions and Public Policy in Presidential Systems." In *Presidents, Parliaments, and Policy*, ed. S. Haggard and M. D. McCubbins. Cambridge: Cambridge University Press, 64–102.

Shugart, Matthew S., and Scott Mainwaring. 1997. "Presidentialism and Democracy in Latin America: Rethinking the Terms of the Debate." In *Presidentialism and Democracy in Latin America*, ed. S. Mainwaring and M. S. Shugart. Cambridge: Cambridge University Press, 12–54.

Siavelis, Peter. 2000. "Disconnected Fire Alarms and Ineffective Police Patrols: Legislative Oversight in Post-Authoritarian Chile." *Journal of Interamerican Studies and World Affairs* 42(1): 71–98.

Siavelis, Peter M. 2002. "Exaggerated Presidentialism and Moderate Presidents: Executive-Legislative Relations in Chile." In *Legislative Politics in Latin America*, ed. S. Morgenstern and B. Nacif. Cambridge: Cambridge University Press, 79–113.

Sigmund, Paul E. 1977. *The Overthrow of Allende and the Politics of Chile, 1964–1976*. Pittsburgh: University of Pittsburgh Press.

Skidmore, Thomas. 1999. "Collor's Downfall in Historical Perspective." In *Corruption and Political Reform in Brazil: The Impact of Collor's Impeachment*, ed. K. S. Rosen and R. Downes. Miami: North-South Center Press, 1–19.

Skowronek, Stephen. 1997. *The Politics That Presidents Make: Leadership from John Adams to Bill Clinton*. Cambridge, MA: Belknap Press.

Smulovitz, Catalina, and Enrique Peruzzotti. 2000. "Societal Accountability in Latin America." *Journal of Democracy* 11(4): 147–158.

Sola, Lourdes. 1994. "The State, Structural Reform, and Democratization in Brazil." In *Democracy, Markets, and Structural Reform in Latin America*, ed. William C. Smith, Carlos H. Acuña, and Eduardo A. Gamarra. Miami: North-South Center Press, 151–181.

Stepan, Alfred. 1971. *The Military in Politics: Changing Patterns in Brazil*. Princeton, NJ: Princeton University Press.

Stepan, Alfred, and Cindy Skach. 1993. "Constitutional Frameworks and Democratic Consolidation: Parliamentarism vs. Presidentialism." *World Politics* 46(1): 1–22.

Stokes, Susan. 1996a. "Public Opinion and Market Reforms: The Limits of Economic Voting." *Comparative Political Studies* 29(5): 499–519.

Stokes, Susan. 1996b. "Economic Reform and Public Opinion in Peru, 1990–1995." *Comparative Political Studies* 29(5): 544–565.

Stokes, Susan C. 2001. *Mandates and Democracy: Neoliberalism by Surprise in Latin America*. Cambridge: Cambridge University Press.

Stokes, Susan, and John Baughman. 1999. "From Policy Change to Preference Change? Neoliberalism and Public Opinion in Latin America." Paper presented at the fifty-seventh annual meeting of the Midwest Political Science Association, Chicago, April 15–17.

Stokes, William S. 1945. "Parliamentary Government in Latin America." *American Political Science Review* 39(3): 522–537.

Sunkel, Guillermo. 1997. "Medios de Comunicación y Política en Chile: Notas a Partir de Datos Recientes." Paper presented at the twentieth International Congress of the Latin American Studies Association, Guadalajara, Mexico, April 17–19.

Szulc, Tad. 1959. *Twilight of the Tyrants*. New York: Holt.

Tanner Hawkins, Eliza. 2003. "Media and the Crisis of Democracy in Venezuela." Paper presented at the International Communication Division, Association for Education in Journalism and Mass Communication convention, Kansas City, Missouri, July 30–August 2.

Taylor, Philip B. 1952. "The Uruguayan Coup d'Etat of 1933." *The Hispanic American Historical Review* 32(3): 301–320.

Taylor, Philip B. 1962. *Government and Politics of Uruguay*. Westport, CT: Greenwood Press.

Thompson, John B. 2000. *Political Scandal: Power and Visibility in the Media Age*. Cambridge, UK: Polity Press.

Tsebelis, George. 1995. "Decision-Making in Political Systems: Veto Players in Presidentialism, Parliamentarism, Multicameralism, and Multipartyism." *British Journal of Political Science* 25(3): 289–325.

Tsebelis, George. 1999. "Veto Players and Law Production in Parliamentary Democracies: An Empirical Analysis." *American Political Science Review* 93(3): 591–608.

Tsebelis, George. 2002. *Veto Players: How Political Institutions Work*. Princeton, NJ: Princeton University Press.

Turner, Brian. 1999. "The 1998 Elections in Paraguay." Paper presented at the twentieth conference of the Middle Atlantic Council of Latin American Studies, March 26–27, Ursinus College, Collegeville, PA.

UNESCO. 1996. *Statistical Yearbook*. Paris: UNESCO.

Ungar Bleier, Elisabeth. 1995. "El Congreso: ¿De la Transición a la Consolidación?" In *Síntesis '95: Anuario Social, Político y Económico de Colombia*. Santafé de Bogotá: IEPRI–Fundación Social–TM Editores, 85–94.

Ungar Bleier, Elisabeth. 1997. "El Congreso Colombiano en 1996." In *Síntesis '97. Anuario Social, Político y Económico de Colombia*. Santafé de Bogotá: IEPRI–Fundación Social–TM Editores, 75–82.

Valenzuela, Arturo. 1994. "Party Politics and the Crisis of Presidentialism in Chile: A Proposal for a Parliamentary Form of Government." In *The Failure of Presidential Democracy: The Case of Latin America*, ed. Juan J. Linz and Arturo Valenzuela. Vol. 2. Baltimore: Johns Hopkins University Press, 91–150.

Valenzuela, Arturo. 2004. "Latin American Presidencies Interrupted." *Journal of Democracy* 15(4): 5–19.

Vallenilla Lanz, Laureano. [1919] 1991. *El Cesarismo Democrático y Otros Textos*. Caracas: Biblioteca Ayacucho.

References

Vanden Heuvel, Jon, and Everette E. Dennis. 1995. *Changing Patterns: Latin America's Vital Media*. New York: The Freedom Forum Media Studies Center.

Vargas, Mauricio, Jorge Lesmes, and Edgar Téllez. 1996. *El Presidente que se Iba a Caer: Diario Secreto de Tres Periodistas Sobre el 8.000*. Santafé de Bogotá: Planeta.

Velásquez, Osvaldo. 1993. *Historia de una Dictadura: De Torrijos a Noriega*. Panama: Litho Editorial Chen.

Verdesoto, Luis. 2004. "¿Hacia Dónde va Bolivia?" *Nueva Sociedad* (191): 38–49.

Verkuilen, Jay. 2005. "Assigning Membership in a Fuzzy Set Analysis." *Sociological Methods and Research* 33(4): 462–496.

Victoria, Pablo. 1997. *Yo Acuso: Un Documentado Pliego de Cargos contra el Presidente Samper*. Bogotá: Ediciones Temas de Hoy.

Villagrán de León, Francisco. 1993. "Thwarting the Guatemalan Coup." *Journal of Democracy* 4(1): 117–124.

Virtue, John, and J. Arthur Heise. 1996. "Controversies over Mass Communication and Professional Education in the Andean Countries." In *Communication in Latin America: Journalism, Mass Media, and Society*, ed. Richard R. Cole. Wilmington, DE: Scholarly Resources, 199–216.

Waisbord, Silvio. 1994. "Knocking on Newsroom Doors: Press and Political Scandals in Argentina." *Political Communication* 11(1): 19–33.

Waisbord, Silvio. 1996. "Investigative Journalism and Political Accountability in South American Democracies." *Critical Studies in Mass Communication* 13(4): 343–363.

Waisbord, Silvio. 1998. "The Unfinished Project of Media Democratization in Argentina." In *Communicating Democracy: The Media and Political Transitions*, ed. Patrick H. O'Neil. Boulder, CO: Lynne Rienner, 41–62.

Waisbord, Silvio. 2000. *Watchdog Journalism in South America*. New York: Columbia University Press.

Weinstein, Martin. 1988. *Uruguay: Democracy at the Crossroads*. Boulder, CO: Westview Press.

Weyland, Kurt. 1993. "The Rise and Fall of President Collor and Its Impact on Brazilian Democracy." *Journal of Interamerican Studies and World Affairs* 35(1): 1–37.

Weyland, Kurt. 1998a. "The Politics of Corruption in Latin America." *Journal of Democracy* 9(2): 108–121.

Weyland, Kurt. 1998b. "Peasants or Bankers in Venezuela? Presidential Popularity and Economic Reform Approval, 1989–1993." *Political Research Quarterly* 51(2): 341–362.

Weyland, Kurt. 1999. "A Paradox of Success? Determinants of Political Support for President Fujimori." Paper presented at the fifty-seventh annual meeting of the Midwest Political Science Association, Chicago, April 15–17.

Weyland, Kurt. 2002. *The Politics of Market Reform in Fragile Democracies: Argentina, Brazil, Peru, and Venezuela*. Princeton, NJ: Princeton University Press.

Whitehead, Laurence. 2002. *Democratization: Theory and Experience*. Oxford: Oxford University Press.

Windt, Theodore. 1973. "The Presidency and Speeches in International Crises: Repeating the Rhetorical Past." *Speaker and Gavel* 11(1): 6–14.

World Bank, 2005. *World Developement Indicators On-Line*. Available from ⟨http://devdata.worldbank.org/dataonline⟩

Yanai, Nathan. 1990. "The Political Affair: A Framework for Comparative Discussion." *Comparative Politics* 22(2): 185–198.

Zadeh, Lofti A. 1965. "Fuzzy Sets." *Information and Control* 8(3): 338–353.

Zamosc, León. 2006. "On Popular Impeachments." Paper presented at the twenty-sixth International Congress of the Latin American Studies Association, San Juan, Puerto Rico, March 15–18.

Zuleta Puceiro, Enrique. 1993. "The Argentine Case: Television in the 1989 Presidential Election." In *Television, Politics, and the Transition to Democracy in Latin America*, ed. Thomas Skidmore. Washington, DC: Woodrow Wilson Center Press, 55–81.

Zúñiga Guardia, Carlos Iván. 1957. *El Proceso Guizado (Un Alegato para la Historia): La Sesión Secreta*. Lima: Talleres Gráficos EETSA.

Index

Index

constitutional procedures, 137–139
in Ecuador, 27–28
in Guatemala, 138
in Nicaragua, 138
in Peru, 184, 185
delegative democracy, 207, 208
Delvalle, Eric, 51
Democracia Popular (Ecuador), 152, 153
Democratic Action (Venezuela). *See* Acción
Democrática
Democratic Front (Paraguay), 162, 164, 165
Democratic Left (Ecuador). *See* Izquierda
Democrática
democratization, 5, 10, 36, 40, 41, 42, 62, 65, 68, 69, 70, 73, 77, 210, 212
disruption. *See* regime disruptions
dissolution of Congress, 44, 47, 52, 58, 60, 62
Dobles, Isa, 127
Dominican Republic, 5, 6, 23, 24, 41, 48–54, 191, 193
DP (Ecuador). *See* Democracia Popular
Drug Enforcement Administration, 22
Duarte, Marcelo, 164
Duarte Frutos, Nicanor, 35
Duhalde, Eduardo, 62, 182, 213

Ecuador
1961 crisis, 51
1963 crisis, 54
1970 crisis, 52
1990 crisis, 191
1997 crisis, 1, 24–29, 38, 48, 106–109, 156, 187
2000 crisis, 10, 47, 183, 187, 189, 196, 202, 211
2004 crisis, 2, 193
2005 crisis, 2
journalism, 79
procedures for impeachment, 136
Estrada, Vicente, 130

Fanego, Julio César, 131
Faria Viso, Augusto, 127
Farias, Paulo César (P. C.), 16, 17, 98, 125, 126
Febres Cordero, León, 154
Filizzola, Carlos, 166
Filizzola, Rafael, 166
Fiuza, Ricardo, 55, 125, 150, 151
Fleury, Penzini, 127
FRA (Ecuador). *See* Frente Radical Alfarista
França, Eriberto, 126
Franciscan politics, 150
Franco, Julio César, 34, 35, 165

Frente País Solidario (Argentina). *See*
Frepaso
Frente Radical Alfarista (Ecuador), 152
Frepaso (Argentina), 177, 178, 182
Fretes, Daniel, 130
Fujimori, Alberto, 2, 23, 26, 34, 48, 85, 86, 184, 192, 195, 197, 201, 226, 230, 233
fuzzy sets, 195

García, Orlando, 127
Gaviria, César, 22, 23, 24, 34, 104, 159, 160, 192
Gomes da Rocha, Zé, 151
Gómez, Juan Vicente, 207
González, Aristides, 164
González Macchi, José Ignacio, 131
González Macchi, Judith, 131
González Macchi, Luis
appointment, 32
economic policy, 33, 34, 111, 113
impeachment, 2, 35, 167, 175
impeachment charges, 34, 166
legislative support, 165–167, 168, 174
presidential approval, 33, 89, 111–114
scandals, 33, 95, 111–114, 130
González Mosquera, Guillermo, 129
González Ugarte, Julio, 131
Goulart, João, 55
Grooscors, Guido, 30, 78
Guatemala
1993 crisis, 53, 182, 187, 196, 199, 202
1994 crisis, 59, 62
newspapers, 70
peace accords, 186
Guerra, Alceni, 125
Guizado, José Ramón, 6, 48, 58, 234
Gutiérrez, Lucio, 2, 29, 183, 192
Guyana Development Corporation (CVG), 101, 126

Hausmann, Ricardo, 157
Heydra, Pastor, 126, 127
Hurtado, Osvaldo, 27, 129

Ibáñez, Blanca, 34, 127
Ibáñez, Carlos, 53
ID (Ecuador). *See* Izquierda Democrática
impeachment
congressional model, 134, 136, 139
constitutional procedures, 133–137
definition, 6, 133
judicial model, 135, 136, 139
model of, 144
outside Latin America, 6
in the United States, 6, 9, 60, 133
wave in the 1990s, 1, 5, 35, 190, 193

Index

Index

Other Books in the Series (continued from page iii)

Michael Bratton, Robert Mattes, and E. Gyimah-Boadi, *Public Opinion, Democracy, and Market Reform in Africa*

Valerie Bunce, *Leaving Socialism and Leaving the State: The End of Yugoslavia, the Soviet Union, and Czechoslovakia*

Danicle Caramani, *The Nationalization of Politics: The Formation of National Electorates and Party Systems in Europe*

Kanchan Chandra, *Why Ethnic Parties Succeed: Patronage and Ethnic Headcounts in India*

José Antonio Cheibub, *Presidentialism, Parliamentarism, and Democracy*

Ruth Berins Collier, *Paths Toward Democracy: The Working Class and Elites in Western Europe and South America*

Christian Davenport, *State Repression and the Domestic Democratic Peace*

Donatella della Porta, *Social Movements, Political Violence, and the State*

Alberto Diaz-Cayeros, *Federalism, Fiscal Authority, and Centralization in Latin America*

Gerald Easter, *Reconstructing the State: Personal Networks and Elite Identity*

M. Steven Fish, *Democracy Derailed in Russia: The Failure of Open Politics*

Robert F. Franzese, *Macroeconomic Policies of Developed Democracies*

Roberto Franzosi, *The Puzzle of Strikes: Class and State Strategies in Postwar Italy*

Geoffrey Garrett, *Partisan Politics in the Global Economy*

Miriam Golden, *Heroic Defeats: The Politics of Job Loss*

Jeff Goodwin, *No Other Way Out: States and Revolutionary Movements*

Merilee Serrill Grindle, *Changing the State*

Anna Grzymala-Busse, *Rebuilding Leviathan: Party Competition and State Exploitation in Post-Communist Democracies*

Anna Grzymala-Busse, *Redeeming the Communist Past: The Regeneration of Communist Parties in East Central Europe*

Frances Hagopian, *Traditional Politics and Regime Change in Brazil*

Gretchen Helmke, *Courts under Constraints: Judges, Generals, and Presidents in Argentina*

Yoshiko Herrera, *Imagined Economies: The Sources of Russian Regionalism*

J. Rogers Hollingsworth and Robert Boyer, eds., *Contemporary Capitalism: The Embeddedness of Institutions*

John D. Huber and Charles R. Shipan, *Deliberate Discretion? The Institutional Foundations of Bureaucratic Autonomy*

Ellen Immergut, *Health Politics: Interests and Institutions in Western Europe*

Torben Iversen, *Capitalism, Democracy, and Welfare*

Torben Iversen, *Contested Economic Institutions*

Torben Iversen, Jonas Pontussen, and David Soskice, eds., *Union, Employers, and Central Banks: Macroeconomic Coordination and Institutional Change in Social Market Economies*

Thomas Janoski and Alexander M. Hicks, eds., *The Comparative Political Economy of the Welfare State*

Joseph Jupille, *Procedural Politics: Issues, Influence, and Institutional Choice in the European Union*

Stathis Kalyvas, *The Logic of Violence in Civil War*

David C. Kang, *Crony Capitalism: Corruption and Capitalism in South Korea and Philippines*

Junko Kato, *Regressive Taxation and the Welfare State*

Robert O. Keohane and Helen B. Milner, eds., *Internationalization and Domestic Politics*

Herbert Kitschelt, *The Transformation of European Social Democracy*

Herbert Kitschelt, Peter Lange, Gary Marks, and John D. Stephens, eds., *Continuity and Change in Contemporary Capitalism*

Herbert Kitschelt, Zdenka Mansfeldova, Radek Markowski, and Gabor Toka, *Post-Communist Party Systems*

David Knoke, Franz Urban Pappi, Jeffrey Broadbent, and Yutaka Tsujinaka, eds., *Comparing Policy Networks*

Allan Kornberg and Harold D. Clarke, *Citizens and Community: Political Support in a Representative Democracy*

Amie Kreppel, *The European Parliament and the Supranational Party System*

David D. Laitin, *Language Repertoires and State Construction in Africa*

Fabrice E. Lehoucq and Ivan Molina, *Stuffing the Ballot Box: Fraud, Electoral Reform, and Democratization in Costa Rica*

Mark Irving Lichbach and Alan S. Zuckerman, eds., *Comparative Politics: Rationality, Culture, and Structure*

Evan Lieberman, *Race and Regionalism in the Politics of Taxation in Brazil and South Africa*

Julia Lynch, *Age in the Welfare State: The Origins of Social Spending on Pensioners, Workers, and Children*

Pauline Jones Luong, *Institutional Change and Political Continuity in Post-Soviet Central Asia*

Doug McAdam, John McCarthy, and Mayer Zald, eds., *Comparative Perspectives on Social Movements*

Beatriz Magaloni, *Voting for Autocracy: Hegemonic Party Survival and Its Demise in Mexico*

Richard Snyder, *Politics after Neoliberalism: Reregulation in Mexico*

David Stark and László Bruszt, *Postsocialist Pathways: Transforming Politics and Property in East Central Europe*

Sven Steinmo, Kathleen Thelen, and Frank Longstreth, eds., *Structuring Politics: Historical Institutionalism in Comparative Analysis*

Susan C. Stokes, *Mandates and Democracy: Neoliberalism by Surprise in Latin America*

Susan C. Stokes, ed., *Public Support for Market Reforms in New Democracies*

Duane Swank, *Global Capital, Political Institutions, and Policy Change in Developed Welfare States*

Sidney Tarrow, *Power in Movement: Social Movements and Contentious Politics*

Kathleen Thelen, *How Institutions Evolve: The Political Economy of Skills in Germany, Britain, the United States, and Japan*

Charles Tilly, *Trust and Rule*

Daniel Treisman, *The Architecture of Government: Rethinking Political Decentralization*

Lily Lee Tsai, *Accountability without Democracy: How Solidary Groups Provide Public Goods in Rural China*

Joshua Tucker, *Regional Economic Voting: Russia, Poland, Hungary, Slovakia, and the Czech Republic, 1990–1999*

Ashutosh Varshney, *Democracy, Development, and the Countryside*

Jeremy M. Weinstein, *Inside Rebellion: The Politics of Insurgent Violence*

Stephen I. Wilkinson, *Votes and Violence: Electoral Competition and Ethnic Riots in India*

Jason Wittenberg, *Crucibles of Political Loyalty: Church Institutions and Electoral Continuity in Hungary*

Elisabeth J. Wood, *Forging Democracy from Below: Insurgent Transitions in South Africa and El Salvador*

Elisabeth J. Wood, *Insurgent Collective Action and Civil War in El Salvador*